P. Buck $ 18⁰⁰

Gender. ~~Cla~~
Rural ~~Tr~~

Agribusiness ~~a~~nd the
Food Crisis in Senegal

Gender, Class and Rural Transition

Agribusiness and the Food Crisis in Senegal

Maureen Mackintosh

Zed Books Ltd
London and New Jersey

Gender, Class and Rural Transition was first published
by Zed Books Ltd, 57 Caledonian Road, London N1 9BU, UK, and
171 First Avenue, Atlantic Highlands, New Jersey 07716, USA,
in 1989.

Cover designed by Andrew Corbett
Typeset by EMS Photosetters, Rochford, Essex
Printed and bound in Great Britain by
Biddles Ltd, Guildford and King's Lynn

British Library Cataloguing in Publication Data

Mackintosh, Maureen
  Gender, class and rural transition:
  agribusiness and the food crisis in Senegal.
  1. West Africa. Agricultural industries.
  Economic development.
  I. Title.
  338.1'0966

  ISBN 0-86232-840-3
  ISBN 0-86232-841-1 pbk

Library of Congress Cataloging-in-Publication Data

Mackintosh, Maureen.
  Gender, class, and rural transition: agribusiness
  and the food crisis in Senegal/Maureen Mackintosh.
      p.   cm.
  Bibliography: p.
  Includes index.
  ISBN 0-86232-840-3. ISBN 0-86232-841-1 (pbk.)
  1. Agricultural industries – Senegal. 2. Agricultural
  laborers – Senegal. 3. Farm tenancy – Senegal.
  4. Food supply – Senegal. 5. Poor – Senegal.
  I. Title.
  HD9017.S42M33   1989   89-5836
  338.1'09663–dc20   CIP

To my mother, Enid Knowles

Contents

Preface and Acknowledgements   xi

Introduction: Food Crises and Development Projects   xiii

1. **Commercial Agriculture and West African Farming: Profiting from Crisis**   1
   Commercial Agriculture before Independence   1
   Senegal before Independence   2
   Drought and Commercial Agriculture after Independence   4
   International Horticulture and Market Gardening in Senegal   10
   The 'House of Bud'   12
   Bud in Senegal   13
   Wage Labour and Smallholdings in Senegalese Market Gardening   14

2. **Estate Agriculture and Small-scale Farming: Analysing Impact and Transition**   20
   The Bud Estates and Senegalese Farmers   20
   Analysing Transition   24
   The Problem of the 'Household'   28
   Households and Farming Systems   30
   Hired Labour, Migration and Class Formation   33
   Women's Work and Class Formation   35
   Monetization, Markets and Transition   37
   Agrarian Transition and the Food Crisis   40

3. **Kirene Village: Economic Adaptation before Bud**   44
   A Homogeneous Safen Village   45
   Households and Domestic Work   47
   Compounds and Matrilineal Kin   49
   Land Holding and Access to Land   51
   Land Shortage in Kirene before 1972   53
   Farming Organization before Bud: the Millet and Groundnut Crops   54
   Vegetable Growing in Kirene   59
   Wage Work by Kirene Villagers before Bud   60
   The Currency of Money in Kirene before Bud   62
   Transition in Wealth and Inheritance before Bud   63
   Economic Transition in Kirene before Bud   64

4. **The Impact of Bud on Agriculture in Kirene**   72
    The Uneven Impact of Land Loss   72
    The Effect of Land Loss on Food and Cash Crops   74
    The Decline of Vegetable Growing in Kirene   75
    Villagers' Participation in Estate Work   78
    Conflict between Estate Work and the Farm Labour Calendar   80
    The Effects of Bud on Collective Millet Fields and Communal
        Labour   82
    The Probability of Future Farming Decline   85

5. **Wage Work, Individualization and Solidarity in Kirene**   92
    Changes in Village Cash Incomes   93
    The Distribution and Scale of Income Losses Attributable to Bud   93
    Distribution of Net Income Losses by Social Group   95
    Incomes and Income Distribution by Household   96
    The Effect of Bud on Spending Patterns   99
    Changes in the Use of Cash within the Village   101
    The Disappearance of Investment   102
    Perceptions of Wage Work: Land and Job Rights   103
    Resistance to Division: the Kirene Stoppage   105
    New Forms of Social Organization: Women, Young People, Trade
        Unions   106
    Conclusion: Economic Division and Social Cohesion   108

6. **Migrant Labour on the Baobab Estate: Labour Market Formation**   116
    Recent Male Migrants at Bud: Migratory Lives   117
    Agricultural Labouring in the Cap Vert   120
    Female Migrants and Wage Work   122
    Bud and the Market for Male Labour   123
    Women's Employment at Bud   128
    Individual Work and Class Formation   131

7. **Wage Work and the Decline of Farming in the Cap Vert**   137
    The Decay of Wet Season Farming in the Cap Vert   137
    Individualization and the Unproductiveness of Wet Season
        Farming   140
    The Economic Organization of the Market Gardens   144
    The Effect of Bud on Labour and Product Markets   150
    Bud and the Future of Market Gardening   152

8. **Wage Labour and the Household: Gender Division and Class
        Formation**   162
    Propertyless Households   163
    The Organization of Domestic Work   164
    Domestic Work and Household Structure   165
    Control and Disposition of Cash Income within the Household   167
    Domestic Work and Sexual Hierarchy at Bud   172
    Female Militancy: the Baobab Stoppage   174

Gender Division and Class Formation   178

9.   **Conclusion: 'Agribusiness', Accumulation and Rural Economic Crisis** 181
     Commercial Pressure and Rural Risk   181
     Accumulation in Europe, Deficits in Africa   182
     State Responses   187
     Small Farmers, Capital and the State in Senegal   190
     Conclusion: What Kind of Agrarian Transition?   195

     Appendix: Research Method   201
     The Choice of Villages for Study   201
     Fieldwork Method   202

     Bibliography   205

     Index   213

Figures

1.1   Senegal: Sources of economic crisis 1961–1971   6
2.1   Bud Estates: average monthly employment   23
4.1   Kirene: First and last dates recorded for agricultural tasks and for
         Bud work 1975/6   81
5.1   Kirene: Income distribution between households   98
5.2   Kirene: Scattergram: Income of household head, and proportion
         spent on millet and rice   98
9.1   Bud-Senegal: net cumulative return cash flow less investments of
         each investor 1972–76   183
9.2   Senegal: The Continuing Economic Crisis   192

Maps

1   Senegal: Regions and Main Towns   3
2   Western Senegal: Location of the Bud Farms   46

Tables (located at the end of each chapter)

2.1   Bud: Area under Crops   43
2.2   Bud: Total Tonnage Sold   43
3.1   Kirene: Farm Labour Organization. Labour on Farm Plots of
         Married Men   68
3.2   Kirene: Farm Labour Organization. Labour on Farm Plots of
         Unmarried Men   69
3.3   Kirene: Farm Labour Organization. Labour on Farm Plots of
         Married Women   70

3.4 Kirene: Farm Operations Performed by Communal Labour
      Parties 1975/6   71
4.1 Kirene: Effects of Land Loss on Estimated Cropping Areas   87
4.2 Kirene: Correlation Coefficients for Determinants of Areas
      Farmed   87
4.3 Kirene: Distribution of Farm Plots by Crop in Sample
      Households 1975/6   88
4.4 Senegal: Output of Millet and Groundnuts in Thies Region   89
4.5 Kirene: Participation in the Bud Labour Force According to Age   89
4.6 Kirene: Farming Practices According to Participation in Wage
      Work – Sample Households   90
4.7 Kirene: Number of Days Spent in Farming – Averages per
      Person   91
5.1 Kirene: Estimated Incomes from Vegetable Farming without Bud   111
5.2 Kirene: Net Cash Income from Vegetable Growing 1975/76   111
5.3 Kirene: Costs and Returns of Groundnut Farming: Male Farmers   112
5.4 Kirene: Cash Income from Bud and from Farming, by Position
      in the Farming Structure (Men)   113
5.5 Kirene: Cash Income from Bud and from Farming, by Position
      in the Household and Farming Structure (Women)   114
5.6 Kirene: Proportion of Total Household Cash Income Held by
      Different Groups   115
6.1 Ponty: Place of Birth, by Ethnic Group, of All Villagers as
      Percentages of Total in Each Group   133
6.2 Bambilor, 1975: Place of Origin of Recent Migrants   134
6.3 Bambilor, 1975: Women's Work, by Age and Types of Work   135
6.4 Ponty: Women's Participation in the Bud Labour Force   136
7.1 The Cap Vert and Thies Region: Production of Main Crops
      1973/4   155
7.2 Ponty: Intersection between Farming and Bud Work, by Sex   155
7.3 Ponty: Costs and Returns to Wet Season Farming   156
7.4 Bambilor, 1975/6: Breakdown of Cash Costs and Returns to Wet
      Season Farming   157
7.5 Land holding by Non-Villagers on Bambilor Village Land, 1975   158
7.6 Cap Vert: Land Tenure and Land Use in the Bambilor/Sangalkan
      Areas, 1975   159
7.7 Bambilor: Labour Use on Market Gardens in Sample, 1975/6   160
7.8 Bambilor: Cash Costs and Cash Returns from Market
      Gardening 1975/6   161
8.1 Ponty: Extent of Transfer of Cash within the Household to
      the Household Head   180
9.1 Changing Ownership of Bud Senegal   199
9.2 Fresh Produce Production and Exports   200
9.3 Indicators of the Food Situation: Millet and Sorghum
      Production; Imports of Rice   200

Preface and Acknowledgements

The core of this book is a study of the agricultural, economic and social consequences of the arrival in two rural areas of Senegal of a large American 'agribusiness' enterprise called Bud Senegal. The book also draws on earlier fieldwork – a year in Senegal studying industrial relations issues – and on research in Europe on agro–industrial and commercial capital operating in the production and marketing of fruit and vegetables. The book attempts to use the case study of this rather notorious but not otherwise well-documented project to illuminate a whole slice of agrarian change in Senegal in the 1970s, and its determinants: the international forces shaping agricultural change, the local agricultural and economic crisis, state responses to the crisis, the nature of the agrarian system and agrarian transition in the areas studied, wage work and the labour market, gender relations and their influence on class formation.

With a sweep of interests of this kind, my debts are naturally very wide. This book is an attempt to repay, very belatedly, the worst debt. I remember all too vividly a Senegalese friend fulminating to me in the mid-1970s about foreign researchers who leave with their research 'under the arm' after drawing so heavily on local support and goodwill. Swearing I would never perpetrate this crime, I nevertheless fell victim to the pressures which create it: academic, economic, social. While I offer no excuse, here at last are the results of the study so many Senegalese people urged me to undertake. My deep apologies for the delay.

The field research in Senegal and Europe in 1975–1977 was financed by a generous grant from the British Overseas Development Administration. The ODA is in no way responsible, however, for the present reworking of the material on which my final report to them was based; responsibility for this version rests entirely with the author. In Senegal the research was undertaken with the kind permission of the *Delégation Générale à la Recherche Scientifique et Technique*.

In Senegal my debts are too many to enumerate. Above all I am indebted to the inhabitants of the three villages studied, and to the numerous other estate workers who answered my questions with such patience and friendliness. I learned a great deal about hospitality and humanity in these villages, and also in Sebikotane, where I lived for fifteen months. In particular, the research owes most to M. Boubacar Soumaré who worked as my research assistant and colleague throughout the years I spent in Senegal, and without whose skills this study would have been impossible. I also owe a very great deal to M. Issa Diop and his family (especially Mme Mariama Diedhou) for the hospitality of their household and for their kindness, friendship and support; and to Mlle Ndeye Diop, of the same family, who also acted as my research assistant for two months. I owe an even greater debt of gratitude to Aladji Sow, a colleague and friend throughout this work, after encouraging me to undertake it, and to the friendship of his wife Sophie. I would also like to thank, inadequately, M. Pape Kane, M. Abdoulaye Sow and M. Michel Parsy of the *Ecole Nationale d'Economie Appliquée* in Dakar: the teaching and field studies undertaken by this institution under the direction of M. Kane were an inspiration and a guide for this study. None of these people are responsible in any way for what I have made of their guidance.

My thanks also to the following: in Kirene, M. Sene, the village head, and his family, especially M. Boubacar Sene, M. Mbaye Ciss and Mme Madjiguene Ciss; in Bambilor, M. Ndoye, the village head, and M. Mamadou Gueye; in Ponty, M. Ba, and Christina Gomis and her household. At the Ministry of Rural Development in Dakar, my thanks to M. Paye and M. Sagna. At Bud Senegal the Managing Director, M. Marschall, allowed me free access to the estates, and provided a great deal of information and documentation on the firm's operations; M. Bathor Diop, M. Zee, M. Mazide Ndiaye, M. Steiner, George Trappan and Sam Armstrong were also very helpful. Many other staff and managers on the estates and the extension projects made a great deal of time to talk to me. Again, none of these people are in any way responsible for the conclusions I have drawn in this book. The same disclaimer applies to those cited elsewhere in the footnotes as having provided advice and assistance.

In Senegal, I also owe thanks to George Scharffenberger, Pat McAleer and François and Brigitte Barbier for friendship and support; in England, my thanks to Biplab Dasgupta and Manfred Bienefeld at the Institute of Development Studies at Sussex for supervision and argumentation, and to Margaret Haswell, a most encouraging examiner; to Henry Lucas for help with programming; to Jo Foster who typed the thesis, and Trisha O'Doherty who typed the book manuscript; to Hilary Standing and Ben Crow who read and commented on the thesis and the book manuscript respectively; and to my friends at the Open University Development Policy and Practice Research Group for stimulation and support, financial and intellectual; to Ann Whitehead for inspiration and friendship, and to all the members of the Subordination of Women Group and the participants in the 1978 Conference at Sussex on the Subordination of Women in the Development Process, for information and inspiration on the subject of gender relations; at Zed Press, to John Daniel for enthusiasm and support for this book; and to Carole Furnivall, Gaby Charing and Mandy Cook for help, caring, patience and encouragement.

Introduction:
Food Crises and Development Projects

This is a book about the way in which large-scale agricultural development projects can breed food crisis. Since the 1960s food crisis and famine in Africa have helped to open that continent to successive waves of agricultural development initiatives. The farmers and herders of the ecologically fragile West African savannah and Sahelian desert fringe have faced greatly increased pressures from foreign-financed interventions in their economic lives: large-scale commercial farming, large-scale irrigated agricultural development projects, 'small farmer' contracting schemes, other projects to organize and transform the technology of low productivity farming, changes in economic incentives and pressures directed at 'smallholders': all these have been generated in good part by foreign pressures and organized with foreign finance.[1] Each new drought has provided motive and opportunity for further foreign resources and foreign initiatives to 'solve' the food crisis. And each fashion in rural development has stimulated further fears, locally and abroad, that many of these initiatives may actually be making things worse: in particular, that the projects may be competing with local food production.[2]

This book demonstrates how large-scale farming projects *can* indeed make food crisis worse by undermining local food farming systems and creating a dependence on dubiously viable wage work. It contains a detailed study of the impact of one big commercial farming project on small-scale integrated farming systems in the Senegalese rural areas. The book argues, on the basis of this study, that long-run changes induced in the social and economic organization of rural life and work are the most important effect of such projects, outweighing the immediate competition for land and labour with local farming, on which most studies have focused. Accounts which concentrate on the immediate income effects of projects, as economic assessment typically does,[3] without an eye to the organization of the existing farming system as it changes under severe pressure, may seriously underestimate effects on food production and local access to food. Stepping back from the point of view of the project organizers, and trying to grasp the effects from the point of view of farmers and wage workers, is the essential starting point for trying to correct this bias.

Characteristic of many of the development projects in the Sahel have been ambitious scale, a mixture of private investment and foreign and local public funding, and a remarkably sketchy knowledge of or respect for the existing farming and economic systems of the areas where they were implanted.[4] Some of the consequences of this last feature for the financial viability of the projects themselves are now widely acknowledged, but the detailed consequences for the local populations are taking longer to emerge.[5]

The project whose effects are studied here – a foreign private venture backed by the International Finance Corporation (IFC), the arm of the World Bank set up to encourage private investment in the Third World – was a characteristic if somewhat extreme example of this 1970s wave of 'agribusiness' interest in one of Africa's most fragile agricultural areas. The firm was a subsidiary, via a European holding company, of a US agribusiness company, Bud Antle – lettuce growers on a huge scale – and it proposed to grow fruit and vegetables on big estates for the European off-season market. Senegal was to become 'Africa's California', as the managers put it (though 'Europe's Mexico' would have been more exact).[6] Arriving in the worst drought year of the early 1970s, the project was at first hailed by the Senegalese government as a source of economic salvation: a new irrigated export crop, not subject to drought, which could supplement declining groundnut revenues. Four years later the project was on the verge of bankruptcy, the target of furious government and public criticism. In 1980, *Le Monde Diplomatique* devoted a whole page to its final demise. In its wake, several thousand unemployed workers marched in protest through Dakar.

The extent to which the project, called Bud Senegal, contributed to unemployment through its impact on surrounding rural areas emerges as a central theme of this book. The management of Bud (as I shall henceforth call the Senegal-registered company except where I need to distinguish it from the European holding company of the same name), initially argued that the estates would cause no detriment in rural areas, since they operated only in the Senegalese dry season, while local farming was chiefly rain-fed. It was the contrary opinion of farmers and some government employees working in the Senegalese rural areas which first led me to study the local impact of the estates.

This book is the result of fifteen months living in, and trying to understand, the villages surrounding the two Bud estates, and of subsequent reflection on the information collected. The core material is a study of agricultural organization and change in three of these villages. This is integrated with a study of labour force formation, patterns of change in domestic work and domestic relations, and associated patterns of change in the aims and self-perceptions of villagers and migrant labourers.

To understand what was happening in these villages, I was forced first to dispose of a number of erroneous preconceptions about 'peasant' agriculture and economy. Economists still tend, despite decades of argument to the contrary from anthropologists, to characterize African agriculture in terms of atomized 'smallholdings' using 'family' labour.[7] This concept of individual household farming is so misleading when applied to West African farming systems that it impedes an understanding of the direction of economic change at village level. I had therefore to replace it with categories and questions which allowed analysis of the web of domestic and wider social relations which held together the complex farming and economic systems. The crucial elements of this change in perspective were the attention I now paid to the pattern of economic relations between individuals within as well as across households; the dropping of the assumptions of a sharp break in social relations at the household boundary and of a household head with unproblematic access to the labour of other household members; the construction of the 'household' as a variable, changing in form and content as class definitions and social relations shifted; and the investigation of the changes in social relations between men and women as a major indicator of economic transition.

The complex farming systems which this approach allows us to analyse can break down in a variety of directions under pressure. One possible outcome is a system based more explicitly on households. In the circumstances analysed here, a frequent and more likely outcome of the disintegration of complex co-operation in farming was the emergence of an impoverished form of individual farming – its poverty was economic, technical and social – which produced little or no food, and rapidly ceased to be viable. It was this agricultural disintegration which helped to create a dependence on wage work at Bud, reinforcing the existing rural migration patterns on which the estates drew;[8] hence Bud had begun to develop a rather stable labour force who saw themselves primarily as wage workers.

The development of this labour force alarmed the Bud management, who had hoped to avoid 'Cesar Chavez and all those problems in Senegal'.[9] The management, faced with labour organization and resistance, and having looked in vain for the 'outside agitators', began to turn instead to mechanization – thus replicating the experience of the US parent company, Bud Antle.[10] Later, with the agreement of the Senegalese government, which was also worried about the social and economic implications of rural proletarianization, they started to look instead towards the increasingly promoted contract farming schemes: managed 'household farming' to tie people to the land, transform the social organization of small-scale farming, reduce labour solidarity, and incidentally increase the share of risk borne by the local producers.[11]

And in the end the question of risk, and who bears it, becomes the central issue. The Bud ventures were high-risk, trying to bring export horticulture, with its stringent marketing and quality demands, into the ecologically fragile and drought-threatened Sahel. The risks were borne chiefly by the workers and the farmers, most obviously through the precariousness of their employment, and most significantly through a further decrease in the productive capacity of their farming systems.

The question of risk and who bears it has been raised sharply in recent years, with the growth of the literature on food security and food crisis.[12] But while it is now accepted by writers on farming systems and by some economists that small-scale African farmers try to minimize risk,[13] there has been less discussion of the implications of agricultural interventions for the distribution of risk, and of ways of developing rural economic systems which reduce farmers' risk. As work on the causes of famine (Sen, 1981) has demonstrated, people in the Third World face a particularly precarious time when older solidarity systems have broken down in the face of the market, yet wage workers and other individuals have no state-based social security system to provide a safety net. Michael Watts (1983) has made a similar point about farmers' vulnerability to famine in northern Nigeria, arguing that it was increased by colonial policy and market development which weakened an earlier 'moral economy' centred on the reduction of individual risk. This book explores this territory further, examining changes in the economic organization of both farming and domestic life which can weaken food production permanently while steering social relations and expectations irreversibly towards an individualized dependence on the market: a slow but cumulative shift in the class composition of the society.

Many millions of African rural people are caught in a pattern of life half-way between integration into small-scale, partially monetized farming systems and individual dependence on the market. The latest wave of prescriptions for African rural development – centred on the freeing of markets (IBRD, 1981) – still does no justice to the complexity and precariousness of the farmers' situation, nor to their own responses to increased risk. *How* the market develops is as important as *whether* it develops: if it undermines non-monetary economic solidarity without raising productivity, then it may make the farmers' situation markedly worse. This book is an attempt to understand one major intervention in farmers' lives – which certainly widened the scope of the market – from the perspective of those most at risk.

The Bud estates, which for a few years (including one of the worst Sahelian droughts) offered an extraordinary spectacle of hundreds of hectares of green amid the brown of the Senegalese dry season, also offer a near caricature of the way in which international capital can shift its risks and benefit from its bankruptcies. The European holding company lost some of its small invested capital but emerged from the wreckage having built up a new European broking firm on the basis of handling the Bud Senegal produce, and ready to seek new African sites to begin again.[14] The Senegalese government lost large quantities of finance it could ill afford. But the people who adapted their lives to try to survive on the basis of the Bud work lost most. Their arguments and explanations as to why, if Bud left, they would find themselves worse off than before formed the starting point for the research in this book.

Notes

1. Dinham and Hines (1983) catalogue commercial schemes in Africa; Swainson (1980) discusses corporate agricultural projects in Kenya; irrigated agricultural schemes in Sudan, Nigeria and northern Senegal are discussed in Heyer *et al.* (1981); the expansion of contracting schemes in Africa is discussed in Watts (1986); investment by international institutions in the search for the African 'Green

Revolution' is outlined in Eicher and Baker (1982); the 'Berg Report' (IBRD, 1981) began a series of World Bank papers promoting market-oriented solutions for African agriculture; Comité Information Sahel (1974) catalogued the rush of private overseas investment into agricultural and ranching schemes during the Sahel drought of the early 1970s.

2. Critiques of the impact of rural development initiatives in Africa include Heyer *et al.* (1981), Richards (1985); popular concern over their effects on local food production was stimulated by Lappé and Collins (1977), Burbach and Flynn (1980), George (1976), Dinham and Hines (1983), Comité Information Sahel (1974). See Chapter 1.

3. For example, Price Gittinger (1982); for a critique of the narrowness of such assessment, see Gentil and Dufumier (1984). See Chapter 2.

4. This was true for example of the project studied here, of many of the farming and ranching projects put forward in Senegal in the mid-1970s, and of a number of large farming projects in Nigeria (Wallace, 1981).

5. Pioneers in analysing interventions from the farmers' side in West Africa include Adams (1981), Richards (1986).

6. Feder (1977) describes horticultural production in Mexico for the US market. The quotations are from the author's discussions with Bud management, 1975–77.

7. Recent examples include Low (1986), and Eicher and Baker (1982:47). Anthropological attacks include Gastellu (1978), Richards (1986). See Chapter 2.

8. West African migration has a huge literature (Amin 1978, Colvin 1981, Lindsay 1985): for Senegal see Chapter 7; for a recent analysis of the effects of migration in Niger see Painter (1987).

9. Discussion with Bud management, 1975.

10. Bud Antle resisted unionization by the UFW and was a pioneer of harvest mechanization. See Friedland *et al.* (1978), Fredericks (1978), and Chapters 1 and 9 of this book.

11. For contracting in fruit and vegetable production see Mackintosh (1977) and Watts (1986). See also Chapter 9.

12. For example, Eicher (1984), IBRD (1986), Sen (1981), Lawrence (1986); see Chapter 1.

13. Lipton (1968) was an early theorist of risk minimization by peasants; Richards (1985) has analysed risk spreading by African farmers and its implications for the adoption of technology; see also Richards (1986), Chambers (1983).

14. The reappearance of Bud in Nigeria is discussed in Jackson (1979) and Horton (1986); see Chapter 9.

1. Commercial Agriculture and West African Farming: Profiting from Crisis

Commercial Agriculture before Independence

There was nothing new, for Senegalese farmers in the 1970s, in external commercial pressures, nor in production or labour for cash. West African farmers were accustomed to produce for exchange and to travel in search of land and work. The big agricultural projects of the 1970s, of which the firm studied in this book is an example, formed merely a new phase in the development, under external pressure, of commercial agriculture in West Africa. This book examines, through a case study, the extent to which the pressures of the 1970s created new problems and insecurities for West Africa's rural producers.

A brief background will set the discussion which follows in context.[1] Elaborate trading networks existed in West Africa long before European colonialism. Short distance trade allowed the exchange of crops, animal products and fish between different West African societies before the eighteenth century. In long distance trade across the Sahara and the Atlantic, the agricultural goods which circulated before the nineteenth century were limited to costly, non-perishable goods such as kola nuts, cloth, leather goods, gum, and later palm oil. Most trade was non-agricultural: in gold, weapons, ivory and people (slaves). It was the European-run Atlantic slave trade which transformed the balance of power between West Africa and those who traded with it.

The devastating effects of the slave trade, which undermined the viability of some West African economies while strengthening the centralization of power within other West African states, were followed in the nineteenth century by the rapid spread of commercial agriculture. In most of West Africa, unlike large parts of central, eastern and southern Africa, this did not take the primary form of European settler colonization, but depended rather on the rapid spread of small-scale indigenous production of cash crops. Pushed along by a mixture of force, taxation and commercial incentives, this cash cropping transformed the relation between African farmers and the market, and provided the profits exacted by European commercial and political domination.

Enormous changes in economic and social organization resulted. As transport improved, and the new crops spread, large-scale migrations began from the interior of the subcontinent to the coastal areas; the migrants provided labour for local farmers, and grew their own crops as 'strange farmers'. The groundnut, palm, and cocoa exports from the Senegambia, Ghana and Nigeria all drew on these migratory labour flows.

Before the establishment of colonial government in West Africa at the end of the nineteenth century, these local crops were bought, processed and resold by European merchant companies operating in West African coastal trading centres. After the imposition of colonial rule at the end of the century, exports of groundnuts, palm products, coffee and cocoa grew rapidly, dominating the export income of most West African states, including Senegal, up to Independence and beyond.

As well as providing sources of raw materials and profits for European firms, these export crops supported through customs revenues and taxes the costs of colonial government, including some investment, especially in transport, to open up new areas for cash cropping. Following these transport links inland, the expatriate trading firms turned themselves through expansion and amalgamation into huge limited companies – of which the most famous is the United Africa Company – and expanded into the inland trading centres, often wielding as much political and more economic power than the colonial administrations. As towns grew, farmers specialized more, the scale and range of food crops as well as local artisanal work declined, and local market networks developed.

At each major economic recession in the nineteenth and early twentieth centuries, as crop prices and supply fell, the Europeans began to consider settler plantations on the subcontinent. In West Africa however, these were rarely viable – Liberia is the only major exception – and were quite rapidly abandoned. In Sierra Leone, Senegal and even the Ivory Coast expatriate plantations were generally short-lived; major irrigation schemes promoted by colonial governments, such as the *Office du Niger* and the Volta River project, showed themselves to be badly planned and unprofitable.[2]

Senegal before Independence

The agricultural history of Senegal before Independence followed the pattern just described.[3] Senegal is a small country on the far western tip of Africa. Most of the country's land area, north of The Gambia, is semi-arid; the single wet season brings a rainfall which varies from 200mm in the far north to about 1000mm near the border with The Gambia; the southern Casamance area is much wetter. The far north is the true Sahel, with an economy based until the coming of cash crops on millet, sorghum, and transhumant[4] cattle keeping; the south supports rice paddies and forests. In the central, sandy savannah area – much more wooded and with more ground water than is now to be seen – and in the south, small-scale farmers working with hand implements developed, like their counterparts in Ghana and Nigeria, a major export crop.

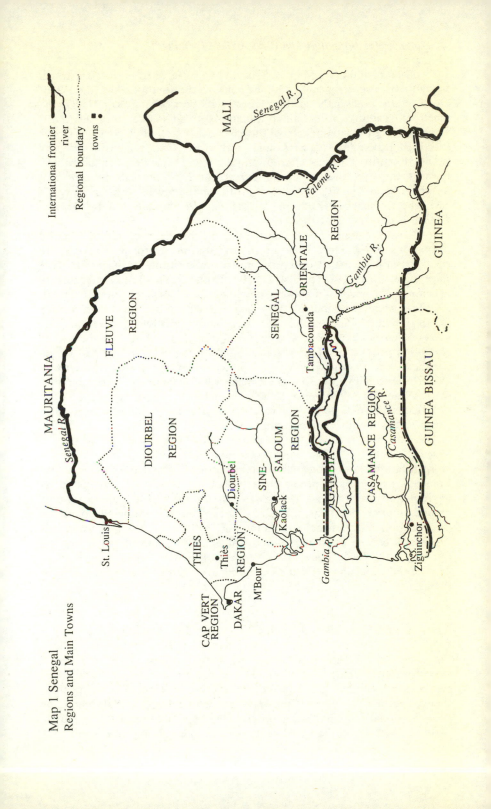

Map 1 Senegal
Regions and Main Towns

A coastal country (see Map 1), Senegal had suffered from the slave trade, though not as severely as the Guinea coast to the south; Dakar (the Isle of Gorée) and St Louis in the north were both slave ports. In the second half of the nineteenth century, groundnut production spread inland from the coast, attracting migrant labourers from the east to the 'groundnut basin' of Cayor (north of Dakar towards St Louis), and to the Casamance. In the early twentieth century the areas of groundnut cropping expanded with the railway towards the east and, as in the forest zones of the subcontinent, big merchant/industrial firms built their profits on the new harvests: in Senegal's case, the *Compagnie Française de l'Afrique Occidentale* and the *Société Commerciale de l'Ouest Africaine*.

As elsewhere, attempts before and during the colonial era to establish settler plantations were a failure. In the north near St Louis, cotton plantations were tried by the French in the nineteenth century as a substitute for the profits of the slave trade. (Barry, 1972: 201, 241ff.) The 'labour problem' cited so frequently in colonial documents – that is, the unwillingness of local inhabitants to work under the conditions and for the wages offered – was a central reason for failure, though not the only one. Similarly, in the early twentieth century, the success of groundnut production by small farmers ruled out an incentive to plantation production. The crop expanded throughout the first half of the twentieth century, sales rising by 7.7 per cent per year in the 1950s (Amin, 1970:1). Already by the 1920s an estimated 60–70,000 people were migrating for each annual rainy season to the groundnut fields of Senegal and the Gambia, establishing a migration pattern which lasted long after Independence and is part of the story this book has to tell.

Revenues from groundnuts were therefore the basis of the colonial state in Senegal. From the 1930s, and especially from 1945, there were some reorganizations in the economic system but no fundamental change. Some French firms began to produce groundnut oil in Senegal, stimulated by metropolitan preference; a *Caisse de Stabilisation* was set up to support groundnut prices (Hopkins, 1973: 285). The soil fertility was being reduced by deforestation and over-cropping in the north of the country, and groundnut production became concentrated in the Sine Saloum, spreading east with the railway. After 1945, a measure of technical change began in groundnut production, with animal traction beginning to spread slowly, and some use of fertilizers.

Drought and Commercial Agriculture after Independence

The pattern of agricultural and economic change just traced – of commercial agriculture developing as a complex response to outside pressures – was continued after Independence in West Africa. But the form of those pressures changed according to shifts in the organization of agro-industrial capital, the prices of primary commodities in different markets, and the relative economic position of Africa in the world economy. As international recession in the pre-colonial and colonial period had brought pressure for large-scale, settler-run agriculture, so the new recession and the drought and famine of the 1970s brought new pressure for large-scale agricultural intervention.

Senegal, with the rest of colonial French West Africa, became independent in 1960. Except in Guinea, which had voted in 1958 not to remain within de Gaulle's 'Franco-African Community',[5] Independence brought few immediate changes to the economic organization of these countries. In Senegal, over 80 per cent of the country's export revenue in the early 1960s came from the groundnut crop. The decade saw little agricultural diversification, and few mineral discoveries of any importance.

The food supply problems of later years were already posed in embryo in 1960, with the pattern of exchanging groundnuts for basic food well established in rural areas and internationally. Dakar, the capital of colonial French West Africa, was already in 1961 a city of about 400,000 people, about 13 per cent of the Senegalese population.[6] Senegal's imports in 1962 included 200,000 tons[7] of rice to feed the city and reduce the food deficit in rural areas. The imports of rice had begun in the 1930s, from what was then Indo China.[8] A taste for bread, produced from imported wheat, had also been developed by the French, and in the early 1970s one could find bread stalls in numerous roadside villages.[9]

In the first decade of Independence a crisis of agricultural and economic policy developed in Senegal;[10] as for other West African governments, that crisis came to a head in the late 1960s and early 1970s, when a series of drought years set in, coinciding in the 1970s with international recession. Like others in West Africa, the Senegalese government reacted by mounting a search for agricultural diversification and reorganization, looking particularly at the large-scale agricultural projects put forward by private capital and international funding agencies as the drought continued.[11]

The Senegalese economic crisis of the early 1970s was rooted in stagnant production and falling real incomes in the countryside, and in changes in international trading relations. For the Senegalese administration, the crisis took the form more particularly of financial and economic policy problems resulting from the agricultural crisis.

The view from Dakar is summarized in the three trends shown by Figure 1.1. Groundnut sales to the state had stagnated after the peak years of the 1960s, and then gone into precipitous decline after 1965. This decline was not primarily because of the drought. The 1968 rains were poor, and both groundnut sales and estimated millet production had declined. In 1969, however, only cereal production appeared to have recovered: groundnut deliveries continued their downward slide. The data strongly suggested a withdrawal by small farmers from planting groundnuts, increasing instead their millet and sorghum, the main food crops. This impression in Dakar was strongly reinforced when in 1970, another year of poor rains, food production appeared to have dropped back no further than its 1968 level, while groundnut sales plummeted to 450,000 tonnes, by far their lowest level for a decade.

Estimates of food crop production are notoriously unreliable in Africa (Harriss, 1979; Berry, 1984). But the figures show the trends as they appeared to

Figure 1.1
Senegal: Sources of economic crisis 1961-1971

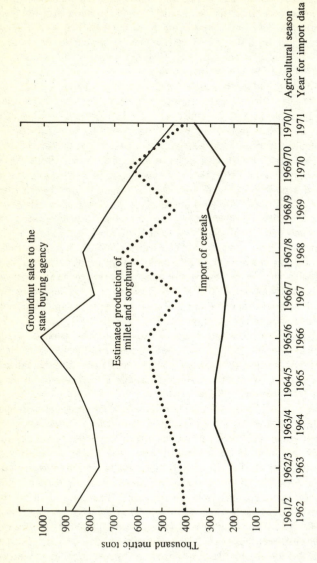

Source:Le Sénégal en Chiffres (1976)

the Dakar administration, backed up by more political evidence. By 1970, the Senegalese farmers were making it clear that the drop in groundnut production was not merely a risk-averting strategy – concentrating first on food crops in the face of the worsening drought – but also a reaction to falling real prices for groundnuts. The government was the monopoly purchaser of groundnuts through a system of 'co-operatives' which were essentially buying agencies. Over the 1960s, it had reduced cash prices to the co-operatives from 22 francs c.f.a.[12]/kilo in 1961 to less than 18f. in 1968, through a period of rising prices for goods purchased by farmers.[13] By 1970, these prices were being criticized fiercely by farmers on the rural radio station, *Disoo*, and religious leaders of the groundnut growers were threatening revolt. The *malaise paysan*[14] represented by farmers' growing, and organized, anger at falling real incomes and rising indebtedness was by 1970 a major subject of political discussion in the capital.

The trends in production and imports in Figure 1.1 therefore summarize the economic trap which the Senegalese government felt itself to be falling into in 1971. Groundnut growing, 70–80 per cent of export revenue up to 1968, was in sharp decline, bringing in only 36 per cent of export receipts in 1971. Estimated food production was rising too slowly in the face of population growth of over 2 per cent per year, was at the expense of groundnuts, and was threatened by drought. Furthermore, soil erosion, long-term desertification, and severe pressure on farming land in some areas were adding to the crisis. Food imports were rising, to over 360,000 tons in 1971. Worse still, export prices for groundnuts had dropped in 1968, when Senegal lost its protected market in France. Thereafter, the chronic balance of trade deficit had worsened sharply. Finally, the groundnut decline threatened government finances: the state monopoly of purchase and resale of the crop yielded a margin, nominally held in a stabilization fund but, as one commentator put it, 'rapidly absorbed by the running costs of national administration' (D. Cruise O'Brien, 1979: 219). The agricultural crisis was producing economic crisis for the Dakar bureaucracy.

This pattern was not unique to Senegal. Many West African countries, including Ghana and Nigeria, Niger and Mali, had seen cash crops and government revenues from them decline, and estimated food production at best stagnate, while food imports rose. And in all those countries, the drought culminating in the famine of 1973 brought the crisis to a head, while focusing the eyes of the world on the problem. That the drought was effect of past agricultural policies, as well as cause of new problems, is undoubted; the famine, similarly, was no act of nature but the result of the way the existing economic and political systems and the aid donors handled the crisis.[15] While food production fell, it was the cattle-herding peoples who were the first to starve. The ecological causes and disastrous consequences for the local population of the Sahel drought are outside the scope of this book, though the long-term development of food production and distribution systems is a major theme. It is the impact of the drought and economic crisis on the government's agricultural policy which particularly concerns us here: the argument of this book is that the new agricultural policies, in one major case at least, represented another turn of the screw in Senegal's food crisis.

By the early 1970s the solution to Senegal's production and trade crisis was thought in Dakar to lie in a reorientation of rural development strategy. This would take the form of crop diversification away from groundnuts to more food crops and new exports. The route to this diversification was thought to lie in large-scale agricultural projects with foreign inputs and finance, especially large irrigation schemes.

This was a big shift in forms of agricultural intervention. Up to this time the independent government had continued the colonial strategy largely unchanged, apart from increased state control of purchasing and transformation of groundnuts. Agricultural extension centres and particularly the groundnut co-operatives provided some technical assistance. The co-operatives gave credit for seeds, and for animal-drawn hoes, seeders and carts, all repaid in kind. Cotton was promoted in the 1960s by an extension scheme involving credit and purchasing. Market gardening, the only other cash crop of any importance in the 1960s, expanded on small-scale plots supplying the demand of the towns, and virtually without state assistance or interference. Even the groundnut resettlement schemes – to settle farmers from the crowded groundnut basin on the *Terres Neuves*[16] further east – involved only the provision of sites, services and financial incentives.

The new direction in rural development policy in the 1970s, however, was much more interventionist. Under the then Minister of Rural Development, Mr Habib Thiam, the 'industrial' option in agricultural development found favour.[17] This option meant a number of different things: an estate using wage labour, a large-scale project based on the close control of work carried out by either smallholders or wage labourers, an irrigation project, a project where the output was planned for local industrial transformation. The early experiments in this type of agricultural change in Senegal took the form of large irrigated projects in the Senegal River valley in the north of the country. These were designed to produce sugar cane, tomatoes, rice and wheat by a mixture of wage labour and closely controlled small-scale farming by resettled farmers, financed by a mixture of public and private funds. The SOCAS project, for example, was approved in 1971: it involved direct tomato production by the canning firm, plus purchase of tomatoes from farmers, organized in co-operatives for marketing and managed by SAED, a large public agency which developed and managed the irrigated areas on which the farmers were settled. Similarly, the Richard Toll sugar cane plantation, a private estate using wage labour, began its first plantings in 1973.

The essence of the 'industrial option', then, was a very sharp increase in intervention, by government and private capital, to manage and transform the labour process in agriculture.[18] Farmers who up to then had retained some power of decision over their farming practices would find themselves incorporated into large projects. Whether they were now classed as farmers or wage labourers, they would find that control of the land, technology and inputs, and management power in general, was retained at the level of the project as a whole. Farmers had previously had little control over prices, but much power of decision over crop mix, area planted, proportion sold, labour use, technology, and planting dates. The aim of the new agricultural strategy was to remove all those latter powers in the interests, it was argued, of higher food production for the cities, and higher production for export. The main recurrent criticism which would be levelled against these proposals was that it was not in the cities that people starved, and that the projects threatened to put these aims, and private profit, above the interests of the rural producers themselves.

These new agricultural development proposals issued from a convergence of two trends: the focusing of international attention on the Sahel, as a result of the drought, and the changes in the international economy then facing Africa. The post-war period had seen the increasing concentration of agro-industrial capital within a number of powerful 'agribusiness' firms.[19] Some of them old plantation companies, some food processing firms or agricultural broking firms integrating or diversifying backwards, some non-agricultural companies diversifying into corporate farming, these big firms represented concentration of control over international agricultural markets in fewer hands. At the same time, the scale of international trade in agricultural goods was rising rapidly, as Third World countries expanded food imports and the US increased subsidy for its food exports. While some of this trade was in food grains and long established plantation crops, other companies were developing production and trade in the new long distance, 'luxury' crops and products, such as meat, fresh fruit and vegetables, and flowers.

These firms had been developing new agro-industrial projects in the Third World, including Africa, through the 1960s. But the African drought gave new impetus to their interest in Africa. They proposed a large number of new large-scale commercial farming activities for the African savannah lands. In this, they were supported and abetted by another group of growing post-war international economic agencies: the multilateral and big bi-lateral 'aid' agencies and development funds.

Many of these agencies have located an important part of their role in forming partnerships with international capital in agricultural development, and in promoting private capital in Third World agriculture. In the African drought regions of the 1970s, institutions such as the International Finance Corporation, the arm of the World Bank set up to promote private capital investment, and US AID played midwife to a wide range of new large-scale agricultural schemes proclaimed as the answer to Africa's problems of low productivity agriculture, foreign exchange shortage, and hunger. And it was not only the Senegalese government which looked at these schemes with interest and even enthusiasm. The schemes included huge cattle-ranching projects in Senegal, Burkina Faso (then Upper Volta) and Mali, enormous dam construction and river basin development schemes in Nigeria and Senegal, new plantation-style export crop projects in Senegal and Niger, cotton-growing projects in Francophone Africa. The list is long, and a large number of these 'projects' were financed by a mixture of African government, aid and private sources with the aid agencies putting the projects together and acting as intermediaries. In addition to the profit motive, another motive emerged clearly at the time from the Western European governments and, especially, the US: in this period of upheaval in the Middle East, and threat to the West's oil supplies. West Africa took on a new strategic importance because of its generally pro-Western governments and its geographical location.

International Horticulture and Market Gardening in Senegal

Of the international firms looking for new footholds in Africa in the late 1960s and 1970s, the promoters of export horticulture, along with the ranchers, stand out as proposing new major products for export. Increasing international trade in both products was the result of rising incomes in Europe, and of better storage on cheaper international transport. Both were to create very serious problems for the ecology and economy of the West African areas where they were tried.

The arrival of export horticulture in Africa had its roots in the transformation of horticulture in Europe after the Second World War. That most local and small-scale of crops, fresh fruit and vegetables, was rapidly transformed into international agribusiness.[20] To the Northern European consumer, the most visible evidence of the transformation included more standardized produce, the replacement of local markets with large retail stores, the drop in seasonality of vegetables and the availability of southern European and other produce brought from long distances, and the rise of frozen produce. The latest addition is irradiation to lengthen 'shelf life'.

Lying behind these familiar changes is an enormous transformation in the fresh produce industry, turning it from a local industry – with a few 'tropical' crops such as bananas – into an international business. The business has seen enormous amounts of investment and a struggle, between farmers and those who buy and sell their produce, for control of production and accumulation. On the whole, the brokers and big retailers have won this struggle in Europe, and the outcome has consequences for Third World farmers.

Investment in horticulture has concentrated on trying to reduce the high risks of the trade, especially from the perishability of the produce. Investors who can reduce this risk gain a greatly increased market size. Innovations include the iceberg lettuce, developed in California, which stays crisp far longer than ordinary lettuce. Then there are all the changes in irrigation, glasshouse production, mechanization, pesticides and packaging which allow control over the look of the product – not to mention the continuing search for the square tomato which can be picked by machine!

In addition, the development of low temperature storage, freezing, and cheaper, faster transport increased market size and scale economies in handling. As a result of all these changes, there was a sharp increase in concentration and a rise in the average size of firms, as the large international firms in processing, broking and retailing competed for market dominance. Big freezers and canners, like Nestlé, Unilever and Libby McNeil began to plan production for a Europe-wide market. Brokers specialized more, and as international communications continued to improve they increasingly bought and sold sight-unseen, bypassing physical wholesale markets altogether. Sharp concentration in retailing created the giant buying power of firms like Sainsbury or Tesco.

All these firms started to compete for 'captive' sources of reliable supply, to provide them with competitive advantage over their rivals. They invested in farming, and retained the return from the investment by eroding the market relations with farmers in favour of some form of vertical integration: either corporate farming (still relatively rare in Europe, but not in the US), or forms of tight forward contracting which transfer decision making from farmer to buyer, and sometimes leave the farmer as a mere 'labour-only' subcontractor. The resultant transformation in European farming is visible in the south of France (where farmers fought off the threat of corporate takeover by Libby's, only to find themselves subcontractors instead), in Friesland in the Netherlands, and in East Anglia. The contracting tentacles also spread to many parts of Eastern Europe.

In the 1960s they were also spreading to the Third World. Like the labour-intensive manufacturing industries, the buyers of fruit and vegetables began looking for cheaper labour, cheaper sources of supply. The 1960s saw a sharp relocation of horticultural production towards the European fringe and the Third World, where labour costs were lower and farmers could resist less effectively, having fewer alternative sources of income and less influence upon weaker national states. Big processors such as Heinz developed supply sectors, through contracting, in Portugal, Greece, Turkey and Morocco; Heinz and Findus shifted supply locations of hand-picked crops to Eastern Europe, and began to look to Africa as a promising source further afield. The pattern is paralleled by the US processers buying through contract from Central America.

In fresh produce broking a similar though fragmentary picture emerged of an active search for new sources of supply. Some overseas supplies came from dealing with state marketing boards, for example those of Israel and Morocco, and some from foreign farmers producing in Kenya, Zambia and elsewhere. But elements within European broking capital were following the US lead and trying to establish their own captive sources, through investment in the Third World. Like the US strawberry brokers whose activities in Mexico were investigated by Ernest Feder (1977), European brokers tried to find backyard 'gardens' for Europe in Africa. In the 1970s, schemes for the export production under irrigated conditions of winter fruits and vegetables for Europe were developed in Nigeria, Senegal, Mali and Upper Volta (Burkina Faso), as well as in southern Africa. This book investigates the implications of one such scheme, organized by a European produce broker, in Senegal.

In developing African sources of supply, the produce brokers behaved as the discussion above predicts: they sought to establish control of the production process. The reorganization of European horticulture had been the concomitant of centralization and accumulation of capital in the industrial and commercial firms: now the same process was extended to the Third World. But here, the brokers and processers faced farmers in an especially weak position after the years of relative drought which began in the Sahel in 1968 and culminated in the famine of 1973. Furthermore, because investment and control operated across national boundaries, the actions of the African states became crucial to the fate of the farmers: and these states too, as already demonstrated, had been weakened by the drought years and the impact through agriculture on their finances. This was a situation which the European firms could exploit. It was not 'market gardening' which they sought to develop, but organized production of standardized crops for a monopoly buyer, eroding the market relation.

The 'House of Bud'

In all these changes, Bud Antle of Salinas, California was a pioneer.[21] Until 1978, Bud Antle was a private, family-owned firm, which had begun by wholesaling produce and integrated backwards into estate farming, specializing in lettuce for the US market. The firm has a reputation for technical innovation, as well as for determined resistance to organization by the UFW in the 1970s. At the end of the 1960s it began to branch out, first into marketing Dominican bananas in the US, and then into produce dealing in Europe. Its European and African operations – regarded as somewhat 'maverick' at first by established dealers – were marked from the start by its American style. From its 1970 announcement that it 'expects to have 10 per cent of the US banana market in the very near future' to its conception of Senegal as the future California of Africa, the tone was consistent, the forecasts (to put it mildly) optimistic.

Bud moved into the European market by lending its name to, and taking a small proportion of the shares in a broking firm called The House of Bud S.A.[22] When the firm was set up in 1968, the majority of the shares were owned by an established German produce broker. The original aim was to import and distribute US produce in Europe, working from Delft, a centre of the European import trade. According to a manager of the firm, sea transport costs made these imports unprofitable, and in order to establish itself the firm began looking around for new sources of winter produce closer to Europe – such as West Africa.

Bud was attempting to break into a highly competitive sector of European commerce. Commercial capital in horticulture consists of those firms who buy in order to resell: wholesalers, retailers, importers, brokers (the categories overlap). The physical markets in fruit and vegetables have declined in importance relative to buying and selling on description alone, through the telephone and the telex. The size of firms has grown, and Europe has become a single market. In the 1970s there was most concentration – that is, the fewest firms relative to market size – in the import trade, especially in the off-season trade in long distance imports.

This off-season trade was regarded as 'difficult' by traders, recognizing the high-risk factors: it needs specialist knowledge of crops and overseas growers, means dealing with difficult long distance transport, and involves selling to the choosy 'luxury' end of the trade. The relatively few specialist importers – used even by big retailers who in Europe increasingly buy straight from producers – resisted new entrants. Hence the importance for a new importing firm of developing a captive source of supply. The House of Bud took the view that it could steal a march on competing importers, who thought dealing with African farmers 'more trouble than it's worth', by integrating backwards, as its American parent had done, and developing African supplies on which to base its business ambitions.

Bud in Senegal

Two Bud directors set off for Africa in 1970 in search of production sites. They rejected most of North Africa ('the government owns everything there', as one manager put the problem, objecting especially to extensive government control of marketing) and thus arrived in the Republic of Senegal, 'the first country [they] came to' as they went south. Senegal appeared to fulfil all their requirements: good climate in the European winter months, sea and air communications, and an existing small market gardening sector which suggested favourable growing conditions. And the government was amenable to foreign direct investment and in need of export diversification.

From the start Bud behaved in Senegal as a hybrid: a commercial multinational in some contexts, and in others a 'development project', drawing on aid funds. The feasibility studies were funded by the FED (*Fonds Européens de Développement*), the European Community Development Fund. After a year of experimental production, funded by Bud, on a 60 hectare[23] site near Dakar, the agreement was signed in 1972 establishing the firm of Bud Senegal. The primary purpose of the firm, stated in the agreement, was to produce fruit and vegetables for export, on sites of up to 3,600 hectares; in addition the firm agreed to contribute to the development of existing market gardening by technical assistance and the purchase of produce for export.[24]

The structure of the firm was designed to keep down the risks to the House of Bud, while maintaining control of production and sale. The House of Bud ('HOBSA') subscribed a bare majority of the equity (51 per cent), entirely consisting of the capitalized costs of the experimentation in varieties and growing conditions already undertaken. The rest of the share capital was put up by the Senegalese state (29 per cent) and by the World Bank in the shape of the International Finance Corporation (20 per cent). HOBSA retained managerial control, the Managing Director of Bud Senegal being the largest shareholder in HOBSA.

In addition, Bud Senegal was given the most favourable terms available for foreign firms operating in Senegal, plus a further concession of its own. The company could import freely, without licence and free from tax, capital goods and raw materials. It was exempt from export tax, was to pay no profit tax for five years from the date of its first export sales, and was permitted accelerated write-off for its capital equipment. Free movement of capital and repatriation of profit were guaranteed. And, particularly important, the marketing agreement gave HOBSA sole rights in Europe as sales agents of Bud Senegal, with a commission of 10 per cent on gross sales.

Next, Bud Senegal was given access to Senegalese natural resources on subsidized terms. Large land concessions were given to the company for periods of five years, renewable, virtually free of charge. Water (a very scarce resource in Senegal, especially as the drought years wore on) was to be sold to the company at a rate lower than that charged to small-scale market gardeners and other consumers. The state also undertook to provide infrastructure for the firm: water for certain sites, and electricity, either by links to the national grid or in the form of generating plant. Many of these investments were to be repaid by the company to the state over a number of years, in line with the depreciation agreement; the company thus kept its initial fixed investments to a minimum. A few were not to be reimbursed but to remain state property: for example, the road and electricity links for the first main site.

Finally, there was a major gap in the agreement: there were no conditions covering the training of Senegalese nationals. As late as 1975, one of the Bud managers commented in an interview that up to that time the training of Senegalese for supervisory and junior management positions had been almost non-existent.

In summary, HOBSA, through a small equity contribution (the total initial capital was only 66 million francs c.f.a., or approximately £100,000), had gained complete economic control of Bud Senegal. The free hand they obtained, and the vertical integration with a monopoly seller, are more characteristic of colonial plantation enterprise or 'free zone' export processing,[25] than of a joint development venture between a national state and a foreign commercial company, based on local resources and aimed at building up a new local export industry. The agreement gave HOBSA – as managers, importers of inputs, and monopoly dealers in the output – the maximum ability to manipulate the balance sheet of the Senegalese enterprise through transfer pricing,[26] to the benefit of their European company, should they so wish. Thus the Senegalese government had signed away virtually all levers of economic control over the firm, despite the heavy financial and resource commitment. The agreement might be used as a case study demonstrating how not to negotiate with a foreign investor. The financial, economic and political consequences of the agreement for the Senegalese state and the other shareholders are examined later in this book.

Wage Labour and Smallholdings in Senegalese Market Gardening

The justification offered by Bud and the Senegalese goverment for favourable treatment of Bud Senegal was that the structure of the agreement allowed the new project to avoid a number of familiar problems of commercial viability.

Export horticulture was, rightly, perceived as a high-risk crop, whose profitability depended heavily on quality, price and timing of sales, and hence on control of production and good marketing. The HOBSA connection was therefore intended to ensure effective selling; the American Bud Antle connection to provide modern technology; the IFC connection to ensure financial strength. As a result Bud, it was argued, would provide the impetus for an agricultural transformation: the agreement was seen by some as a recognition that, as even one of Bud's opponents within the Senegalese administration put it, 'nevertheless, [Bud] has allowed us to understand the importance and potential of market gardening in Senegal'. It was also a statement of faith in top-down transformation of small-scale agriculture in Africa.

Up to the arrival of Bud, horticulture, or 'market gardening', was not seen by the Senegalese government as a major potential source of exports, nor as a candidate for the 'industrial option'. Vegetables were grown for market on two types of plots. First, a range of local vegetables was grown on small plots, alongside cereals and other cash crops, for home consumption and for sale in small local markets. These included cherry tomatoes, local sour aubergines (called *jaxatu* in Wolof,[27]) and a type of sorrel (*bissap*).

Second, the whole range of vegetables familiar to Europeans was being grown in the dense network of rural smallholdings (discussed later in this book) which surrounds Dakar in the rural Cap Vert,[28] and which runs north up the coast through the area called the *niayes*. In this belt of land a high water table allows gardening in damp depressions behind the coastal sand dunes for most of the year. Most of these vegetables were being sold on urban markets by traders who circulated through the *niayes* buying the crops. Apart from potatoes and onions, bought by the state through the co-operative network, there was no regulation of fruit and vegetable markets. The gardeners might join a co-operative and grow a few groundnuts in order to obtain, for example, a cart. Otherwise, they purchased their inputs and sold their output through the urban market, and the sector had grown without state assistance.

Bud's arrival radically changed the Senegalese government's plans for the crop, to the alarm of the market gardeners. Bud was being given, in effect, the task of fitting the gardeners into the industrial option. The plans envisaged nucleus estates, using wage labour and mechanized cultivation over large areas to build up rapidly to high enough volumes for profitable export. These were later to become the focus for managed outgrower (contracting) schemes, and extension work with and purchase from existing gardeners. The volumes of exports envisaged by HOBSA were ambitious: 100,000 tons by 1977/78. (Exports in 1971 were 3,335 tons). At 1971 vegetable prices, the 100,000 tons would have meant a gross export income of 6,600 million francs c.f.a., which was more than half the value of the 1971 groundnut exports. Hence, the Senegalese government was hoping for a radical diversification of exports when it signed the 1972 agreement.

This was presumably the reason why the government originally allotted to Bud a quasi-governmental role within the market gardening sector. The new agricultural development strategy for Senegal in the 1970s included giving to large agricultural project development agencies, with outside funding, not merely control over projects, but also *overall* hegemony over agricultural development within their areas. Irrigated farming, managed by SAED in the Senegal River valley, was an example of this approach (Adams, 1981). Bud was being offered a similar role in the western coastal areas where market gardening was the main crop: the 'industrial option', in other words, was becoming partly a corporate-based agricultural development strategy, with Bud straddling the role of private company and 'development agency'.

The existing market gardeners were alarmed by these plans, because they saw their independence and their profits potentially vanishing to the benefit of a corporate-government agency. They were worried both by the proposals for big estates, which they were convinced would take over land and flood urban markets, putting them out of business, and by the proposals to incorporate them into 'outgrower' schemes, which would reduce their independence, and make them more subject to effective taxation. The consequences of state intervention in groundnut growing, just traced, reinforced their fears that they would lose from any such proposals to control the market gardening sector. Up to the 1970s, market gardening, where land was suitable, was a substantially more profitable use of labour in small-scale farming than was groundnut growing (see Chapters 3–5 and 7).

Bud appears to have been given by the government a choice of estates or outgrower schemes. They chose to begin with wage labour estates, arguing that these would allow a more rapid build-up of sufficient volumes for profitable export. The volumes necessary to attract ships to stop at Dakar were quite large, and the management thought estates easier to set up from scratch. Later they intended to experiment with outgrower schemes in the hope of switching the bulk of production towards these: they thought them more politically acceptable, less likely to create labour problems, and better in promoting individual work incentives. The evidence of the experimental scheme which was set up after 1972 inclines one to add that contracting on managed small grower schemes would also allow the firm to lower labour costs by sidestepping minimum wage laws, of which the farm management complained constantly, and enforcing the use of unpaid household labour. The system would also allow the company to divert much of the managerial and financial risk to the small growers.

Given the history of commercial farming just discussed, one might have expected serious problems in establishing wage labour estates. Up to the 1970s estate agriculture based on wage labour had not been a success in Senegal. Cash cropping, whether migrant or settled, competed successfully with wage work. But by the 1970s, when Bud arrived, the conditions for labour force formation were substantially different. It is a measure of the decline in the returns from Senegalese small-scale agriculture relative to the payment for even seasonal agricultural wage labouring, that when Bud opened its two main estates, it found no difficulty in hiring a labour force: there were queues at the gates, especially at the larger farm which was closer to Dakar.

Bud, and initially some members of the Senegalese administration, attributed this ease of recruitment to the fact that Bud operated in the dry season. Senegal's rainy season, in the summer months, was regarded as too difficult for vegetable growing, when in any case prices in Europe were low: the Bud growing season, using drip and sprinkler irrigation systems, was to run from October to May, through the Senegalese dry season. Hence, it was argued, all Bud's operations were a net gain to the economy: providing seasonal work and production in an idle period of the year for those who spent the rainy season on their own farms.

Early doubts about this thesis of a pure net economic gain – doubts among farmers, gardeners and people working in rural extension – provided the initial motivation for this study. The research set out to assess the balance of gains and losses from the estates. The book concentrates particularly on the gains and losses to the farmers and wage workers, balancing in particular short-term cash gains against longer-term agricultural problems. In doing so it examines the detailed changes in gender and class relations which resulted from Bud's recruiting from local settled farmers and from the large numbers of desperate people which the drought and famine in the north of the country were bringing to the Dakar areas. While it is almost a commonplace that the provision of wage work can transform class structure, precisely how this occurs is much less widely studied in Africa than in either Europe or Latin America.[29] This book sets out, as the next chapter explains, to unpick one example of this transition process and to explain it for one African situation, by close attention to the – largely irreversible – changes in farming relations, and household and gender relations, which constitute a transition in class structure.

Notes

1. References for the pre-Independence economic history include: Hopkins (1973), Barry (1972), Suret-Canale (1964, 1972), Amin (1970, 1971a), Klein (1968, 1979), Curtin (1975), Rodney (1970), Meillassoux (1971), Helleiner (1966), Hill (1963), Diop (1965).

2. The Volta River project was designed under colonial rule (Hopkins, 1973: 284) but pursued only after Independence.

3. In addition to the reference in Note 1, material on Senegal before Independence is also taken from Pélissier (1966), Vanhaeverbeke (1970) and Diarrassouba (1968).

4. 'Transhumance' is the system whereby cattle drovers make long circuits of West Africa, following the grass north in the rainy season, and south as the land dries out.

5. The voting process and its implications for post-Independence policies in Francophone West Africa is discussed briefly in Crowder (1962) and Deschamps (1968).

6. The population of Senegal in 1961 was approximately four million; by 1985 it was about 6.5 million (*Le Sénégal en Chiffres*, 1976, République du Sénégal, 1985).

7. 'Tons' implies metric tons throughout unless otherwise stated.

8. This food dependence distinguishes Senegal from, e.g., Ghana, where Accra was fed more successfully from its hinterland before Independence (Hopkins, 1973: 245).

9. For a case study of the long-term implications of wheat dependence, see Andrae and Beckman (1985).

10. For the post-Independence agricultural and economic problems of Senegal, in addition to the previously cited references, see R. Cruise O'Brien (1979), Dumont (1972), IBRD (1974), D. Cruise O'Brien (1971, 1975), Amin (1971b, 1978), Reboul (1973), Gellar (1982), Gakou (1987) and the various official and statistical publications cited elsewhere in these notes.

11. On the Sahel drought, and the wave of proposed large-scale projects, see Copans, ed. (1975), Comité Information Sahel (1974), Dalby and Harrison Church (1973), Dalby *et al.* (1977), Ball (1976), Franke and Chasin (1980), Dinham and Hines (1983), Meillassoux (1974).

12. The franc 'c.f.a.' is the local currency of Senegal and most of Francophone West Africa. Tied to the French franc, it was and is worth F.Fr.0.02. References to 'francs' or 'f.' refer to the franc c.f.a. henceforth, unless qualified.

13. There were for this period no good estimates of consumer and producer goods prices facing farmers. An estimate based on the 'European' cost of living in Dakar would show inflation of over 30 per cent in total over the period 1961–1968. See also Gakou (1987: 68) on the fall in the producers' share in final groundnut prices.

14. The 'peasant troubles' of declining incomes and incipient revolt were analysed by Dumont (1972); see also Copans (1975) for a summary of farmers' views expressed on the radio; the religious leadership of resistance to groundnut policy is discussed in D. Cruise O'Brien (1975, 1979).

15. For the origins and handling of the drought and famine, see also Sen (1981).

16. The 'new lands' developed by the government for groundnut settlement, using animal traction, east of the old groundnut basin.

17. The phrase comes from a broadcast by the then President Senghor, which I heard in April 1976.

18. By 'labour process' I mean the organization, technical and social, of work. The phrase originates in the Marxist literature on industrial change; see, for example, Brighton Labour Process Group (1977).

19. By 'agribusiness' I mean corporate-owned, or corporate-run, farming. The literature is huge. See for example Horst (1974), Harle (1978), Turner (1973); for Africa see, for example, Dinham and Hines (1983), Swainson (1980); for the relation of food industry multinationals to the UN and development agencies, see George's (1976) description of the Industry Co-operative Programme, and for the firms' views see Lipton, ed. (1977).

20. The discussion of international horticulture is based on, among other references, Goldberg (1974), Lauret (1973), INRA (1974), Butterwick and Neville-Rolf (1968), Hinton and Housden (1973), Morrissey (1974), CENECA (1969), OECD (1974), Crubelier (1977), Montigaud (1975), LeBihan (1964), Lauret and Montigaud (1974a and b), Friedland *et al.* (1978); it also relies on journal literature, including the *Fruit Trades Journal, International Fruit World, Economic Review of Agriculture, Acta Horticulturae*, and the publications of the Tropical Products Institute in London. Finally, it draws on discussions in the 1970s with people who knew the trade well, including John Winter and Felicity Proctor of the Tropical Products Institute, Mr Koler of the Dutch Commodity Board for Fruit and

Vegetables, Mr van Pelt of Bud Holland in Delft, M. Aube of the Centre Technique Interprofessionel des Fruits et Légumes in Paris, and Jan Smit of Wageningen University; none of these people are responsible for my use of the information provided. A more detailed paper on this subject is Mackintosh (1977). The market situation for overseas exporters to Europe has recently been changed for the worse by the accession of Spain and Portugal to the EEC.

21. I owe my understanding of Bud Antle to the assistance of Bill Friedland (Friedland *et al.*, 1978, 1979), Anne Fredericks (1978), Robert Thomas, and Don Watson who took the trouble to send me material about the company and its labour relations.

22. 'S.A.' stands for *Société Anonyme*, limited company. This discussion of Bud's organization, aims and opinions, and the material on Bud's search for sites which follows, I owe to discussions with Bud and HOBSA managers between 1973 and 1977, in Senegal and Holland. Mr Marschall and Mr Gert Zee were particularly generous with assistance. The summary of the information is, of course, my own responsibility; direct quotations are from these interviews.

23. 1 hectare (ha.) = 2.471 acres.

24. Details of the Bud agreements are taken from discussions with Bud management and with Senegalese civil servants, from documents supplied by Bud management, and from agreements published in the *Journal Officiel de la République du Sénégal*; see also Catala (1977).

25. 'Free zone' processing refers to an overseas firm producing for export, generally in a designated zone in a Third World country, free of tariffs or restrictions on import or export of goods, and often in conditions where labour regulations are waived or weakened.

26. 'Transfer pricing' refers to the prices a vertically integrated firm charges itself for transfers of goods between processing stages or companies within the firm; these prices are frequently manipulated to avoid or reduce taxes and restrictions on profit repatriation.

27. Wolof is the local language which operates as a *lingua franca* throughout a large part of Senegal. It was used as the medium for many of the interviews, including many where the first language of the interviewee was not Wolof.

28. The Cap Vert is the Senegalese region which includes the capital city, Dakar. See Map 1.

29. For Latin America, see Goodman and Redclift (1981).

2. Estate Agriculture and Small-scale Farming: Analysing Impact and Transition

The Bud Estates and Senegalese Farmers

Wage labour estates can help to create their labour force by transforming the society around them; in the process they can undermine local agricultural systems, and increase the vulnerability of the rural population to food crisis. This book argues that these were the effects of the Bud estates in Senegal, and that this conclusion has implications for the way we analyse the impact of large agricultural projects elsewhere in Africa.

The Bud estates had this effect in Senegal because the employment they offered, the loss of land their presence imposed on rural communities, and the potential competition they offered to small growers, combined to *catalyse* longer-term changes in the economy and society of surrounding villages. The form these changes took depended of course on what had been happening before, and on how the villagers reacted, severally and collectively, to the new pressures. The future consequences of the changes depended on what other pressures came after Bud. But the villagers who were caught up in the Bud estate labour force could never simply return to where they were before; in that sense, the changes were long-term and irreversible.

This chapter begins by describing the Bud estates, and the scale of their immediate demands on land, labour and other Senegalese resources. It then examines some of the methodological problems of studying the effects of the estate, sets out the main theoretical concepts used to analyse change, and discusses the general conclusions which emerged from the research about organization and change in West African farming systems. This chapter therefore provides the basis for the detailed analysis of the impact of the estates in the Chapters which follow.

The impact of Bud came mainly from the two big estate farms. Bud never did come to dominate Senegalese market gardening as it had planned. Its experimental contracting scheme never found aid funds for expansion, and its buying scheme from small gardeners remained small-scale. These schemes may have had a longer-term impact on the fate of small gardeners, by demonstrating the potential profits from control of the sector. But the main influence on the rural economy came from the estates, established in 1972/3 and run by HOBSA, and later under government control, until the firm's bankruptcy in 1979.

Even on the estates. Bud came nowhere near its ambitions. It proposed to have 3.600 hectares under crops in six years. with virtually no local knowledge of production and labour. with almost all the infrastructure to be created (including water supplies in the midst of a very severe drought), with managers some of whom spoke very little French let alone local languages, and in a situation where some of the land the government had given them was occupied by Senegalese farmers. This was hopeless. In practice, two estates were established by 1975, with a total area of less than 600 hectares (Table 2.1, p. 43). But these were large enough to have a major impact.

Neither of the Bud estates was far from the capital city. The Baobab estate, so called after the forest of famously grotesque trees within which its land was cleared, was in the Cap Vert Region only 50 kilometres from Dakar (see map 2). From Bud's point of view this site offered several advantages: close to the port and airport, with good road communications, a climate cooler in the dry season than any of the sites further east, and a clay soil which was also felt to be particularly suitable near an existing reservoir. It was on land virtually abandoned by arable farmers, though used for cattle. This farm covered 450 hectares by 1975, and its offices housed many of the farm management functions for the two estates.

The second and smaller estate, called Kirene after the nearby village which supplied most of its labour, was beyond the borders of the Cap Vert in Thiès region. It had a rather hotter climate and a less accessible site, and its establishment involved the dispossession of a number of farmers from part or all of its land. The Kirene farm had reached 125 hectares by 1975/6.

The estates operated in the Senegalese dry season from approximately October to April or May. When I first visited Bud in 1973[1] only the Baobab farm was in production, growing green beans, bell peppers, strawberries, melons, tomatoes, aubergines, courgettes and flowers. By 1975 when I returned, the crop range had narrowed considerably: Baobab was producing peppers, melons and small areas of green beans, while Kirene, then in its second year, grew only tomatoes.

These estates affected the local economy in three major ways. They influenced land holding and land use, by taking land from other uses, and by affecting the land market, or other forms of land transfer, in nearby or potential estate farming areas. Second, they employed large amounts of seasonal labour and small numbers of skilled and more permanent workers. And third, the estates affected the local markets through the sale of their produce.

When Bud began production it assessed its potential profitability only in terms of export sales. Not only were local sales bound to be unprofitable, given high cost levels and a restricted market, but the government was also concerned to ward off the impact of local Bud sales on prices obtained by small gardeners. Therefore in the early years produce below export quality was dumped or ploughed in. As a small gardener near the estate ruefully acknowledged, the later increase in Bud's local sales (Table 2.2) was in part a response to pressure from the local population, who saw food rotting, and in particular from the local traders who saw profit opportunities in buying and reselling the produce. The local uses of the Bud produce were sometimes ingenious: some women, for example, bought the red bell peppers, unknown in the local diet until then, cooked them with a little tomato, and sold them as 'tomato paste', a product widely used in cooking in the area.

Bud production grew quite rapidly in the period 1971–76 (Table 2.2). Most of the local sales in 1975/6, were of tomatoes, and 1,000 tons went to the canning factory. They also included some aubergines and peppers, and a varied collection of vegetables in small quantities from the buying centre and the experimental scheme. The effects of these sales on the small gardeners is discussed in Chapter 7.

The decisive impact of the two estates was felt through seasonal employment. The estates were quite highly and increasingly mechanized, apart from picking and packing, and until 1976 Bud could make decisions on technology and farm organization unhindered by government policy on these issues and with a blanket right to import equipment. The result was an increasingly peaked seasonal pattern of employment. Figure 2.1 shows the peaking of employment in 1975/6 at around 1,500 workers present on average on the farms each day; after April employment fell off very rapidly. There exist no data on how many jobs for how many people these figures represent: there was considerable turnover, some tasks ended before the end of the season, and several tasks, such as packing, were done by several shift teams which did not work every day. So far more people in total than the peak numbers of over 1,600 came to work on the farms at some time over the season.

The estates employed both men and women: most of the packers and some of the pickers were women on both estates. In earlier years there had been far more people employed than the numbers shown because hundreds of pickers were employed each day on the green bean harvest. After 1974/5 green beans had largely been given up because they used so much harvest labour that they were regarded as difficult to manage and expensive. Similarly, between 1974 and 1976 the use of herbicides had reduced the labour for hoeing by two-thirds, according to the production manager. And in 1975, packing shed labour had been reduced by the introduction of a machine to make boxes. The green bean pickers had been women, as had the box makers; the production workers, men; there are no reliable figures by gender, but rather more than one-third of the total workforce was probably female in 1975/76.

This work influenced the local economy by changing people's incomes, competing with other work they would otherwise have been doing, altering their social and economic relations with each other, and changing the way they saw themselves. It also affected the wider economy by encouraging migration. The siting of the big Baobab estate in the Cap Vert region made it inevitable, as will be shown, that much of its labour would be supplied by seasonal or permanent migrants. The decision to put the farm close to the capital implies that the aim of a rapid increase in production and exports took precedence over rural development considerations. The firm was sometimes commended in Dakar as providing off season employment for settled farming populations to

Figure 2.1
Bud Estates: average monthly employment.
Seasonal and casual workers

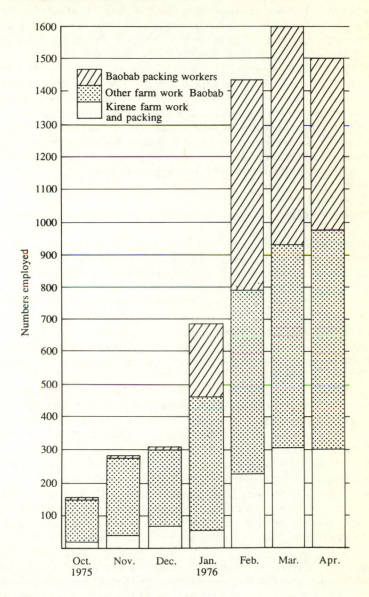

Legend:
Baobab packing workers
Other farm work Baobab
Kirene farm work
and packing

Numbers employed

complement their own dry season production. But most of the employment was being provided, as will be shown, in a region where the wet season agriculture had largely decayed, and where people migrating to work rapidly became dependent on the seasonal farm wages for their entire subsistence.

Finally, Bud in Kirene took substantial areas of farmers' best land, with consequences which will be examined in detail. At Baobab, much of the heavy clay land was no longer farmed, and the only people who felt that their land use had been squeezed were the cattle herders. However, Bud also influenced the small gardeners' hold on their gardens in the area of the *niayes*[2] near the Baobab farm by encouraging (illegal) land speculation. This area had long been affected by the Dakar élite purchasing land for 'Sunday gardens' (weekend homes outside the city); to this Bud added a second motive for land speculation by demonstrating a new and potentially profitable use of the land.

Bud, then, influenced the Senegalese economy through its effect on land, labour and produce markets. But to understand the effects of this impact, particularly within the rural economy, we first need conceptual tools which will allow us to analyse the direction of rural economic change.

Analysing Transition

This study of the impact of Bud was undertaken in the first few years of its existence. Its results provide an unusual view of a rural society in the process of becoming more dependent on wage labour; unlike most studies of company villages,[3] commenced long after the arrival of the estates, this one highlights, for once, the early stages of impact and transition. The fact that the Bud estates had been in operation for only three years provided an opportunity, as well as posing methodological problems. It both demanded and allowed the development of a method for identifying strains, tensions and conflicts which determine change, and which therefore indicate the direction of the long-term impact of the estates.

If a satisfactory method can be developed of identifying the direction of change, then it provides a more satisfactory methodology, of wider application, for studying the impact of development projects. The most common method for studying the economic effect of a new estate or development scheme[4] is to compare the total incomes created by the project with the incomes lost to people as a result of the project. This is misleading, since it assumes a once-for-all impact on livelihoods, normally without consideration of any underlying transformation of the organization of production which may produce further, cumulative change. But if the effect of the project is to transform the social organization of farming, then that in the long run will be far more important than the immediate gains and losses in income.

The central theoretical problem for this study, therefore, was to find a method for analysing the direction of change in rural economic systems. And this in turn raised the danger of teleology: the analysing of observed processes as contributions to an assumed end point, such as rural proletarianization.

To try to avoid this, detailed research was undertaken, over fifteen months, in three villages supplying labour to the Bud estates.[5] The research included a study of the organization of farming and other economic aspects of life in the three villages in 1975/6, plus detailed interviewing about changes in farming and economic and social organization over the previous three years (for farming data) and the previous five to ten years (for other aspects of life). Out of this material, answers to three distinct questions were extracted. First, what had been the *pattern* of evolution of the economy of the villages (including their links with the wider Senegalese and international economy) before the arrival of Bud? Second, what had been the *immediate* changes wrought by Bud? And third, what *pressures* for further change had Bud set up?

The answer to the second question was a matter of disputed facts, but raised few problems of interpretation. The first question was methodologically more straightforward than the last, though it raised some complex problems of research design and conceptual choice addressed further below. The last question raised some difficult issues of how to identify the pressures and conflicts which were likely to direct the evolution of the villages' economic systems in the longer run. This in turn raised some of the most interesting and debatable methodological issues addressed in this study.

Since the whole study concerns the micro details of change in village economies, the theoretical concepts had to be flexible enough to capture the small-scale alterations which led to major long-term transformation. I rapidly found, as have many other field researchers, that the then-popular model of the articulation of modes of production (Meillassoux (1964, 1975), Terray (1969), Rey (1971, 1973), Hindess and Hirst (1977)) was too blunt an instrument for this purpose. The tightly structured concepts – whether of a 'lineage' mode of production, or more atomized 'domestic' production forms – when applied to the variable detail of real world situations, tend either to breed a proliferation of different interacting modes, or to produce unhelpful oversimplification.[6] The focus tends to be shifted by this rigidity from the patterns of conflict and gradual change in real farming systems, to a concept of change as a sharp break with past production relations.

Finally, this sociological concept of modes of production creates a misleading image of West African farming systems as relatively remote from the influence of national and international markets. As traced briefly in Chapter 1, the impact of commerce on West African farming has been long and deep. It is more helpful, in understanding its effects, to treat the capitalist mode of production not as a closed system, but (Banaji, 1977) as a concept at the level of the 'laws of motion' of capital accumulation and production for the market, or economic dynamics.

The implication of this approach is that once the capitalist mode of production becomes dominant, the forms of production for capitalist markets become contingent: small-scale, relatively uncapitalized farming does not form a separate mode of production, any more than do *latifundias*; to call them such is to confuse levels of analysis. These are rather forms of production, different from wage labour, through which people *may* be exploited by capital. The question for analysis then becomes, as in this study, one of the direction of rural change catalysed or influenced by a major change in the operation of capitalist production and markets (such as the arrival of a big plantation). Whether it is creating the conditions for a rural proletariat, as opposed to some other form of exploitation of rural labour, becomes a question to be answered, not an assumption of the research. This was a question in which the Senegalese government itself became increasingly interested.

To try to define and answer that question, through a study of the precise forms of rural production and their relation to market formation and large-scale capital investment, became the focus of this study. Proletarianization, however, is a highly problematic concept in the West African context, where few people can afford wholly to lose their connections with land and the rural areas. What does seem clearly identifiable, and definable, is a pattern of greater or less distance of individual people from involvement in viable small-scale farming systems. This study defines economic change along two axes: individualization of economic activity, and commercialization (or monetization) of economic activity, and then examines the viability of the changing farming system and the resultant 'distance' of people from a farming base.

It is the argument of this book, then, that the Bud estates increased both the individualization and the commercialization of both farming and overall economic activity in the villages. Thereby, it is further argued, it threatened the viability of small-scale local farming, in the sense of its ability to adapt to pressure and continue to support the rural population, and strengthened the dependence of local people on Bud work. Over time, furthermore, people were adapting their domestic lives and ideas to the new dependence in ways which would cement that new distance from the land. But Bud did not create these patterns on its own: it fitted into and amplified existing tendencies within the Senegalese economy, while giving them a new twist.

The fieldwork on which this argument is based therefore began with a detailed analysis of the relations of production and consumption at village level. By this phrase I mean the whole web of economic relations between people through which agricultural and non-agricultural production is organized, its products sold or consumed or invested for different purposes, and the economic relations themselves reproduced: including identifying the places where this process escapes the boundaries of the economy of the village.

I concentrated on understanding four aspects of the relations of production within the village economies: the forms of property and possession of land[7] and other means of production; the forms of command over labour, and of the appropriation of the product of the labour of others; the disposal and consumption of the product, including markets external to the village, the extent of commoditization of the products of village labour and the development of money forms of exchange within the village; and, finally, the forms of wealth and accumulation at the village level where such existed, and the reasons for their absence where they did not.

Based on this understanding of economic organization at the village level, I constructed a description of patterns of change before Bud, and cross-checked this within the interviews. I then looked for processes of change in the existing situation created by the advent of Bud, and in particular for points of contradiction: points at which stresses were occurring which might lead to a break with previous forms of production and consumption. Such stresses included, for example, incompatible labour demands on individuals, and the choices they made; or new uses of money and conflicts over such innovations. They included major price changes. They included the emergence of apparently wholly new institutions such as labour unions among the villagers. And among the indicators of underlying conflict was the divergence between different people's understanding and description of what was happening, and attempts to expand and reorder old concepts to include new processes. Out of this analysis emerges a pattern of sharp pressures for change: in some cases overt, in some lying under an apparently stable surface.

This approach implied a research method drawing on anthropology, including Marxist economic anthropology, and on the 'village studies' tradition within development studies.[8] The central concern is with economic issues: with the organization of production and consumption. But I have attempted not only to measure, as economists generally will, but also to listen, as they will less frequently outside the traditions just cited. I have tried to grasp how people in the villages understood what was happening to the economic organization of their lives; what forms of resistance they organized to the changes which threatened them; and how they tried, successfully or unsuccessfully, to organize their response to Bud. I have looked particularly for the gaps between people's perception of what was happening to the material organization of their lives, and observed changes, for example, in patterns of land and labour use. Gaps and conflicts of this kind in people's perceptions of economic trends are strong indicators of areas of contradiction and transition.

How does an analysis of this type relate to concepts of class? There is a sense in which this study is concerned with the micro-economics of change in the nature of the working classes. It does not reveal a shift in which peasants become proletarians: those distinctions are too sharp for a society of the West African type, where the market for hired labour[9] is so large and varied, and people rely so extensively on having a foot in both camps. Rather, it is a study of change in the nature of these camps, and hence in the options open to the rural-based labouring classes: and of the way they adapt themselves to those changes.

When we speak of transition, then, we mean not only a sharp break in a production system, but also a process of change which seems sufficient to threaten, if it continues, the reproduction of important elements of existing relations of production, and to create different patterns of economic and social organization. This does not happen all at once, but unevenly through the economy of a village. In the areas around the two estates, I identified changes which, although still in process, were significant enough to indicate a transition under way. I have not assumed that all these changes were the result of Bud, but have tried to separate out and explain those which were.

This is not an exact method of studying impact and transition: there are no experimental conditions within social science. However, to extrapolate changes in economic and social organization, and argue through their likely effects in this way, is an improvement on methods which concentrate on incomes distributed and incomes foregone. The function of income depends upon who holds it, and within what social and economic system. In some cases, increases in wage incomes may reinforce existing farming systems;[10] in others, they may break them down. In some cases, they bring the market into intra-village relations; in others, that effect is successfully resisted. In this case, it is argued in the chapters that follow, the changes wage income brought threatened food production; that effect potentially dominated, in the medium term, the cash income effects. Extrapolation of this kind has its dangers, but it is a great deal more satisfactory as a method of predicting outcomes than a method which ignores changes in relations of production. And I have tried to make my own data and deductions sufficiently transparent to allow readers to draw their own conclusions if they are not satisfied with mine.

The Problem of the 'Household'

The concepts used in analysing economic structure and change in the villages inevitably altered as the fieldwork proceeded. I began from an attempt to develop concepts to analyse the social organization of farming: where, how, and under what constraints decisions are made; who has access to which resources, and why; who works for whom, and why. In doing so, I immediately ran up against the problem of the 'household' as an analytical concept and research tool.

Economists had in the 1970s, and still have, a commitment to the idea of the African household as the basic unit of farming and consumption. Recent examples run from Hopkins's (1973) economic history of West Africa, through Cleave's (1974) use of the 'smallholder' concept in his survey of African farming, via the rediscovery and application of Chayanov's work to Africa (Hunt, 1979), to Low's (1986) wholesale application of the 'new household economics' to Swazi farmers and wage workers. As Jane Guyer (1981: 98) has suggested, this commitment stems in part from the need economists have to find an analogue to the 'firm' as a basic unit of decision making, in order to apply their apparatus of theories based on the premise of atomized decision takers. Because of the dominance of the framework of thought of neoclassical economics, even economists working in the village studies tradition, influenced by anthropological or sociological categories and aware of the patchy nature of rural markets, have tended to start their studies by looking for and defining the farming enterprise, based on the domestic unit.

By the household enterprise, economists generally mean a household-based farm, or 'smallholding', operating independently, with a given labour base, and under the domination of a single head, usually characterized as a patriarch. This unit becomes the unit of production and consumption, and also of accumulation to the extent that this takes place at the village level. The crucial assumption, whatever the variations, is the unequivocal hierarchy of power and decision making over resources, which implies in turn that all labour is available 'unpaid', at its opportunity cost, to be disposed of by the household head as 'he' thinks best. This model is highly misleading when applied to Senegalese farming systems: and indeed, anthropological studies suggest, to a wide range of farming systems in West Africa. Senegalese farming is not characterized by corporate units of this kind, and predictions which rely upon such conceptualizations are potentially inaccurate.

If one begins by defining 'the household', in the tradition of the anthropological literature on Senegalese rural areas (for example Gastellu *et al.*, 1987; Roch, 1972), as a residential unit of people who eat from a common pot, then in all the villages studied this was an easily recognizable unit to which people readily referred. Living arrangements consisted of one or more such households, living within compounds marked out by a common boundary wall.

In one village studied (Kirene) this residential group formed in any farming year an important basis for farming cooperation: that is, a substantial proportion of the farming on fields whose product was appropriated by people within the household was carried out by a complex pattern of co-operation among some members of the household. But it is a very long step from such a qualified statement, to the image of a 'household' farm, for the following reasons. First, the residential units themselves were changed in the farming season – by amalgamating households – in order to provide a wider basis for farming co-operation. Second, the farming system also included important elements of farming co-operation among individuals across household boundaries, chiefly in the form of co-operative work groups. And third, the farming organization among the household members was complex, with dependent household members having varying rights as well as obligations, and retaining control of their own incomes from cash cropping.

The scope for internal conflict among household members was therefore considerable, and the internal 'settlement' which held a household residential unit together could easily be undermined by new pressures or opportunities.[11] The household head – usually but not always male – had considerable capacity to manage and influence farming activity. But that capacity was based, first, on the head's ability to fulfil demands such as that for land and, second, on the options open to other members of the household, including the women. It is a serious mistake, in analysing West African farming systems, to assume that male household heads always have an unchallengeable right to the unpaid labour of women or other members of the household.[12]

The approach taken to 'the household' in this study is therefore the following. I start from a distinction between the living (or domestic) unit and the farming system, treating the relationship between the two as a matter for research, rather than conflating them conceptually. The domestic unit, furthermore, is defined, not simply as a food consumption unit, but as the *unit of consumption of domestic work*. By this is meant the unit within which a division of labour is established, generally between women, for the performance of the classically female tasks of cooking, cleaning, child care and care of the sick; the unit also includes the group of people who benefit from their output. By association, this 'household' is generally, in the societies studied here, the unit of consumption of meals in common – but not necessarily a unit of common food stocks.

This definition[13] allows a working definition of the household which has several advantages. It focuses attention on the domestic work which produces the 'common pot' which is more generally used as the definition of the household (as if, almost, the pot grew unaided from the granary).[14] It allows me to demonstrate, in the chapters which follow, that changes in the organization of this work, and the resultant shifts in the nature of the household, are an important facet of rural change, which is not passive, but interacts with the organization of the farming system and other non-domestic work. The definition brings into focus the sexual division of labour, and the relations between the genders as crucial variables in the analysis of change. Finally, it is a consistent and, as the following chapters show, an illuminating way to grasp the household as an economic institution, without confusing it with the farming system.

Households and Farming Systems

Defining the household in this way then allows one to ask, without creating fresh confusion, what is the relation between household and farming system? Within the village studied in Senegal there were two quite distinct types of farming system, which nevertheless had in common the absence of any simple household-based production unit.

The first, in the village called Kirene,[15] conformed in general pattern to farming systems in Serer[16] areas studied by anthropologists in the 1970s (Gastellu *et al.*, 1974; Gastellu, 1981). The farming system had a complex set of 'farms', or fields. The farming of these fields involved extensive co-operation, but the cash crop revenues were individually appropriated. The food produced – reduced by the Sahel drought to the short-cycle 'early' millet crop – was managed by the person I have referred to throughout as the 'millet farmer'. This person was also generally the household head, but the identification was not complete: an elderly household head might be living in a household where the food farming was wholly managed by an adult son. Again, clarity is helped by separating domestic and farming arrangements.

As a result of these arrangements there was in this village no identifiable 'family labour product'[17] available to the household as a whole for consumption purposes. Only the millet crop was all jointly consumed, though other resources owned by various members of the household also went into the common pot. There was no direct calculated reciprocity, so that the labour of some household members went, without direct or cash payment, into the product appropriated by the members of other households. Accumulation was by the individual, not the household group, and there had previously been accumulation by non-household units, centred on maternal kin, though this system had largely disappeared by the 1970s.

In Kirene village, as later chapters will argue, millet farming was the linch-pin of this farming system. Food farming and food provision formed the link between household structure and farming system. The millet farmers were able to play their managing role in village farming by virtue of their food provisioning role. And the unit of food provisioning underpinned the pattern of farming co-operation. The link between millet farming and food provision created the close connections between residential organization and farming co-operation, which in turn gave the system some of the appearances of a 'household farming' system. And it was this organization of food farming which had allowed the village to combine a considerable responsiveness to external commercial opportunities, in the development of new cash crops, with a pattern of labour organization which ensured the continuing provision of a village food base. The next three chapters argue that Bud's arrival threatened this food farming system, and hence threatened the central link holding the farming system together.

What might happen when that structure was threatened was suggested by the entirely different farming system being practised around the Baobab estate, only 30 kilometres away. This could best be characterized as individual farming, undertaken by the individual for private (cash) gain. That individual might be aided sometimes on his or her fields by other household members, but such aid was occasional rather than regular: it could not be counted on, and the demand for it could arouse considerable conflict. In this situation, farming was only viable as a means of livelihood for the farmer where labour productivity was high, and particularly where wage labour could be hired at a wage which could be paid from the returns on the crop. A single productive unit could be identified in this farming system, but it did not consist of the household.

It is not argued in this book that the Kirene farming system displays the earlier history of the farming system in the Cap Vert around the Baobab estate. On the contrary, both farming systems had undergone very considerable and specific adaptations to the pressures of the mid-twentieth century before the arrival of Bud. But it is proposed that the juxtaposition of the two systems, and the evolution of the Kirene farming system once under pressure from Bud, raise a serious question about the direction of evolution of farming organization in this area when forms of unpaid labour co-operation are broken down.

One form of this unpaid labour co-operation in Kirene was the communal labour party, that is, a co-operative work group of individuals drawn from a number of households, carrying out a single farm operation on the fields of one farmer. Analysis of such cross-household co-operative labour in the context of change in African farming systems has been very limited. Economists have generally been concerned with communal labour parties only to predict their demise on the grounds of their supposed inefficiency in commercial farming. Anthropologists and historians have documented their continuing and widespread existence in African agriculture.[18] But we remain without an analysis of how important these work groups are to these agricultural systems. To what extent does the collapse of such work groups threaten farming organization? How does it change crop choice and why? A historian (Tosh, 1979) has proposed that the type of pre-existing communal labour party strongly influenced the economic effects of the introduction of cash crops into African savannah agriculture. The form of introduction of groundnuts into Kirene agriculture, discussed below, tends to bear this out. But we are still left without an analysis of the causes and consequences of the collapse of communal labour. The Kirene example show clearly that it is not commercial crop production as such which destroys the communal labour party.

For a household farming system to emerge from one based on wider co-operation, two processes have to occur. The household head has to be able to assert control over the labour services and product of the family members, and in order for this to be viable the household head has to have access to sufficient resources to provide for the household. For certain Wolof areas of Senegal, Roch (1972) has proposed that animal-drawn equipment has effectively replaced mutual aid, leaving a household-based farming system. In the case he studied, higher productivity from more extensive farming taking in spare land has provided the base for more restricted labour co-operation; even in such Wolof areas, however, sub-units continued to exist within the household in terms of appropriation of the product (Benoit-Cattin and Faye, 1982). In Kirene the emergence of such a system tended to be blocked by the continuing importance of matrilineal ties outside the household, the lack of spare land to allow increased labour productivity through increasing acreage, and the tendency of the decline in communal labour to reduce total food production.

There is thus a danger, in the West African context, in assuming that unpaid labour services within the household are somehow privileged, less subject to disintegration, than unpaid labour between households. The second farming system just described illustrates the alternative outcome of a collapse of wider co-operative work ties. While in Kirene there were virtually no paid labour or other cash exchange relations among members of the village as a whole, in villages a few kilometres distant market relations permeated even the relations among houehold members. There had been a disintegration of unpaid labour relations within households as well as between them, and this had been associated with a decline in millet growing. Here only high-value cash crops, cultivable with the use of wage labour – that is, irrigated market gardening – remained to the farmer as an alternative to seeking wage work.

It follows that communal labour parties should not be understood as co-operation among households, but rather as an important and integral part of the wider pattern of 'unpaid' social relations among individuals which organize farming in many West African areas. When communal labour breaks down, there is no necessary evolution towards a household system. In the West African context, with its complex pattern of intra-household and individual cross-household economic activities, an individualized commercial farming – successful or unsuccessful according to the economic conditions and technology available – is an at least equally plausible outcome. Where dependent potential household members identify a range of alternative options for cash income earning, it becomes a highly probable result.

Finally, this argument is related to a wider discussion in the anthropological literature. Anthropologists have proposed (Guyer, 1981: 97ff.) that it is still an open question whether commercialization in West African farming systems produces an evolution towards a farming system based on what Goody (1976) has called the 'conjugal estate' of the classic peasantries. While not addressing directly the terms of this debate, the material in this study is highly relevant to the many open questions in this area. Furthermore, in recognition of definitional complications, and the images conjured up by the word 'peasants', I have avoided as far as possible references to African 'peasants', referring to the farmers as such, or as 'small-scale' farmers to distinguish them from Bud.

As a result of these reflections, the relation of farming system to domestic unit is not treated in this book as an unquestioned assumption, but as a subject for research. This distinction undermines not only many neo-classical economic analyses of farming systems, but also Marxist theories which analyse change on the basis of an irreducible 'domestic unit' (Meillassoux, 1975) which, as such, is the subject of exploitation, for example by forced production or cheap purchase of crops. Such 'units' are a product of empiricism (an observed relation between production and consumption in some cases) and romanticism (an unwillingness to treat domestic production as itself complex and contradictory) (Mackintosh, 1977). To abandon these starting points leads to a much more interesting set of questions about the relations between gender, domestic work, farming change and class formation.

Hired Labour, Migration and Class Formation

I have said that changing economic organization is examined in this study along two axes: individualization and commercialization of economic activity. It will be argued that the Bud estates, by their impact on land use and labour markets, shifted the working lives of people in the villages around them in a direction that was both more individualized and more commercialized. Increasingly, people lost their connections to a network of unpaid labour relations in farming, and came to rely more on hired labour and individual commercial farming for survival. Given the lack of viability of most individual farming, dependence on wage work increased as the cost of not finding such work rose. In that defined sense, Bud might be said to have pushed the rural inhabitants in the direction of greater proletarianization.

The concept though, needs to be used with care. On the one hand, it is argued that Bud, through its impact on farming, increased people's 'distance' from involvement with and primary identification with farming. This 'distance' involved, among other factors, access to land, and possession of agricultural skills. More precisely, it included all the aspects of access to farming as a mode of livelihood: in the Senegalese conditions studied, it is argued that preconditions for successful farming activity were either insertion into a farming system which provided access to the labour of others without prior payment, or access to the capital, including land and cash, necessary to make a success of commercialized farming. In the second case, those who farmed did not produce food. If neither of these preconditions existed, people were no longer able to be farmers as their primary means of survival, even if they grew a few crops by exclusively manual methods to supplement other sources of income. In so far as Bud was helping to create people without the preconditions to farm effectively, it was encouraging proletarianization.

On the other hand, there is more to the process of labour force formation than the disintegration of other options. Bud fitted into and drew on an existing labour market whose extent has frequently gone unrecognized in the literature on West African agriculture and rural areas. A central theme of a later chapter is the geographical and numerical scale and complexity of the Senegalese labour market from which Bud drew its labour. Hired labour, and dependent non-kin farmers of a variety of types, have long been common in West African agricultural systems: one more serious problem with the 'family labour' image of the farming system. Senegal has been estimated to have contained 300,000 foreign nationals in 1975 (Zachariah and Condé, 1981), as well as very large internal migration flows. The pattern is repeated elsewhere (Hill, 1986).

Most of the existing literature treats the 'strange farmers', working for local farmers in return for a plot of land, and the farm and non-farm labourers as migrants, concentrating on the flow of people from place to place within the West African subcontinent, and between West Africa and Europe. This literature then focuses on the effects of these migrations in sending and receiving areas, distinguishing circular and permanent migratory patterns, and staged migrations towards the cities. This whole literature fails, in my view, to capture the element of labour *market* development through migration within West African countries, and its impact on patterns of economic activity: one element of that history of African labour, especially outside the few centres of industrial employment that still waits to be written.[19]

Seen from the gates of Bud, the migratory patterns looked rather different. What emerged from the working life histories of Bud workers was the extent and continual nature of the wandering in search of work. There were, certainly, patterns of established circular migration, notably between the south of Senegal (the Casamance) and the Dakar area. But many others seemed to have become launched on much longer, semi-permanent wandering, and had taken a wide variety of 'jobs': farming a patch of land in return for labour services to a farmer; labouring for cash; working for food only; casual work in Dakar; and labouring and street selling in France. Some felt their ability to return to farming had been fatally undermined by the drought. Bud, for these workers, offered just one more option: a relatively better-paid one, for which it was necessary to stay in the area to compete.

The Bud workers, then, were not a 'new' rural proletariat: for none of them was wage work an unfamiliar idea. 'Semi-proletarianization', in the sense of reliance on paid work for others at different stages of people's economic lives (especially but not only in youth), is very widespread in Senegal. The particular focus of this study is the way in which rural societies adapt to or incorporate the cash income and experience of wage work. Three arguments about this are central to the discussion of class formation to be pursued here. First, it is possible for rural societies to stall the impact of cash incomes and monetization on the borders of farming organization and intra-village economic life. This had happened for years in Kirene before Bud. Bud, however, for reasons to be explored, was bringing individual economic relations expressed in cash into the heart of village economic organization, and hence threatening to transform it. This form of individualization and monetization of social relations is part of the meaning of rural proletarianization in Senegal.

Second, a strong indicator of transition in economic systems is a change in the position of women. This takes two particular forms in the case studied here. First, the adaptation of domestic work organization and related living arrangements (household structure) to the changing demands of dependence on wage work. And second, the creation of new categories of 'women's work': an indicator of a shift in the nature of an economic system.

And finally, social organization in response to wage work, notably unionization and labour conflict, is another indicator of people's changing perceptions of themselves and their options. This study demonstrates the rapid emergence of labour organization on both Bud estates, and examines the reasons for the form it took. Interestingly, the results belie a common view in the literature[20] that labour organization and militancy is likely to be greater and more effective, the more run-down the rural economy. On the contrary, in this case the most effective labour organization was in the area where that organization could draw on a solidarity based on farming.

Women's Work and Class Formation

One of the most general results of feminist-inspired research in the last ten years[21] has been the understanding that class experience – and class change – is gender-specific. This book provides evidence for the view that, not only do men's and women's experiences of class differ, but changes in the relations between men and women, including the sexual division of labour, is one of the ways in which new class structures become established.

This process is clearest in the village where people were most dependent on wage work, and the decay of wet season agriculture had gone the farthest. Chapter 8 discusses domestic organization in this village – which was called Ponty – and argues that it is in the social relations of domestic work, and other economic relations between men and women living in the same household, that indicators of class change are most clearly found. The composition of the household, in this village of migrant workers, was becoming increasingly influenced by the women's need to undertake both domestic and wage work. The gender division of domestic work remained rigid – women still did virtually all of it – and hence households were beginning to become more female-centred, with men moving into the households of women they married in a way they would not have done previously. Women tried to organize to have other women to share housework, and to be able to take in lodgers.

As a result, economic relations among members of the household, unmediated by insertion into a wider farming system, became centred on relations of disposal of individual incomes for consumption: who should consume the results of women's domestic work, and at what price, and who should control the expenditure of whom. The question of control of women's incomes by their husbands became a subject of dispute, and of open appeal to conflicting sets of principles, in a way that it was not in Kirene; so did the issue of disposal of the incomes of young unmarried men.

Changes such as these are the micro-processes of class formation. Such changes in domestic patterns of life signal the end of an old order for a group of people: though domestic relations may change again, the process cannot easily be reversed. In Kirene, where the domination of an integrated agricultural system had been much stronger before Bud, though that agricultural system was threatened, nevertheless the changes in the form of the household and the relations between men and women were traceable only in embryo. Many villagers took the view that the huge economic changes had brought no social changes, and used the stability of domestic life as their example.

Simultaneously, and with great rapidity, there was emerging on the two estates that familiar category of 'women's work': jobs done largely by women, lower paid than those where men predominated, less stable over the season, with poorer working conditions in many cases. In three short years, a complete and quite rigid sexual division of labour had appeared on the estates, interacting in ways that will be described with the rigid sexual division of labour within domestic work.

This process, it is contended, is a characteristic part of new patterns of labour force creation and class formation throughout the world. Changing class structure threatens existing economic relations which embody and maintain the subordination of women.[22] New forms of economic activity produce new forms of female subordination as an inherent part of their structures: and that process does not always or even usually go unchallenged by women. It is typically a painful and conflict-ridden process.

In addition to the conflicts already traced over domestic economic relations, the pattern of labour conflict also demonstrated the perceived importance to management and workers of gender relations within the workforce. The rapid development of trade unionism and workplace labour organization was another indicator of the speed with which people came to see themselves in new lights, and to develop new social responses to huge and unexpected new pressures. But the differences in the way unions were formed and operated round the two estates were sharp, and again the best indicator of the type of change is in relations between the genders.

In both areas, there were strikes on the Bud farms in the year of the study: in both cases, it was the women who first came out on strike. This was in part a result of the division of labour just traced. But there were very different responses in the two areas. In Kirene, where the villagers held on to a strong sense of village-wide solidarity, and tried to give it new meaning in the face of Bud, the rest of the labour force came out in sympathy. In Baobab, the women were left to struggle on, and negotiate, alone, and a number of the male workers were openly hostile to them. The difference, it will be argued, can be explained by the way in which, in the workplace and the villages around Baobab, a much more immediate conflict of interest was developing between men and women as they competed for scarce jobs and tried to survive.

Treating the nature of the household as a variable, and gender relations as a major subject of investigation, is therefore very productive in trying to understand class change. Both factors are crucial to the small changes in economic and social organization, self-perception and patterns of resistance which make up a transformation in class structure. It should not need saying – but probably still does – that this does not mean that this study is concerned with the question of whether gender division is more or less 'important' than class conflict. That is simply not the question at issue. The argument is rather that one cannot understand the making of a class without understanding how male–female relations change in the process, since those changes are integral to the way classes are structured and reproduced – and experienced.

Monetization, Markets and Transition

It was argued above that the best way to escape from the excessive rigidity of the 'modes of production' approach to change in African rural areas was to focus instead on the pattern of change in farming and other rural production systems, including domestic production, and on the related shifts in the relation of those systems to the market and to the wider processes of capital accumulation.

These issues are addressed in this study in two ways. First, it examines in detail the uses of money, and the organization of the market, within the economies of the villages studied. This issue again demonstrates, on the one hand, the small cumulative changes brought about by the pressures from Bud in each area; and, on the other, the very sharp break between the forms of production in the area studied which was nearer to Dakar and those of the village of Kirene, 30 kilometres further into the interior.

Consider, for example, the land market. The legal framework enacted by the Senegalese government after Independence implied the virtual abolition of legal land purchase and sale. The law, referred to in the chapters which follow as the '1964 law' was the *Loi No. 64.64 relative au domaine national* (the national land law). Its effect was to establish several categories of land holding in Senegal: land held by the State, land which had been registered as private property before the 1964 law came into force or was so registered within a stipulated time limit, and land not falling under either heading which became therefore part of the *domaine national*. In principle, in all areas including the Cap Vert the national domain land was to be put under the control of a local rural council (*counseil rural*), elected from the villages in each area, and having the power to allocate any land not effectively in use to someone willing to farm it. Land effectively in use remained with the farmer in 1964. Land within the *domain national* could not be legally bought and sold: the aim of the law appears to have been to change the nature of local communal land management, while preventing the emergence of a private rural land market. By 1975 the rural council prescribed by the law existed in Kirene, but had never been set up in the Cap Vert area.

The limited effect of this law upon the actual situation of land tenure and disposal is illustrated by the organization of land holding in the areas of the two Bud estates. Though close together, they had totally different land holding structures. In Kirene, land had not been bought and sold before 1964; the arrival of groundnuts as a cash crop had not commoditized land at all, and in 1975 land was still not exchanged for cash. In the Cap Vert area, on the other hand, land had been purchasable long before Independence, and continued to be bought and sold, not to say pledged and hijacked. In this area, closer to the city, the rise of land sales had been closely associated with the rise of commercial farming, particularly market gardening in the valuable *niaye* land;[23] it had also been associated with migration to the area and with proximity to the city.

In Kirene the commoditization of land, along with the monetization of other internal relations within the village, appears to have been consciously resisted by the villagers up to the time of the arrival of Bud. The villagers worked for wages outside, but not in the village. Goods were rarely bought and sold among villagers, and cash earned from cash crops was used in such a way that it did not monetize village economic relations. The market was held at the boundaries, not of the household, but of the village (or even, it appears, at the boundaries of the group of closely related Serer villages in the area).

When Bud arrived, the Kirene villagers attempted to deal with the work and the cash income it brought in the same manner, integrating it in the existing organization of economic relations within the village as they had done with other sources of cash. But the attempt was essentially artificial because of the scale of the wage incomes paid relative to incomes from agriculture, and their destructive effect on the dynamic of the agricultural economy; there were already some indications of intra-village monetization by 1975.

Given the pressures from the state and from the farmers to limit the scope of the market, and given the very disparate patterns of commoditization and levels of capitalization in agriculture, it is evident that there was no such phenomenon as *the* market in these Senegalese rural areas. Markets in Senegal were 'patchy', because they depended for their operation on how they were structured, on their scale (international, national or local) and on the nature of the influence exerted by the national state. As a result markets were fragmented, half-concealed, and operated in conditions of some ignorance on the part of participants. There still exists little research on the operation of land, labour and even product markets:[24] even in the case of migrant labour, there is much more work on migration to France and to the city than on the extensive seasonal migration within the rural areas. It is clear from the fieldwork for this study that wage rates varied enormously in the area of the Baobab estate; hired workers were in a highly dependent position on the small farms and might even not be paid at all. Similarly, with the exception of fresh fruit and vegetables, product and land markets in this area were fragmented and hidden.

What, in such a situation, constitute indicators of transition? One such indicator is a change in the scope of the market, a considerable extension or retraction of its scope. Another, marked in the case of Bud, is the phenomenon whereby a market of previously local scope, in which prices are dominated by the productivity of the local economy, becomes dominated by influences from a market of much larger scope and higher capitalization. Bud provides an example of this in both land and product markets: dumping produce on the local market, because local prices were not the determinants of its profitability but merely a bonus on top of export sales; and causing speculation in the local land market which meant that land prices became further disconnected from the returns offered by market gardening. It was this sense of conflict between the dynamics of two disconnected markets, and the knowledge that if Bud were successful, the market which it served could easily swamp the prices in their own local market which caused the farmers to say frequently, 'Bud is beyond us' or 'Bud will take us over', even when they were not in direct conflict with the estates for selling produce or hiring labour.

The patchy and fragmented product and labour markets, the virtual absence of an open private market for credit or equipment, and the focusing of credit, marketing and equipment purchase relations on the state-dominated co-operatives are all indicators of the virtual absence of indigenous capitalist development within Senegalese agriculture in the areas studied at the time of Bud's arrival. The market gardeners of the city fringes were genuinely commercial gardeners, but on a very small scale, with low levels of capital investment. There were no capitalist farmers like the Bugandan 'men of profit' (Richards *et al.*, 1973); accumulation in indigenous agriculture had been largely blocked by a combination of government policy and resistance by the farmers themselves. The effect of Bud, furthermore, was *not* to loosen this constraint or develop 'the' local market. On the contrary, Bud produced a complex mixture of encouragement and suppression of local market exchange, of which the overall effect was to undermine further the viability of local agriculture.

The most important of the extensions of the market were: the extension of the scope of the wage labour market; pressure to extend the market in consumption goods; and pressure to extend the land market in ways which reflected perceived potential export profitability. In terms of restrictions, the arrival of Bud restricted the scope of the market in produce for export, in the sense that Bud held the monopoly sales contract for its production; the government, meanwhile, continued to suppress the market in both groundnuts – where it had long held a monopoly – and millet. By 1976, private transport and resale of food grains had effectively been suppressed by government monopoly of purchase and licensing of movement. The small market gardeners' most serious fear was that the arrival of Bud might focus attention upon them and herald the arrival of just such a domination of their market by Bud or by the government.

Typically, schemes which incorporate small farmers or agricultural wage workers into production for international produce markets set out to elide the relations of those producers to the market for their goods. They become cogs in a larger production scheme, where prices are set to locate returns further up the chain of production and sale. As Arthur Lewis (1955) among others has pointed out, the poorer the food farming by the farmers-turned-export producers, the fewer the gains which stay with the workforce. Large agricultural export enterprises, whether or not they call themselves 'plantations', have a particularly poor record in returning the benefits to country or workforce (Beckford, 1972; Kemp and Little, 1987). Too often, as in Senegal, few of the benefits of mechanization go to the remaining workers, though the risks of production are effectively borne by them. As signalled in the last chapter, the position of Senegalese farmers was inevitably much weaker than their French counterparts who had fought to keep their land when threatened by the large companies dealing in fresh produce.

In one way or another, involvement of small producers in export crops tends to mean, not the extension of 'the market' as such, but rather a reduction of the scope of produce markets – through vertical integration with international capital – and an increase in the scope of the market for local consumption goods, including food. The labour market may increase in scope – in terms of numbers of jobs – but be reduced in competitiveness, as the dominance of a few employers increases. Land may not be commercialized so much as transferred administratively from one set of interests to another. Reflection on these lines led Jean Copans (1980: 97) to argue that a true peasantry in Senegal was disappearing, to be replaced by a more 'bureaucratic' farmer, obedient to orders of technicians, 'no longer a peasant'.

These reflections are all relevant to the question of what came after Bud, as well as to understanding Bud's impact. We return at the end of this book to review in this framework the small farmer schemes and proposals for the integration and extension of the national market which followed the big wage labour schemes of the mid-1970s.

Agrarian Transition and the Food Crisis

The African food crisis is properly understood as a crisis of the access of African rural people to sufficient food to sustain them from year to year. As experienced in the semi-arid Sahelian and savannah areas of West Africa, it has a series of interlocking aspects: production decline, market problems (including cycles of debt), labour problems and migration, and food distribution issues.

This study offers a contribution to understanding how this cycle of problems may derive from the frequently suggested link between large-scale export farming and decline in the production of and access to food. The next three chapters examine in detail how the arrival of a large estate did not merely reduce total production in a farming system that previously was relatively viable, though pressured. It also changed the production structure, notably by undermining labour co-operation in agriculture.

Initially, the reaction of Kirene farmers was to try to maintain food farming despite the problems. But, these chapters argue, the impact of Bud in the longer run was to promote an individualization of farming relations which sharply reduced the incentives to produce. Furthermore, there was a shift towards relying on cash for food: this, as so often occurs,[25] put particular pressure on women to find cash for food, and very sharply increased women's workload. A process of internal monetization of village relations was encouraged, beginning with consumption goods.

One plausible outcome of such a process of farming and consumption change was suggested by the farming system a few miles away from Kirene, near the larger estate. There, as the following three chapters show, labour co-operation had almost completely collapsed, to be replaced by a commercialized system. As a result, food farming had almost completely disappeared: the economics of millet farming by hand would not sustain wage labour; nor would groundnut farming. Only small-scale market gardening generated enough revenue to be viable.

While Bud was there, the workforce, especially women and older men, spent much of their income on food. The chief immediate impact of Bud, therefore, was to increase the market demand for food while somewhat reducing the supply. People did not, for reasons explored, grow their own food in the wet season around the bigger estate. In the longer run, when Bud collapsed, as it did, the implications were more serious: the Senegalese countryside had experienced one more major pressure towards the undermining of its wet season, low productivity agriculture, which was still producing foodgrains, but had not seen any associated improvement in farming productivity which might have allowed food farming to survive in more individualized forms. The long-run implications, therefore, were a further decline in the country's food production base, a further impoverishment of rural farming, an increased dependence of the rural population on wage work, and a further decrease in the resistance of the rural population to the next drought.

Had Bud succeeded, it might at least have provided the foreign exchange to buy the increased food required. But the problems of this export-oriented approach to food availability are twofold, and both are illustrated by Bud: it can worsen the problem it is supposed to help resolve, and it is a high-risk strategy where the risk is borne chiefly by the rural poor. We return to these issues of international capital and the shifting of risk in the last chapter of this book.

Notes

1. This visit is discussed in Mackintosh (1975). All the data on Bud's activities come from my own field research unless otherwise stated.

2. The *niayes* are hollows, with almost year-long ground water, where small-scale market gardening is pursued. For the area, the gardens, and the land speculation, see Chapter 8.

3. See Kemp *et al.* (1987) and Kirk (1987) for recent work and a bibliography.

4. This is the approach of social cost-benefit studies; social impact analysis, a recently expanding area, covers a much wider range of effects; see, for example, Derman and Whitford (1985) which includes a case study on Senegal.

5. For a brief discussion of the choice of villages and fieldwork method, see Appendix. The three villages studied were Ponty and Bambilor, supplying labour to Baobab, and Kirene, the almost sole source of labour for Kirene estate.

6. As Jane Guyer puts it (1981: 94), the attempt to tighten up modes of production theoretically tends to 'mangle the ethnography', while adding new modes 'rapidly becomes difficult to manage'.

7. The distinction is taken from Bettelheim (1970: 58): 'property' is the power to allocate goods to uses; 'possession' is the power to put means of production to work.

8. For example, among the Marxist anthropologists: Meillassoux (1964), Terray (1969), Rey (1971, 1973); among the village studies and related literature, Norman (1967), Hill (1972), Haswell (1953, 1963), Berry (1975), Longhurst (1984).

9. For a discussion of the problems of this concept in West Africa, see Hill (1986: 106).

10. A number of authors (Hunt, 1979; Collier *et al.*, 1984) have identified this effect in Kenya.

11. Richards (1986: 95) makes this point strongly for the area he studied in Sierra Leone: 'The "farm family" does not have definite form but is responsive, even in the short run, to farming conditions and shifts in the balance of male and female economic interests.'

12. Dey (1981) discusses this issue for The Gambia; Wallace (1981) makes an identical point for Nigeria concerning the access problems of household heads to the labour of younger dependent men, and the failed predictions which arise from ignoring those problems.

13. This definition first emerged from a reflection on the problems of understanding change in the sexual division of labour: see Mackintosh (1979); but at that stage I was still treating the farming as 'household-based', which I now think is misleading.

14. This definition is from Gastellu *et al.* (1974), and was my working definition during the field research.

15. 'Kirene' (pronounced Ki-*rene* to rhyme with 'fen') is the real name of the village – or, strictly, the formal name of the whole village for postal purposes, and of a major part of it to the villagers. I have not changed the villages' names, since they are in any case easily identifiable; but I have used no names of villagers, and hope in that way I have avoided distressing any of those who provided me with so much help. Obviously, all interpretations of events and statements are my responsibility alone.

16. The Serer are one of the major ethnic groups in Senegal.

17. The phrase is from Chayanovian models of rural economies: see Hunt (1979), Harrison (1975).

18. See for example Tosh (1979), Gulliver (1971), Meillassoux (1964). Haswell (1953) also documents co-operative labour in The Gambia: an exception among economists.

19. For West African migration studies see Lindsay (1985), Stichter (1985), Amin (1978), Zachariah and Condé (1981); for Senegal and The Gambia, Diop (1965), Colvin (1981), Swindell (1982) and especially Faye's careful (1981) study of local rural migration patterns. For labour history focusing largely on urban workers, see Sandbrook and Cohen (1975), Cohen *et al.* (1978), Lloyd (1982).

20. For example, Stichter (1985: 194).

21. For gender and class in Africa, see Roberts (1984) for a review, and the other papers in *Review of African Political Economy* 27/28 1984; also Bryceson (1980), Obbo (1980). For a general review of gender and class in development, see Sen and Grown (1987).

22. See Whitehead (1979), Young *et al.* (1981) for a discussion of the concept of 'subordination'.

23. See Note 2.

24. The rise in interest in liberalizing agricultural markets has encouraged work on cereals markets in Senegal; see, for example, Ross (1979); for an assessment of the poor state of research on such markets in the 1970s, see Harriss (1979).

25. Whitehead (1981) provides a complex and fascinating examination of this issue in the context of the food crisis in Northern Ghana.

Table 2.1
Bud: Area under Crops

	1971/2	1972/3	1973/4	1974/5	1975/6
Area farmed (ha.)	60	357	425	575	575
Including double cropping (ha.)	60	357	427	590	676

Source: Information supplied by Bud management.

Table 2.2
Bud: Total Tonnage Sold (Metric Tons)

	1971/2	1972/3	1973/4	1974/5	1975/6[E]
Tonnage exported	n.a.	2200	2590	4803	8483
Tonnage sold on local market	n.a.	894	3300	6806	5253
Total tonnage sold	n.a.	3094	5890	11609	13736

Source: Information supplied by Bud management.
E: Estimate.

3. Kirene Village: Economic Adaptation before Bud

In 1972, the beginning of the worst year of the 1970s drought in the Sahel, Bud Senegal arrived in the village of Kirene and began measuring and staking out the village land. They appropriated, without negotiation or prior compensation, a large tract of the best village land, and by 1975 had come to employ most of the adult village population on a seasonal basis.

Initial interviews with the villagers to elicit the effects of this incursion on their lives produced a curiously contradictory picture. From one point of view – exemplified by but not limited to the views of the younger people – the impact had been enormous. More cash income was being earned from wage work than from farming, and the income distribution had changed considerably, bringing many social changes. From another point of view – put forward by some older villagers – nothing had changed. The farming organization was much as before, socially the village was unchanged – only the source of some of the cash income had changed, and the village had apparently adapted to changing cash incomes without losing its fundamental character.

This and the next two chapters explore this contradictory picture. This chapter examines the organization of the Kirene village economy *before* Bud, concentrating on the ways in which the organization of the farming economy had adapted to land shortage and to pressures to produce higher cash incomes. Such a reconstruction provides a necessary basis for an understanding of the changes that followed; it needs to be rather detailed in order to avoid the mistaken impression that the Kirene economy had been static until the arrival of Bud. Furthermore there appears to exist no detailed study of the social and economic organization of the Serer Safen, the Senegalese ethnic group who make up most of the population of Kirene.[1] Since the evolution of the Kirene village economy was really very markedly different from that of villages only a few miles away, a difference resulting in large part from the specific social organization, and deliberate social isolation, of the Safen population, the ethnographic information forms an important element in understanding the economy.

The central theme of this and the next two chapters is the exploration of economic solidarity and its limits in Kirene, before and after the arrival of Bud. As the last chapter argued, the question of the extent to which commercial pressures on African farming systems reduce the forms of mutual support and solidarity within those systems is an important one for an understanding of food crisis and food security. In Kirene, the villagers' social solidarity and integration was immediately evident to an outside enquirer, and stood in sharp contrast to the social organization of non-Safen villages not far away. These chapters examine the ways in which that social cohesion continued to be rooted in forms of economic organization which, though far from egalitarian, did spread risks and rewards: notably forms of communal and co-operative labour in farming, and a resistance to internal monetization of economic relations among individuals in the village. We then explore the ways in which Bud was tending to undermine those patterns of non-commercial economic structure, the response of the villagers to those pressures, and the likely long-term outcomes.

A Homogeneous Safen Village

A number of the special features of Kirene's economy stem from the ethnic homogeneity and the consciously preserved social isolation of the village from the wider society, up to the arrival of Bud. In 1975, 94 per cent of the villagers said that they were Serer Safen, members of what ethnographers refer to as a 'sub-group' of the Serer, speakers of the Safen language which is quite different from the language of the largest Serer group, the Serer Sine. From scattered references in the literature and from the villagers' own account, the Safen were an independent group without a centralized political structure (in sharp contrast to the hierarchical social structure of the Serer Sine), having a social organization based on named matrilineal clans, and without endogamous castes.

Before colonization the Safen lived in a forested and hilly area, and were highly resistant to attempts by the Guelowar kings[2] and by the Wolof monarchy of Baol to the east at establishing control over them. They took their resistance to domination into the colonial period, and the area where they live therefore had until quite recent years a pattern of considerable residential instability. The elderly men in the village[3] trace the origins of the village back no further than their fathers' or grandfathers' times; furthermore, they describe a village founded three separate times. Kirene, they say, was formed by the migration of individuals to the area from the east (Diobass), the north (Pout) and the south (beyond Diass). Its history was marked by inter-clan violence and boundary disputes, and its population dispersed by attempts to avoid conscription into the French army by hiding in the bush.

By the 1970s the area around Kirene, the *arrondissement*[4] of Nguekhoh, was densely settled,[5] ethnically diverse, and intensively cultivated. Nevertheless, away from the ethnically mixed villages along the roads, there was still a predominantly Safen area in the triangle (see Map 2) bounded by the Dakar-Thiès and Dakar-Mbour roads where they diverge at Diemnadio. The area is uncharacteristically hilly for western Senegal, and there were no roads between the villages, only tracks which were frequently difficult to use because of sand

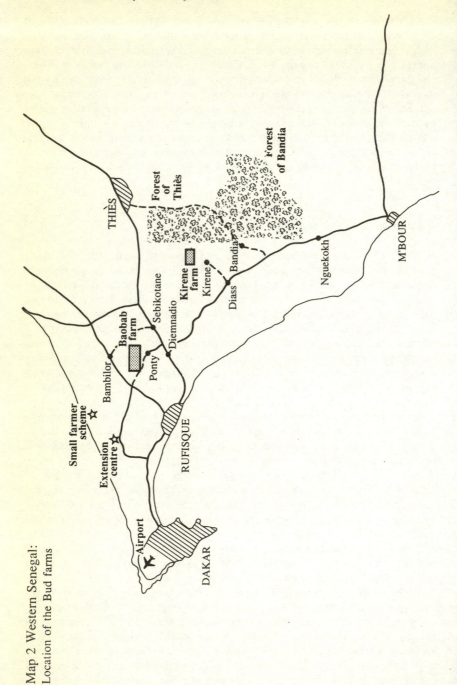

Map 2 Western Senegal:
Location of the Bud farms

or mud. The villages resembled one another greatly, and had retained a strong Safen identity. Although the distance as the crow flies from the Baobab farm in the Cap Vert to Kirene was only about twenty kilometres, one felt much further from Dakar.

Kirene itself lay about five kilometres north of the main Dakar-Mbour road. Bud had laid a laterite road to the farm: this ran over a rocky hill, from which one could see across the valley in which the village lay strung out in scattered hamlets. Bud had chosen the fertile land in the valley bottom for its estate. By the time of Bud's arrival the valley, which had been thickly wooded up to the end of the last century, had been cleared and intensively cultivated. Despite quite a large number of fruit trees and acacias, it had by then the open, domesticated appearance of a settled farming area.

Households and Domestic Work

The residential pattern of Kirene village, including the social organization of household and compound, and the settlement pattern with respect to village land are important for an understanding of the farming organization and of the impact Bud had on the village. The Kirene population was 1,150 in 1976[6] (and Bud had brought virtually no immigration to this village); this population lived, as in other nearby Safen villages, not in a nucleated settlement but in a string of small hamlets, spread out along the valley floor for a distance of more than two kilometres. None of these hamlets were themselves called 'Kirene': each had its own name, its own specific history, and by the 1970s its own small mosque. While the villagers said the name 'Kirene' was their name for the area, predating the government's creation of an administrative unit, and while there was no dispute as to which compounds did and did not belong to the village, nevertheless 'Kirene' was more a centre of gravity than a place; the village was constructing a new village mosque in the 1970s, near the geographical centre of the village, and near the compound of the village head, and when going to this area, people from the most distant hamlet spoke of 'going to Kirene'.

The hamlets of Kirene were clearly the product of considerable residential fluidity in the village until the recent past. Even at the time of Bud, one could not precisely identify the hamlets: some compounds seemed to be at a half-way stage to forming their own hamlet, and in the centre of the village, where distances between hamlets were shorter, compounds might seem to have ties to more than one hamlet. Nevertheless, on the basis of geographical proximity, and attendance at the local mosque, there were in Kirene in 1975 six hamlets each having between three to nine compounds, and a population ranging from 135 to 258 people. Bud had uprooted no houses, taking only farming land.

Within the hamlets, the smallest residential unit was the household, varying in size from 2 to 37 people. The household was composed of a group of people who ate meals together, jointly consuming the cooking of some of the women in the household. Most households had a common granary, and each had housing set closely together within some form of marked boundary. A compound, encircled by an outer wall, might contain one or many more such households.

Marriage was the most important of the social relations which both organized the performance of domestic work and determined the residents of the household. Marriage in Kirene was virilocal, a woman joining her husband generally in his father's household or compound. The dispersal effect of this on matrilineal kin was however tempered by a very strong tendency for people to marry within the village. Thus 92 per cent of the people living in Kirene in 1975 claimed to have been born there, and of Safen women aged over fourteen, 90 per cent had been born there. Furthermore, most of the Serer women who had been born elsewhere had married into compounds at the two geographical extremities of the village, having moved only a short distance, such as from the next village, at marriage. This reinforces the picture of Kirene as forming something of a continuum with the nearby Safen villages, with marriage an essentially local affair, often within the same area of the village.

Most children in Kirene in 1975 were growing up in their parents' household. Kirene villagers said that there had been in the past a practice of sending a male child to live with his mother's brother, but that this was dying out. It is not clear however that this had ever been a common strategy concerning inheritance. The Kirene data bear out studies of Serer groups elsewhere[7] which showed that male matrilineal descendants living with the household head had generally been brought there by female kin, particularly divorced or widowed mothers returning to their own kin, or had moved to join matrilineal kin after being orphaned. Only 1 per cent of boys under fifteen in Kirene were living in the household of their mother's brother.

All but two of the household heads in Kirene were male in 1975. Girls married between fifteen and twenty-five, and shortly afterwards moved out, while boys stayed on in the household, and married later, most often in their thirties. Men, once married, would frequently stay for a few years in the household, then move out to found their own. However, as the household head became elderly, one or more of the married sons stayed permanently with him, taking over the household when the old man became infirm. The widow of a household head, if she was elderly, was likely to remain with her married son (or her husband's married son by another wife), even though she would formally remarry.

There were few households with more than two married men in Kirene and one married son tended to move out when another married. The pattern of growth and fission of Kirene households, unaffected by recent immigration to the village, gave a smooth distribution of households by size, with a modal size of nine and a median size of six, and few households larger than thirteen. The very few large households tended to be special cases: married brothers working in the city, for example, leaving their families in the village. Within these households, marriage relations also structured the organization of domestic work. Domestic work – especially cooking and fetching water and firewood – was hard physical work which was organized entirely on the basis of a division of labour among women within the household, with virtually no cross-household co-operation. A young unmarried girl in a household would assist her mother with her domestic work. After marriage, when she went to live with her husband, she would take over the husband's mother's work completely: any further domestic work the mother-in-law did would be understood to be voluntary. Later, if her husband took a second wife, the two wives would share the work by turns. Only care of her own children remained the individual wife's responsibility.

By contrast, adult female kin of the household head had no domestic work responsibilities; for example, a divorced sister of a household head was doing no cooking except as an irregular favour to another woman. The domestic responsibilities resulted from the marriage tie and kin relations between men. Hence a woman living in her husband's house, but whose bride-price was not fully paid, was doing no housework. And in some cases the rules were adapted to free older women: hence, a young woman marrying the younger brother of a household head had moved into the joint household and taken over the housework of the oldest wife of that older brother.

It was, then, the preparation and common consumption of food, organized on the basis of marriage relations, which constituted the household. This same unit was also an important element in the organization of farming, especially of the millet crop which the household consumed in common. The household did not form in itself, as will be shown, a single farming unit; there was, however, a great deal of intra-household farming co-operation and the household head took an important organizational role in farming.

Indeed, farming and domestic work relations were distinct but closely interrelated. It had been common in the farming season, right up to Bud's arrival, for groups of separate households to amalgamate into larger households in the period of heaviest agricultural work, allowing the women to share the food preparation, and establishing a wider basis, as will be seen, for farming co-operation.

Compounds and Matrilineal Kin

While there was considerable regularity in the size, organization and internal structure of Kirene households, compound structure was another matter, and a testimony to wider relations of social organization. The 31 village compounds, defined by an exterior boundary wall, varied very greatly in size from one to seventeen households, with three containing ten households or more. The compound was not simply a residential unit, any more than was the household: the organization of both was linked to land use and farming organization in ways which are discussed below. While the households were largely structured on the relations between fathers and sons, the relations among household heads in the larger compounds were as likely to be based on matrilineal kinship as on paternal ties.

The operation of matrilineal kinship ties is important to an understanding of the Kirene economy because these bonds were a major means of spreading resources and support beyond the household. Matrilineal kinship relations in

Safen society are based on the clan, and on the 'mother's house'.[8] Every adult we questioned in Kirene could say to which of the named clans he or she belonged, and membership was passed down through the mother. Clan membership extended beyond the village boundaries, and the clans were neither corporate units nor units for inheritance purposes. Only the smaller matrilineal descent group, called the 'sub-clan' in some of the literature on the Serer, and the 'the mother's house' by the villagers, had had implications for inheritance. It was the unit within which certain land rights, cattle and certain other valuables had been inherited, the oldest male overseeing the goods in trust for the other members of the sub-clan. It was also this matrilineal descent group alone which was and remained exogamous: people drew a distinction within the clan between those from whom one might inherit, and those whom one might marry:

> X is of the same clan as his wife, that is not forbidden. He married his younger sister in his father's house. He could not have married his sister in his mother's house.[9]

> . . . two children who have sucked from the same breast can never marry.

Both the 'mother's house' and the wider clan membership ties appear to have had an influence on compound membership in Kirene. How this happened is not easy to identify because, beyond the immediate groups of their mother's siblings and their children, and father's siblings and their children, people in Kirene were often vague about precise lines of descent. There was no detailed tracing back of descent for generations, and many men whose fathers had come to the village as adults could not give the precise relation between their fathers and those with whom they came to live,[10] saying, 'I only know that they were kin.' This always meant matrilineal kin.

Compound membership suggested a history of movement of people, often as adults, to joint matrilineal kin. Thus, over half the household heads in compounds with at least three households were matrilineal kin of the compound head or of his father. Analysis of some of the largest compounds suggests that most sons, earlier as later, had stayed in their father's compound; however *if* one moved it was almost always to join matrilineal kin, sometimes fairly distant clansmen. Many stories of the beginnings of particular compounds in Kirene begin with the arrival of a clansman or clanswoman of someone already there. It also happened that childless adults might request the man's matrilineal descendants as wards:

> In the past, the child followed his father. For the nephew to go to his uncle, the father had to agree. The uncle could ask for the child, saying he had no one: he brought drink and asked for his nephew. The father might agree; if not, the child stayed with his father.

On the other hand, a woman might remain with her own kin, and the child grow up there:

> My mother was from Diobass, and she stayed there, she did not come here. My father brought me here after my mother died.

In general people in trouble, especially women, tended to turn to, and to return to, their 'mother's house'. Therefore, the more mobility there was within the society at any time, the more likely that there would be 'nephews' who remained to found households within a compound. Through these mechanisms of marriage in close proximity and residential mobility based on matrilineal ties, Safen society had long reconciled the view that one's kin were one's maternal kin, with virilocality in marriage and a continuing – *not* new – emphasis on the father–son link in terms of agricultural work and residence. The ideological importance of father–son relations had been considerably strengthened by the conversion of the village to Islam in the 1920s and 1930s, but the duality was certainly not removed.

The effect of this duality was to spread quite widely the net of kinship and potential support and obligation within Safen society. It gave men and women – but most notably women – strong ties outside their own households. As one man explained it:

> X, the old man, was the only real kin of my mother in the village; they were of the same clan. It was always there that my mother went when she had problems, all the time that she was alive.

These ties contributed in ways explored further below both to the farming organization and the wider patterns of economic solidarity within the village.

Land Holding and Access to Land

This same duality in social relations emerges in the determinants of access to land in Kirene, and was important in determining how the farmers responded when they lost a large area of their good land to Bud.

Land use patterns in Kirene remained, up to the arrival of Bud and beyond, highly concentrated geographically: compound members generally farmed land fairly close to the compound, and where they had to walk some distance to their fields this was usually in a direction which did not bring them close to another compound in the village. A major reason for residential mobility and the division and reforming of compounds seems to have been movement of new household heads to settle where there was land to farm.

The Kirene villagers drew a distinction, common in Africa, between two sets of principles of land inheritance in their society: on the one hand, the inheritance of land through the female line, 'so that one may say, the land of so-and-so'; on the other hand, the principles of transmission of usage rights over farm land, based chiefly on residence. Both principles had influenced the actual land use pattern in 1972.

Inheritance of land usage rights in Kirene depended generally on residence, especially residence in youth. Farm land was held largely (but not solely) by the heads of households, who distributed its use between the food crops and their own and other household members' cash crops. A young man who grew up in the household and worked for the household head had a claim on the latter to be found land to farm in adulthood. Once he established his own household the land he had was his to use. Of the heads of the sixteen sample households,[11] eleven had had the bulk of their farm land from their fathers; four had had land from their mother's kin with whom they had lived when young. The last was a cattle herder for the head of the village[12] who had provided land for him to farm.

On the other hand, the villagers could cite many cases where a household head had had insufficient land for division, and young men had moved away to find additional land. In this case he might have turned to a clansman who had inherited through the female line pre-eminent rights over an area of land which he oversaw on behalf of his descent group. Adult men in Kirene distinguished four men of their fathers' generation who had been land holders in that sense, the guardianship of the land passing between maternal brothers, and then to sisters' sons. Such land holders might not use the land themselves, but had, before the 1964 law, the right to levy an annual payment (called a *redevance* in the French literature) from users of the land outside the immediate descent group. The father of one household head interviewed had inherited land in this sense outside Kirene, but in Kirene paid a *redevance* to farm land belonging to another: when the father was disabled in an accident, the son took over the land with the associated payments.

These payments – according to one elderly man, they were formerly made in indigo for dyeing cloth, later in cash – had previously formed part of the marriage funds. The son cited above had had his marriage costs paid by his uncle from such returns on land. Whether such payments had been in decline before Independence was impossible to tell, but the villagers all claimed that they had been ended completely by the 1964 *Domaine National* law. Everyone was aware of this law, which was widely interpreted in the villages as stating that 'the land belongs to the person who farms it'.

Whatever the precise effects of the law, it is clear that the disjunction between land 'owned' and land farmed had long existed in Kirene. People who needed more land than their household heads could give them tended to turn first to their descent group for help. In the sample households in Kirene, several household heads had received land to use without payment in this way from close matrilineal kin. Several others had had land on a long-term basis from more distant kin, against payment of the *redevance*, and all three said that they had simply kept the land, but paid no more, after 1964. In addition two household heads had added to their land by destumping land regarded as ownerless, 'with the agreement of the head of the village'.[12]

Finally, the flexibility of land use in Kirene had long been increased by short-term borrowing and by land redistribution within the compounds. Each household head within a compound held his or her own land, but land borrowing among household heads or dependants on an annual basis within the compound was frequent and free of any payment.

In general the system of transmission of usage rights in land in Kirene had been a flexible one, and the principles had continued to serve up to the 1970s with no development at all of a market in land. But the flexibility in this system depended on the availability of land to permit mobility of residence where necessary. And land had ceased to be abundant in Kirene before the arrival of Bud. Well before 1972, the growing scarcity of land was forcing changes in the Kirene agricultural system.

Land Shortage in Kirene before 1972

There had been increasing pressure on available land in the Kirene area before the arrival of Bud. The farming histories convey the greater ease with which land could be found by previous generations. One man described a division in his compound in his father's time, when his father's nephew had moved a short distance away to found his own compound: 'That was perhaps twenty years ago';[13] 'then there were more fields and people could move more easily'. Another man, then elderly, had come to Kirene when already adult to join his sister and act as the Imam for the village. He married into the village, and was given by his in-laws land to clear and use, sufficient for his household and quite close to the centre of the village.

More recently, households with insufficient land had become more common. Another household head described how, at the death of his father, the sons and his father's matrilineal descendants had divided the land in two and moved apart. The compound of the sons had never had enough land after that, and they had had to borrow land from kin within the village each year. In 1975/6 members of several households which had not lost land to Bud still had to borrow land to farm.

The population of Kirene had increased quite rapidly over the last two generations. The older men and women conveyed memories of a much smaller village when they were young. The histories of the sample compounds show a pattern of growth and fission, and a number of households seem to have arrived about forty years previously, when wells had dried up nearby as a result of drought.

The drought which began in 1968 had added to the pressure on available land. Much of the higher land around Kirene has laterite in it, which makes it, the villagers said, poor millet land. With enough rain, it was good for tomatoes and groundnuts, but not for millet. The drought made it practically unusable. Furthermore, the drought meant that late millet could not be grown, and it was difficult to grow early millet a long way from the compound because it is very vulnerable to birds: hence there was greater pressure on land close to the village.

Another indicator of land pressure was absence of fallowing. The evidence on this is difficult to interpret because the villagers manured their millet fields by keeping their cattle on them for a period, and the Serer have long been accustomed to continuous cultivation of land near the compound (Pélissier, 1966). Farmers said, however, that fallowing of fields had been done in the past away from the household, but that there was no longer enough land. It is likely that the arrival of groundnuts as a cash crop soon after the turn of the century destroyed an older pattern of millet and fallowing on bush fields, a speculation that lies beyond the scope of this essay. At the time of Bud's arrival the commonest pattern seems to have been, apart from the vegetable fields, a rotation of millet (manured) and groundnuts (sometimes fertilized), year on year, with little fallowing.

Changing agricultural techniques in groundnut growing had not relieved pressure on land. Since the early 1960s, every compound in the village had acquired some agricultural equipment, typically a seeder and a hoe to be drawn by horse or donkey, and occasionally a cart. The effect was to increase the area which could be cultivated by an individual, or to reduce labour input, rather than to increase output per hectare, especially since use of chemical fertilizer was low: this is likely to have increased pressure on farm land.

This incipient land shortage had been one reason for the progressive fragmentation of land holdings. Increasingly, land was held by heads of the households, rather than kept by the head of the grouping of households for wet season farming and redistributed each season, as villagers maintained had been usual in the past.

> When the *Domaine National* happened, they said that where someone farms is his land. But by then we had already divided up the compound lands.

Where the head of a new household had to find land on his own initiative, he would hold that land himself, though he might lend it within the compound or outside. Where he did not have enough, dependent household members might also borrow each year.

The effect of this fragmentation was to reduce the land holding within which the rotation of crops was undertaken. Land use in Kirene by 1972 presented a fragmented patchwork very unlike the large areas of rotated crops described by Pélissier (1966) for Serer villages in this area in the early 1960s. The situation was already shifting towards that described by Sow (1975: 76) for a Safen village nearer Dakar in 1974: 'a mosaic of micro plots', decreasing fallowing, growing individualization of land holding, with farmers assembling a holding which was then internally divided between crops with a decreasing respect for the suitability of the soils for various rotations – in other words, a deterioration of farming practices.

The introduction of the vegetable crop into Kirene in the 1940s (discussed below) had been a partial palliative to the problem of land shortage. Vegetables were a crop with a higher value/land ratio, and therefore available cash crop land, if damp enough for vegetable growing, could be more minutely subdivided than if it were used for groundnut plots.

Farming Organization before Bud: the Millet and Groundnut Crops

In addition to the limited but genuine flexibility in residence and land use patterns in Kirene before Bud, the village economy had also displayed another kind of flexibility and adaptability in the way it had integrated cash crops into its farming organization. In 1975/6, the main village crops were early millet[14] and groundnuts. Late millet and sorghum, previously widely grown, had largely been abandoned before 1972 as a result of the drought. The millet was grown, in association with a type of bean, as the main subsistence crop; it was kept in household granaries and very rarely sold for cash. The groundnuts were sold to the government buying agency for cash. In addition to the groundnuts, before 1972 the villagers had been selling substantial quantities of vegetables and tree fruit for cash, and a number of other less widespread cash crops such as henna and cassava.

Most adults in Kirene farmed cash crops on their own account. The household head in Kirene had considerable influence over the cropping decisions of all the household members, a factor which was to be important in determining the response to Bud. This influence was exercised not by giving orders, but through land distribution and through access to seeds. Most land used by the household members was held and distributed by the household head. If land had to be borrowed to allow dependent members of the household to farm, this borrowing was usually done by the household head; sometimes dependent household members, especially the women, would themselves borrow from maternal kin, but household heads who could not provide land for their dependants found this a very painful situation.

Each farm plot had someone who 'farmed' it, in the sense that they were responsible for the work on it, oversaw the disposal of the crop and appropriated the revenue if it was a cash crop. Each household, in 1975 as in 1972, had one and generally only one millet farmer: normally the household head, sometimes a younger married or unmarried man supporting the household of an elderly man. In addition, most households belonged to what I have called a household grouping. These groupings were organized as a single household during the wet season. In addition to the millet fields of the separate dry season households, the senior household head would also plant a common millet field. The crop from this common field was stored separately, and kept for common consumption during the following wet season. This system continued in the compounds studied, right up to the arrival of Bud.

The cash crops were grown by the household heads, by other adult men in the household, and by older married women. Newly married young women rarely had plots, unmarried girls never, but young men would be given plots for cash crops from their late teens. Availability of seeds was an important constraint on crops grown in Kirene and the household heads dominated the supply of seeds. Groundnut seed was obtained on credit from the local government store, and this required membership of the co-operative, generally held only by married men. Otherwise groundnut seed might be kept from year to year, by household heads and others, or occasionally bought for cash. Seed was distributed by the household head to younger men and women, though older women were sometimes given seeds by kin outside the household.

Although each plot within a household had a 'farmer' responsible for it, that person never worked for the plot alone, and was not necessarily the person who did most of the work. Agriculture in Kirene was marked, as already suggested, by a very considerable amount of labour co-operation within farming, both within and across the household. Furthermore, by the 1970s, the bulk of the work on the millet and groundnut fields was being done by the men: in 1975/6 my estimates show 90 days per year on average being spent in agricultural labour by men with farm plots, but only 28 days by women. Although Bud may have reduced the totals, and although the total for women is more likely to be an underestimate than that for the men, due to better reporting of men's work despite my efforts to redress the balance, nevertheless this balance of work accords with observation during the farming season. The ratio of male to female labour had been increasing over the previous twenty years, since the women never used the equipment involving animal traction. The women therefore did little of the seeding or early hoeing, although they did most of the later hoeing by hand on their own fields. There is no evidence to suggest that Bud had changed this sexual division of labour.

The principles on which farm labour was organized in Kirene in 1975 had not changed from the period before Bud, although as will be shown in the next chapter they were coming under very considerable strain. This lack of rapid change in the principles of farming organization – the basis of the 'nothing has changed' school of thought about Kirene three years after Bud – was exactly what one would expect in a village where farming was the main economic activity up to 1972, where there were no non-farming households, and where the organization of farming was central to the social organization of the village. The farming organization still observable in 1975 closely resembles that described in other studies of farming among the Serer (Pélissier, 1966; Gastellu *et al.*, 1974): an emphasis on co-operative labour based on the residential units of household, compound and neighbourhood, with very little paid labour, especially by one village member for another.

The tables in this chapter show the organization of work on the farm plots of the sample households in Kirene in 1975/6. Two features emerge sharply: the extent of co-operative work on individual fields, and the sharp sexual division of labour in farming.

All households in Kirene – with the exception of a single-household compound – were part of household groupings. Within households and household groupings, the adult men frequently worked co-operatively, sharing horse-drawn equipment and moving from field to field. Men undertook all the operations, from sowing to harvest and threshing, on the men's fields and often but not always on the women's fields, too. The women sometimes undertook those operations (by hand) on their own fields, and always did the transporting and (usually) the winnowing of all the crops.

On the millet fields, 20 per cent of the farming operations done by men were done by co-operation across the whole household grouping, and this understates the extent of this co-operation before 1972. Co-operation had been particularly common on the collective millet fields of the grouping, and Bud, as will be shown, was undermining these collective fields. But, strikingly, co-operation across the grouping was even more common on the groundnut fields of the married men (29 per cent), and was also quite usual on the women's and the young men's groundnut fields. The grouping was a basis for co-operation in cash crop farming, not simply for growing a common food crop. Including intra-household co-operation, and the communal labour parties discussed below, far more farming was done co-operatively than was done alone.

In addition to the co-operative unpaid labour within household and grouping, there was another form of collective labour upon which the farmer called, which was more costly in terms of resources in cash or kind: this was the *dahira*. The *dahira*, a supra-household communal labour party whose membership was based on age group and residence rather than kin ties, represented a type of labour system much referred to, but little analysed, in the literature on African agriculture.[15] In other Serer areas, the person who called such a work group together provided a meal: in Kirene this had already by 1972 been turned into a more than token cash payment,[16] but the cash, instead of going into individual pockets, was put into a fund at the mosque for festivities and religious events (and possibly for charity). The *dahira* was a fairly formal male work group with an established membership based on the small local mosques: one *dahira* for each hamlet. Participation in the group work constituted an obligation for members, non-attendance being sanctioned by fines. There was, in addition, a village-wide *dahira* for the benefit of the central village mosque, still under construction, and a *dahira* for single and recently married young men, where the cash went to a fund for festivities, for buying a record player, or for construction of a village youth centre.

A majority of the *dahira*s in 1975/6 were on the groundnut fields (see Table 3.4), especially for the lifting of the groundnuts, physically the hardest task of the year. Fifty per cent of the groundnut plots of the married men were lifted by *dahira*, 65 per cent of those of the women[17] and 30 per cent of those of single men, who often performed this task themselves on their own plots. On average, the millet farmers participated in five *dahira*s during the season, and the other male farmers in seven. In 1972 the distribution of the use of the *dahira* among tasks – not among individuals – seems to have been much the same as is shown in these figures, although the villagers said that in comparison with, say, twenty years previously these groups were used for fewer operations in the farm cycle, in part because they had been replaced by the sharing of agricultural equipment.

Finally, there were a number of cases of paid labour of individuals on the fields: this category of work appears to have been higher in 1975 than in 1972, but was not unknown before Bud. Over half these jobs, paid by the task, were done by strangers: Peuhl[18] or Serer from the Sine who came through the village looking for work in the late agricultural season, and had done so for many years. As for paid work within the village, the Safen, in common apparently with other ethnic groups having a non-centralized social organization in Africa (Tosh, 1979), expressed an aversion to paying for work among themselves. There were however fourteen cases of such intra-village paid work in the sample, falling into two types. Some women paid young men a relatively small sum to thresh their groundnuts; other instances were the result of a crisis, particularly illness, where someone in the village was paid to come and perform a particularly urgent task, generally bringing his equipment with him. Scattered work of this kind had been known before Bud.

One of the most important features of this farm labour organization is the way in which the groundnut cash crop had been integrated into the farming system. My findings on this are exactly the same as Gastellu's research (1974) among the Serer Ol: more co-operative labour of all kinds (co-operation within household and grouping, and *dahira*) was used on the groundnut fields than on the food crop. In other words, the cash crop had been integrated into the farming system by distributing plots whose produce would be appropriated individually to all village members regarded as needing cash, while the plots were nevertheless farmed co-operatively at all the seasonal stages. By this means income from groundnuts was widely distributed to those who 'had needs'[19] within the village, and the income was also somewhat skewed towards those who already commanded most labour within the existing agricultural system, rather than undermining that system. Groundnuts became a means of obtaining agricultural equipment for established millet farmers, or cash bridewealth for younger men. The equipment, once acquired, was shared, thus reinforcing the wide distribution of benefits from the cash crop, though by the 1960s the groundnut harvest was no longer very remunerative.

The early operations on the fields were those most commonly undertaken co-operatively by married and unmarried men: planting, which had to be carried out rapidly after the first rains, and the early hoeings. In 1975/6 both of these operations were usually performed with animal-drawn implements, and the co-operative labour was closely related to the sharing of equipment. In four of the six household groupings observed, the equipment was held by the senior household head in the grouping; in the other two, ownership of hoes, seeders and animals was spread across the grouping; but in all cases it was both co-operatively used, and more generally shared, thus increasing efficiency in the use of equipment, and decreasing the cost of the equipment for each household. The general balance and distribution of labour between household and household grouping, and between tasks, had been much the same before Bud, with the exception of the extent of the collective millet fields (although the number of people farming and the income gained was changed considerably by Bud, as the next chapter will show).

There was no payment involved in this mutual aid within the household grouping, and no strict accounting or strict reciprocity of obligations. The mutual assistance thus permitted a household temporarily without an efficient millet farmer (for example, because of illness of the household head) to be 'carried' by the group in any year. In 1975/6 one grouping, a household with an old, infirm man at its head and a son still unmarried doing the farming, had all its fields, including the women's fields, planted and hoed by men from the other households in the grouping. The grouping thereby provided an insurance against the effects of temporary disaster, and a pool of co-operative labour on which a household head could rely if in need. In the long run, however, a household which was not viable in terms of food production would tend to disperse, and its members to join other households.

Vegetable Growing in Kirene

To this highly integrated millet- and groundnut-based farming system there were progressively added, before 1972, a number of other cash crops with more individualized production processes. The most important of these were vegetables and tree crops, and as the real returns from groundnut growing fell in the 1960s, increasing emphasis was put on these new crops, especially in areas of the village where the land was most suitable.

Vegetable growing had come to Kirene just before the Second World War. It was introduced by a few men of the generation of the head of the village, in 1975 in his eighties. Two men in the sample households, both then in their fifties, had spent time working on market gardens in the Cap Vert, the main vegetable growing area near Dakar: they had worked there for wages, and brought back techniques and seeds to Kirene. Like most of the Cap Vert market gardeners, the Kirene growers had had no help from government extension services and no credit. They took their vegetables to Dakar or Kaolack for the local market; they had never grown for export. A number of the biggest growers also acted as sellers on behalf of the village, dealing with other market dealers, or *banabanas* (travelling traders) from Dakar, and also bringing back seeds and inputs for the village. As a result small growers, men and women in the village, could operate with low overhead costs, and the crop became established in any household with suitably damp, valley-bottom land.

Within the sample households, of the 26 male adults who had been effectively engaged in farming in 1971, only four had not been vegetable growers before the drought: all at the higher end of the village where the land was least suitable. Only two of the vegetable growers, however, had vegetables as their only cash crop; the others also grew groundnuts. This is partly because membership of the co-operative, and deliveries of groundnuts, were the preconditions for obtaining credit for agricultural equipment. Certain men, for example a son of the head of the village who used equipment held by his father and made available to the whole household grouping, were under less pressure to plant groundnuts for this purpose, and this man said that from the early to the late 1960s he grew only vegetables and millet. Of the married women, those who lived in households where the men were not vegetable farmers had tended to grow only a few local types for household consumption. In the households where the men grew vegetables for sale, the women tended to do likewise.

One cannot deduce the organization of work on vegetable plots before Bud from the evidence in 1975 because Bud, as will be described, had virtually destroyed this cash crop. But the interviews suggest that the men's vegetable plots had been farmed in a more individual manner than the groundnut plots, mainly by the gardener himself. A sexual division of labour by task had been almost absent. The women had worked their own gardens, with assistance from other women in the household (rarely from the household grouping) and with much less help from the men than on their groundnut plots. The type of work involved was different: piecemeal work in the wet season, then fencing, care and regular picking.

Finally, there had been, especially in the late 1960s, considerable investment in fruit trees, at the lower-lying end of the village where the land was most suitable. These trees were individually owned, investments which would be passed on like agricultural equipment to whoever farmed the land afterwards – normally the men who had grown up in the household, and usually the sons. Two thirds of these trees had not reached maturity when Bud uprooted most of them; from the mature trees the fruit was sold each year on the Dakar market.

Vegetables and fruit trees were cash crops which brought in a great deal more cash per hectare and per farmer than groundnuts, though requiring a longer season of work. As land shortage developed in the village, the crop allowed cash incomes to be maintained and increased in the face of declining land availability, particularly for compounds in the central area of the village; it also spread labour use through the year, since the crop could be picked well into the dry season without watering in the low-lying areas, and made the best use of the land at the bottom of the valley. As the farmers switched to vegetables, the effect of the crop within the economy as a whole was to lessen the weight of co-operative labour in the farming system and to widen considerably the distribution of current income from cash cropping. The vegetables were thus producing a shift to a more individualized cash cropping system in the 1960s, without apparently reducing the collective nature of the work on the other crops, or the continuing importance given to the food crop.

This complex evolution of farm labour organization in Kirene, with a continuing and developing collective labour system, reinforced rather than undermined by the animal-drawn equipment, side by side with a more individually produced crop, is mirrored in other areas of the village economy. In particular, by the 1970s, a major change had occurred in the inheritance system, which lessened the collective and redistributive elements of wealth holding and inheritance. But this change had not been paralleled by any development of internal monetization of the village economy: on the contrary, the cash income from wage work before Bud, like the cash income from crops, had been used by the villagers in such a way that it did not encourage further internal differentiation through monetization of intra-village economic relations.

Wage Work by Kirene Villagers before Bud

The experience of wage work was not a new one for Kirene villagers, male or female, in 1972. What was new was the presence of wage employment within walking distance of their own homes. As is true of other Serer groups (Lacombe, 1977), Kirene villagers had a history of migration to the towns in search of work. This history goes back many years: for example, one man in his sixties had worked as a labourer on road building before the Second World War; his son, twenty-seven and just married, had spent several seasons as an apprentice in Dakar, learning dressmaking and tailoring. For the men, there had been three types of jobs: labouring in the towns (generally Dakar) or on the roads, apprenticeships, or working in the market gardens near Dakar. A number of men in their forties and fifties in 1975 had learned vegetable growing in this way and passed it on to younger men.

The most striking feature of these Kirene work histories is that the villagers, male or female, did not continue to migrate after marriage: they either departed definitively, or returned to settle in the village. The work histories of the men in the sample households show that of twenty-two men over twenty-five years of age in 1975, thirteen had worked away from the village for a period before marriage. All had ceased to migrate on marriage. It was a frequent comment that, once one had a family, one could not think of leaving the village for long periods. This pattern of migration before marriage continued up to 1972, though there was a shift from seasonal to all-year migration, the young men no longer returning each year for the farming season.

The past extent of permanent out-migration is of course more difficult to assess, though conversations with older villagers suggested it had been considerable. One woman in her thirties said, 'all my brothers are in Dakar', and a man in his fifties, 'all my age group went to Dakar, only some returned'. Demographic data for the village show some drop in the proportion of men to women in adulthood. In the sample households, four men who were working permanently away from the village had retained sufficient links for their names to be recorded on the census forms; two of these had wives living in the village.

From Kirene, as from other Serer villages, young girls also migrated to the towns in search of work, generally as maids in Dakar. Girls migrated much younger than the boys, often having a period of work in Dakar in their middle to late teens before returning to the village to marry. Of 52 women and girls of twelve years and over in the sample households, 29 (56 per cent) had been a maid in Dakar, generally in an African or Lebanese household, for a few years before marriage. Virtually none had worked after marriage, the exceptions being one woman who had gone away to work between divorce and remarriage, and one elderly woman who had once done so in the year of a disastrous harvest some time before.

There are two implications of this migratory pattern for the Kirene economy. First, once men were married and farming to support a household, the dry season was not seen as time 'free' for migration in search of work. The male farmers were present in the village all year, and saw the dry season work, including hedging, house maintenance and vegetable growing, as important. And second, when young men and women migrated before marriage they did not send substantial sums back to the village, but retained their incomes as a fund, in the boys' case for the marriage payments, in the girls' for clothing and other needs when they married. The village economy, in other words, was not dependent on remittances from migrants for its daily standard of living; the cash incomes had instead become part of a fund of resources for marriage costs, and occasionally for purchasing such items as a sewing machine.

The Currency of Money in Kirene before Bud

In Kirene, unlike some other West African societies, goods and labour were not exchanged for cash within the household. Money did not act as a medium of exchange within the household boundaries: it circulated instead as gifts and donations, from parents (especially mothers) to children, from the unmarried to household elders. Adults tended to retain their cash incomes and use them for well-defined areas of expenditure, depending on their position within the household. Otherwise resources were redistributed in kind: men buying cloth for their wives at ceremonies, women buying food, one woman giving cloth to a co-wife who had done some of her housework while she was at Bud.

Strikingly, given the proximity of Kirene to Dakar, these limitations on the use of cash did not stop at the household boundaries. Cash was little used as a means of exchange between individuals in the village as a whole, serving chiefly as a means of purchase (of cloth, kitchen utensils, metal goods, cement, animals) outside the village. Few people within the village exercised a non-farming activity which brought in a cash income from sale of goods or services to other villagers. The Kirene villagers were almost as averse to paying for goods produced by other villagers as to paying directly for their labour. The Safen had no endogamous artisanal castes, and no other ethnic groups practised trades in the village. Our census listed the following trades among the villagers' part-time non-farming activities: 2 bricklayers, 1 carpenter, 2 tailors/dressmakers, 3 woodcutters, 3 charcoal makers, 1 midwife, 2 shopkeepers, 3 vegetable sellers/fish sellers, 1 trader in old clothes, toiletries, etc. There were also four Arabic teachers who received gifts and donations, and two cattle keepers who had the right to the milk. One man was an actor/dancer, frequently away from the village.

This is a short list for a West African village of over one thousand people, as later chapters of this book will make clear. The absence in Kirene of the small-scale sale of cooked foods and other goods was really very striking, and such a trade made little headway during the first few years of Bud. Many goods sold in other villages were in Kirene fabricated by each household or purchased from elsewhere. Blacksmithing, and the large water pots used in the village, were both bought elsewhere; each household collected and wove its own straw for house building, as compared to a village discussed later, where people specialized in collecting, weaving, and selling it.

Instead, cash circulated as gifts and donations, within the village as within the household. Just as payments for the *dahiras* went, not into the pockets of the participants, but into a fund at the mosque, so formal gifts at ceremonies such as funerals were made in cash to the elderly, and to important individuals within the village. The better-off individuals received a great deal; they also gave a good deal in return. This circulation of cash played a considerable role in the wealth of powerful individuals: receivers of gifts and givers of aid in times of necessity. Indeed, one man defined a *khilifa* (an important man, a notable) as someone who received more than he gave when he attended ceremonies. The circulation of cash as gifts within Kirene implied, not equality, but an elaborate pattern of status and obligation. Islam, with its emphasis on gift giving and charity, had been integrated into this pattern without upsetting it.

Transition in Wealth and Inheritance before Bud

While the role of money in the village economy was not changing radically, the form of wealth and its inheritance was in transition in Kirene long before the arrival of Bud. Gastellu (1974) describes a pattern of accumulation of cattle within the 'mother's house' as current in the Serer area he studied in the early 1970s. In Kirene they described the system in the past tense, the time when 'wealth was cattle', speaking of a period before the arrival of the animal-drawn hoes, before the cement block houses, around the time of the coming of Islam. A man in his fifties recalled:

> Previously, if for example my sister's daughter married, my sister would give me the bridewealth to be invested in cattle. It would become a good which was held in common, and if I, my sister or her daughter had needs, we could seek help from that wealth.

Herds of cattle constituted in this way become the 'wealth of the mother's house', passed down in the maternal line, and to be looked after by the eldest of the brothers in that line for the benefit of all.

There still existed in 1975/6 herds of cattle which had been passed down through the mother's line, but their constitution through marriage, villagers said, had entirely died out, and with it the responsibility of older members of a descent group for young men's marriage costs. Men in middle age had saved cash for their own marriage, and the bridewealth was distributed in cash to the girl and to her parents and mother's kin.

> No one holds goods in common in the way in which they did before. That is dying. When you see it here, it just means that in places it is not yet finished. But when those old collections of wealth, those herds of cattle are finished, well that will be all, the system will be finished.

People attributed this change to many factors. But this was one of the most thoughtful assessments:

> You must understand that it is the goods themselves that change. The old wealth finishes and it is not replaced. People no longer give their goods into the control of others as they used to. For example, if you give your sister in marriage then you can no longer keep in your hands the money of the bridewealth if your sister needs it herself.

Cattle remained important in 1975/6. Their possession was still widespread, and one man in the sample spent a considerable sum on the purchase of cattle. They remained a form of saving, provided milk and manure, and were a source of prestige. But the form of possession and inheritance had changed.

By 1975/6, while goods a person had inherited through the maternal line might be passed on that way, 'new' goods, which someone (generally a man) had acquired on his own account, were passed mainly to the sons.

> When my father died[20] his mother's goods, the goods he had from his mother, went to the nephews. But that which he 'worked' himself went to his son.

This transition in inheritance, largely complete by 1972, had been associated with the arrival of cash cropping, constraints on land availability and the changing legal status of land holding, and the conversion to Islam.

> When I was young I farmed, and my father gave the proceeds to my uncle. When he was converted he stopped doing that.

Apart from cattle, the durable goods to be inherited by heirs included agricultural equipment, draught animals, cement block houses and furniture, and – a form of investment in land – fruit orchards. Farm land, of course, a different category, had long been passed on to those who had worked with the previous user.

In the 1960s, the proceeds of groundnuts and vegetables had been used to acquire agricultural equipment and draught animals, and to build cement block houses. There was a rather higher rate of equipment ownership per household at the end of the village where groundnuts had remained the main cash crop, as might be expected. In principle, these goods were sold at death, and the proceeds distributed among the sons. In practice, the sons might share out the equipment.

In 1975/6, 54 per cent of Kirene households had at least one cement block room. In the sample, these had been built mainly in the ten years to 1972, from the proceeds, the owners said, of vegetable growing. This is confirmed by the fact that there were more such rooms per household at the vegetable-growing end of the village. At this end of the village, furthermore, there was a significant tendency for those with no cement block rooms to own no equipment: in the sample, the household with insufficent land was in this position. Because of the system of borrowing equipment, standard of housing and furnishings was probably the best indicator of past cash income. The housing was inherited by the descendants who remained in the household at the old householder's death.

It was a frequent comment that when people inherited cash, they did not usually turn it back into durable wealth: 'People who inherit now just spend what they have inherited, and then it is gone.'

Economic Transition in Kirene before Bud

Kirene was, and remained, a poor village, and therefore to talk of accumulation within the village economy is to talk of small and limited processes. Nevertheless, despite the strains and pressures on the agricultural economy, what stands out from this survey of the evolution of Kirene before Bud is the continuing viability of the Kirene agricultural system, its capacity to adapt under pressure, and the fact that the village was still generating internal sources of accumulation from vegetable and fruit growing, rather than depending on cash income from outside.

If one wishes to characterize in general terms the transition which had occurred in patterns of transmission of wealth generation and control of income in Kirene before Bud, then one must necessarily be prepared to speculate about the organization of the economy several generations back, on the basis of the scattered existing information. My impression of the quite recent Safen past was that this was a society which was relatively egalitarian in the political sense: leaders among the older men, and sometimes the older women, who had both wealth and power, emerged as much as the result of personality and ability as through birth. Such people could construct large compounds around them, collect large herds, and become for a time receivers, and redistributors, of large amounts of income. But to some extent this wealth 'died with'[21] its owner or recipient, the rest becoming part of the collective goods.

The inheritance system tended to disperse access to the wealth in the following generation, and once the personality at the centre of the large compound died, the compound would tend to divide, and some households to move away. Thus the fluidity of the society, the dispersal effect of the inheritance patterns, and the scope for individual pre-eminence of people with 'strength' led to the rise and decline of large compounds, and contributed to the mobility of the population. Compound, and to some extent household size was a variable responding in any generation to relative economic success.

Such an 'egalitarian' situation is compatible with considerable differences in current real living standards, involving much circulation of cash in gifts, not payments. In 1972 elements of this remained in Kirene, of course, allied to a different inheritance pattern. The establishment of such wealth involved the ability to call upon the labour of others in farming. In one generation, real income differences would be wide, but the differences were somewhat transient, tending to be dispersed through inheritance patterns.

Much had changed in this pattern before 1972. The shift in inheritance, virtually complete, had been not simply from the mother's to the father's line, but above all from collective to individual property. Within farming, the control of the individual household head over farming had been reinforced in some ways by government pressures (the rules for access to credit), by the new agricultural equipment, and by Islam. But it had been threatened in other ways, notably by the increasing shortage of land. Access to the farm labour of others in the household was closely associated with ability to provide resources for those dependants to use in farming on their own account. It was also predicated on household heads producing from their farming the basic subsistence crop for the household's consumption. And household heads were closely embedded in a network of obligations which ran beyond the household and could not be maintained without access to cash.

Kirene villagers had attempted to square these circles by developing a crop – vegetables – which made a more limited demand on both land resources and access to the labour of others while providing an input of cash to communal labour and other village activities. This had not created a monetized economy, but had generated assets from gardening – houses, hoes, horses and cattle, vegetable land, fruit trees – which could be passed on to individuals within the confines of household or compound. Depending on the pressures of population on land, and the level of outmigration, this might have led to the creation of a more lasting, self-reproducing stratification within the village, the resources to maintain it being passed down across generations within the household. But there were still major income-dispersing forces at work.

In this shift to individual inheritance within household boundaries, women had been losers: though they had a small share in inheritance, they lost their access to shared resources outside the household, and saw their rights and possibilities becoming ever more dependent on their husbands. Young unmarried men faced a comparable effect, but their earning capacity, eventual inheritance and scope for farming were greater. Though from one angle the Kirene farming system had taken on something of the appearance of a household farming system, the true pattern of intra- and cross-household rights and responsibilities was more complex, as the response to wage labour makes clear.

Up to the time of Bud's arrival, the village economy of Kirene had retained considerable viability by adapting to land pressure through pre-marriage migration and cropping changes. The farming system was producing most of the villagers' basic food; it was producing a surplus, though small, for reinvestment in agricultural development; and the dynamic of change within the village was still being generated from within the agricultural system. Furthermore, despite developing differentiation, the form of production of millet and groundnuts and the absence of monetization had mitigated the effects of the changing inheritance pattern by retaining considerable elements of mutual farming assistance and current income redistribution. Into this system came Bud in 1972, and we now turn to the effects of land loss, wage labour and wage incomes on this village economy.

Notes

1. There is substantial literature on the Serer Sine, the largest and most hierarchical of the Serer groups (Pélissier, 1966; Reverdy, 1964; Lericollais, 1972; Klein, 1978; Diagne, 1967). There is some work on the Serer groups in the Baol (Gastellu *et al.*, 1974; Gastellu, 1981), but no detailed studies of the Safen. The following account is assembled from scattered references in the literature, especially Pélissier.

2. This was the royal lineage of the Serer Sine, of Mandinka origin.

3. All quotations and references are from my own fieldwork unless indicated. I have not used the names of village informants, since I had not requested their permission to do so in print.

4. This is a local administrative area, a sub-division of a Region (in this case, Thiès Region).

5. The density was 75 inhabitants to the square kilometre of land (not including forest reserves and urban areas) by the early 1960s, one of the highest rural densities in the country (Pélissier, 1966: 187).

6. The figures are from the village census taken for the fieldwork.

7. See particularly Dupire *et al.*, (1974: 428–39).

8. The 'mother's house' is the group of people born of the same woman, or of maternal sisters. Gastellu (1974) found this expression in use among other groups of the Serer; he refers to this small descent group as a '*sous-lignage*'.

9. The 'father's house' here is the matrilineal descent group to which the father belongs. The speaker is a man in his forties.

10. This is common in many matrilineal societies (Schneider and Gough, 1961: 491) and distinguishes them sharply from patrilineal societies where descent is traced back for many generations.

11. All the detailed data on economic and social organization are drawn from these sample households; the research method is briefly described in the Appendix. For full details see Mackintosh (1980).

12. The village head in Kirene played an administrative and leadership role which involved adjudicating in land questions. He was given the title of *Lamane* by the villagers (a title which had carried the connotation of large landowner or 'priest of the land'): he himself was not a large landowner in the old sense, though his father had been. There seems in Kirene to have been a substantial element of collective consent in choosing (and deposing) village heads.

13. The period referred to is, from other evidence, nearer forty than twenty years before.

14. The millet *Pennisetum gambicum*.

15. For example Cleave (1974) dismisses the work groups as inefficient for commercial 'smallholders', but offers little analysis. Gastellu (1974) analyses their composition for the Serer Ol, another non-hierarchical Serer group, and confirms the pattern described here of membership based on neighbourhood, not kin ties.

16. See Table 3.4 and Chapter 4.

17. This is not clear from Table 3.4, because the *dahira*s are recorded according to the farmer who requested them; married men often used the same *dahira* to lift their wife's groundnuts, though women might also call them on their own account.

18. The Peuhl are another of the Senegalese ethnic groups, known elsewhere as Fulbe; they supply many of West Africa's nomadic herdsmen.

19. This phrase recurs in all the villages studied; the farming of individual plots was seen as a recognition of people's responsibilities to look after their own needs and fulfil their own obligations.

20. A death which occurred a couple of years before the interview.

21. There was a saying in the village, repeated to me several times, to the effect that when a rich man died, half his wealth died with him.

Table 3.1
Kirene: Farm Labour Organization. Labour on Farm Plots of Married Men (Number of Cases) (Millet and Groundnuts Only)

	Self or self + young boys	Self + other men in household	Self + other men in household grouping	Women in household	Male relative outside household	Dahira	Paid labourer
Land clearance	32	18	6				2
Millet							
Seeding	15	8	8				
First hoeing	14	9	8			2	
Second hoeing	16	8	7			2	
Harvest	16	6	3			8	
Transport of harvest				33			
Sub-total	61	31	26	33		12	2
Groundnuts							
Seeding	5	2	12		2		2
First hoeing	9	2	10				2
Second hoeing	11	3	8			1	
Third hoeing	9	2	6			3	
Lifting	5	2	4			12	
Threshing	10	4	2				7
Winnowing	1	2		13			7
Sub-total	50	17	42	13	2	16	18
Total	143	66	74	46	2	28	20

Number of fields: millet 33; groundnuts 23: total 56   Number of individuals: 19

Table 3.2
Kirene: Farm Labour Organization. Labour on Farm Plots of Unmarried Men (Number of Cases) (Millet and Groundnuts Only)

	Self or self + young boys	Self + other men in household	Self + other men in household grouping	Women in household	Owner of borrowed land	Dahira	Paid labourer
Land clearance	6	3			1		2
Millet							
Seeding		1	1				
First hoeing		1	1				
Second hoeing		1	1				
Harvest		1				1	
Transport of harvest				2			
Sub-total		4	3	2		1	
Groundnuts							
Seeding	1	2	6				1
First hoeing	2	2	5				1
Second hoeing	4	4	2				
Third hoeing	4	1					
Lifting	5	1	1			3	
Threshing	6		1			1	2
Winnowing	1			9			
Sub-total	23	10	15	9		4	4
Total	29	17	18	11	1	5	6

Number of plots: millet 2; groundnuts 10; total 12   Number of individuals: 9

Table 3.3
Kirene: Farm Labour Organization. Labour on Farm Plots of Married Women (Number of Cases) (Groundnuts Only)

	Self or self + small girls	Men in household	Self + Men in household	Men in household grouping	Individual male, unpaid aid	Owner of borrowed land	Self + other women in household	Dahira	Paid labour
Land clearance		12		4		1			
Millet (no cases)									
Groundnuts									
Seeding	1	9		5	2				
First hoeing	2	11		4					
Second hoeing	10	4	1	2					
Third hoeing	10	1	1						
Lifting		2		1				1	3
Threshing		6			1			11	6
Winnowing	5		3				7	4	2
Total	28	45	5	16	3	1	7	16	11

Number of fields: 17   Number of individuals: 17.

Table 3.4
Kirene: Farm Operations Performed by Communal Labour Parties, 1975/6 (Number of Cases)

	Performed for:					Average no. of participants	Average cash payment (f. c.f.a.)
	Married men (millet)	*(Groundnuts)*	*Single men*	*Married women*	*Total*		
Dahira 'of the mosque':							
village or neighbourhood	3	8	1	4	16	23	2767**
Youth group:							
village or neighbourhood	6	8	2	4	20	14	1964
Less formal groups							
Age group	1				1	15	kind
'Mas poche'*		2		1	3	5	1025
Informal assistance		1	1	1	3	8	1000***
Total	10	19	4	10	43		
Of which harvest	7	15	3	7	32		

* Literally, work group 'for the pocket'
** One payment in kind not included
*** Two paid in kind, not included

Note: These numbers do not tally with those on Tables 3.1 – 3.3 since this table counts number of work groups organised; Tables 3.1 – 3.3 count number of fields worked, which will be larger.

4. The Impact of Bud on Agriculture in Kirene

The development of a mixed farming system, including food crops, cattle keeping, and market gardening for the nearby towns, had been a rather successful use of the economic and ecological resources of Kirene up to 1972. Bud Senegal entered this still viable village economy in late 1972, when the wet season crops, such as they had been in a serious drought year, were already harvested, but the vegetables still in the fields. The Bud estate, once established on Kirene land, effectively cut off, as this chapter will show, the pattern of evolution of the local farming system. It destroyed the most lucrative, and developing, cash crop, and undermined elements of the co-operative labour system. At the same time it created sharp divisions between farmers who lost their land and those who did not. In that sense it identified the limits of economic solidarity in Kirene and pushed the farming system beyond them: there were no redistributive mechanisms within that system which could make up for the loss of good farming land at one end of the village, given the existing shortage of land.

This chapter explores the immediate impact of Bud on the Kirene farming system in terms of appropriation of land and competition for labour.[1] It also examines the way in which this impact was mediated through the villagers' response to the estate. It shows that they attempted to maintain their wet season farming, rather than giving up, even where the loss of land had been worst, and that the principles on which farming was organized did not change. Rather, the implications of the principles altered. As the co-operative labour forms were progressively weakened, and the surplus generated within agriculture removed, the farming system, which had been notably adaptable, was becoming rigid, static and increasingly fragmented. Bud was undermining, in other words, the farming system which it had supposedly been intended to complement.

The Uneven Impact of Land Loss

The immediate impact of Bud on the farming system in Kirene came through the loss of farm land to the estate. Bud took 50 hectares in the first year, and 150 hectares in all, of the best land: low-lying, heavier soil that was therefore the most fertile in a drought. This loss of farm land close to the village was very unevenly distributed among Kirene farmers because of the geographical concentration of farming around each compound. The compounds closest to the Bud farm lost a great deal of their land, while households at the other end of the village lost none. Similarly, the loss was unequally distributed across village crops. The area taken by Bud included most of the market gardening land, since it had been the compounds with access to the suitable soil at the bottom of the valley which had taken up market gardening, and this land was almost all appropriated.

Thus, of the sixteen households studied (spread geographically across the village) six had lost a great deal of land, three had lost some land, and the rest none.² Of the first six households, two were planting in 1975/6 only land acquired or borrowed since 1972, two had found since then between a third and a half of their planted area, and two were still using their remaining land. All said their planted area had been reduced by the losses, and the last two said that they had been pushed from good to poor land. Of the three households which lost some land, two had acquired a small proportion of their planted area after 1972. Of the seven other households, only one (which had four adult males farming) had borrowed some land in 1975/6, and some of the others had lent land that season. Of all these households only one had been seriously short of land before 1972: when Bud came, it was one of the six which suffered major loss.

Bud paid no compensation to the villagers for the loss of land (which was their source of livelihood) but it did pay some belated compensation for vegetables and tree crops destroyed by its bulldozers. No grain crops were in the ground at the time. Bud's lists of those paid compensation confirm the land losses claimed by the members of eight of the households interviewed.

As the above cases show, after Bud's arrival there was some redistribution of land towards the members of households which had lost most, but it came nowhere near spreading the losses evenly across the village, and much of it was in the form of very temporary loans. The existing land distribution and redistribution mechanisms in the village, discussed in Chapter 3, contained few intra-village as opposed to intra-compound redistribution mechanisms apart from the palliative of moving away to new land. It had already become clear that these principles of land distribution would tend to produce increasing inequality in conditions of land shortage and inability to move: Bud worsened the situation drastically. A reallocation of land in the village on a more equal basis after Bud's arrival would have gone against the existing principles of organization of the village economy, and it did not occur. In the question of land access, as in all other aspects of farming organization, the villagers atte.·pted to maintain their existing principles of organization despite Bud's incursion.

There was little unused land in Kirene, and borrowing land outside the compound became far more difficult after Bud. The head of the compound most affected by land shortage said:

> This compound does not have enough land. Before we used to borrow land for millet and groundnuts, where Bud is now, from X. Now he has none to lend.

In 1975/6 the speaker borrowed land from three separate people, all living in his hamlet or nearby. The loans were generally for a year only, then the land would be taken back, and in no year since 1972 had he been able to borrow enough for his household members as well as himself. Before Bud, he said, loans had been easier, and for much longer periods.

Ability to borrow depended heavily on the personality and position of the household head, who would borrow first within the compound, then from maternal kin and near neighbours. One man said that there was land at the other end of the village, 'but that is too far': presumably too far socially as well as geographically. The borrower was supplied from land already in use: in addition, three of the household heads who had lost most had cleared some land which had lain long unused, with the agreement of the village *Conseiller Rural*.[3] This land was not very fertile ('not good'); it was 'red land', containing laterite. The restricted scale of these clearances, in relation to need, confirms that there was little land unused at Bud's arrival, at least in the relevant part of the village. One young household head said tersely, 'It is not worth looking for more land, there isn't any.'

The Effect of Land Loss on Food and Cash Crops

The Bud estate operated in the dry season, and the Kirene villagers continued to plant crops in the rains. This indeed was the basis for the argument advanced by some observers (not the villagers) that Bud incomes were a net gain to the village. This could not be so, because of the loss of land. Nevertheless, most of those who had farmed before Bud continued to do so, the exceptions being some women and single men for whom no land could be found.

In 1975/6 all the sample households in Kirene planted both millet and groundnuts. Furthermore, as Table 4.1 shows, the heads of households which had lost most land attempted to maintain the areas of millet planted, at the expense of a drop in the acreage of cash crops. The heads of households with insufficient land were allocating what was available first to millet, then to their own and other married men's cash crops, then to wives, and last to unmarried men. As the head of one of these households said:

> For the first two years the women had no land for groundnuts. Only this year have I found land for them, and the children[4] still have no land.

This was the view of the wife of a man who lost all his lands to Bud:

> Now I can only farm if someone gives me land. The last two years I did not farm; this year my mother's older brother has given me a small patch of land for tomatoes.

This emphasis on food crops appears to be in part a risk aversion strategy; it also reflects the existence of a cash income from Bud as an alternative to cash crops. In addition, it results from the social importance of millet growing in this society.[5] The household heads were able to make this decision because they controlled the allocation of land to people, and therefore generally to crops, within the household, and in the circumstances of acute land shortage their dependants had little hope of finding land elsewhere.

The land loss also broke the link between size of household and the area of food and cash crops grown, as Table 4.2 shows: whereas for the households which had lost little or no land there was quite a strong positive correlation between the area planted with each crop, and both size of household and number of male adults farming, for the subset of the sample which had lost a great deal those correlations were weak and non-significant. The land loss had apparently been serious enough to break the relation between area farmed and the needs and the possibilities of the household.[6]

Those household heads who had lost no land to Bud said, unanimously, that they had not reduced their own millet area after 1972. However, these statements leave out of account the effect of Bud upon the collective fields cultivated by household groupings. I return to this below in the discussion of conflicts in labour use. In households with enough land however, groundnut planting actually rose after 1972 because of the effect of Bud on the vegetable crop.

The Decline of Vegetable Growing in Kirene

> Groundnut growing is increasing here now. Some people who planted 1.5 hectares before are planting 2 or 3 hectares now because they have no vegetables to sell. (The Kirene *Conseiller Rural*)

The most spectacular effect of Bud on Kirene farming was the destruction of the profitable vegetable crop. People in surrounding villages commented on this fact.

> Kirene, instead of advancing, it is going backwards. Previously they really grew a lot of vegetables. For three months there were trucks in the village loading vegetables. Now there is nothing.

> Before we were always hearing about Kirene, about how rich it was. Now we hear that no longer.

These remarks were made by villagers of Soune Thiambokh, a village lying on the opposite side of the estate from Kirene, in the context of a discussion with them about why, in 1974, they had strongly resisted the expansion of Bud on to their lands. They emphasized that the Kirene villagers had been far more successful vegetable growers than themselves before Bud.

In 1975/6 there remained few vegetable growers in Kirene (Table 4.3). The land taken by Bud included the best land, according to the villagers, for fruit trees and vegetable growing, and the households at the opposite end of the village had never been, their members said, vegetable growers on any scale. In the interviews in Kirene there was a fair degree of independent agreement as to which households contained the people who had been the main market gardeners in the village before Bud, and they all lived in areas where people had lost some or all of their land. In 1975/6 the few remaining vegetable plots were mainly on land immediately bordering the Bud land.

Bud's compensation lists also show that in late 1972 the Bud land was used for fruit trees (272 producing trees and 512 young trees), vegetables and fields of henna and cassava. Virtually all were cash crops, to be sold in town. One could not, however, use these compensation lists to measure the average loss of cash crop income as a result of Bud, because they were drawn up for the very worst year of the drought. The drought had begun in 1968, and already by 1971 three gardeners in the sample had given up for lack of water. Vegetables in Kirene were a wet season, non-irrigated crop, planted during the rains. The low-lying soil remained humid in normal years, so that vegetables could be picked for several months after the rains had stopped, without further watering. The short, inadequate wet seasons of the drought years dried out the land and reduced its suitability for this crop.

The first impact of the drought seems to have been on the fruit trees. Here, as in the area where I lived closer to Dakar, the pawpaw trees were the first to go, and then many other trees also died. Kirene had been accustomed to sell fruit as well as vegetables on the Dakar market, and many young trees had been planted before the worst of the drought. The ground had already dried considerably when 1972 arrived. Table 4.4 shows the disaster of the 1972 harvest in the Thiès Region which includes Kirene. Bud therefore arrived in Kirene just after the worst harvest in the memory of most of the villagers. It was a year when the millet harvest had been non-existent, and the vegetables had died in the fields on transplanting.

> That year, there was no rain, and very little was growing in my fields when Bud arived.

> That year I transplanted my aubergines, and they all died because the gap between the rains was too long.

> 1972 was a *very* bad year, the worst here. That year no one paid their debts at the co-operative.

The arrival of Bud in Kirene at this serious moment for the village economy partly explains the contradictory mixture of responses to the firm's arrival. It had an air of the providential, despite the fact that it proposed to take over village land. Allied to the exaggerated promises of income from employment, made or believed to have been made by the firm, this helps explain both why people were more accepting of its arrival than they might otherwise have been, and why they hoped for more than it could deliver.

Not only did Bud take most of the good vegetable land, it also competed for male labour with the needs of the vegetable crop in particular, since vegetables had been picked into the dry season. Furthermore the men within the sample whom we had identified as having been the vegetable growers on the largest scale were all among those who were taken on for the better (that is, longer lasting) seasonal jobs at Bud. They had shared the high expectations of the income Bud might provide and during one year (1973) some of them even worked into the wet season at Bud, thus jeopardizing their millet crop. As it had become clear that Bud would never offer permanent employment for more than a couple of people, these men had retreated from their commitment to wage work. Some (two in the households studied) had left Bud by 1975, and said that they would try to return to market gardening, finding new land. One was trying to combine work at Bud with at least some vegetable gardening.

For those who had not gained so much in the past from vegetable growing, whether household heads, dependent men, or women, several processes were at work. For them too, wage work at Bud constituted a disincentive to continue with this cash crop, because of the alternative source of income the wage provided. This was especially true of the young men. One of them explained:

> In 1971 we did not know that Bud was going to arrive, so we worked very hard at farming. Since then we have somewhat neglected our fields . . . We all neglected our vegetable fields after Bud's arrival.

> In 1972 I sowed vegetables and lost them all. Since then I have no more seeds. My feelings have cooled towards vegetables.

This last quotation points to what I think was the process by which Kirene vegetable growing effectively ended. A combination of the drought, loss of much of the suitable land, and the competition of Bud jobs meant that the big market gardeners in the village mostly gave up the crop. This meant that the smaller growers, men and women, had no access to seeds, advice, or easy sale of this highly perishable crop. As the vegetable economy of the village broke down, those of the smaller growers who wished to continue found it very difficult, and were pushed instead into groundnuts as their cash crop. This last effect was particularly marked in the case of women, for whom vegetables had been a quite lucrative cash crop. Only a few determined older women succeeded in continuing. One of those who had given up said:

> I could find other land, but I have no seeds. We used to get seeds from people in the village, but they have all stopped growing vegetables.

Many other women repeated this explanation. The women's cash crop was dependent not only for land but also for its other inputs on the men's vegetable growing.

There is one final reason which was put forward by the villagers for the decline of vegetable growing. As one former market gardener confirmed, the vegetable fields had been farmed more individually than the millet and groundnut fields. With little collective labour, and the hiring of wage labour virtually excluded, it was very difficult for farmers to replace their own labour while they were at Bud in the way some managed to do on their millet and groundnut fields. We return to this issue below in the discussion of conflict between Bud and farm labour.

Villagers' Participation in Estate Work

The issue of conflict between estate and farm work arises because the participation of Kirene villagers in the Bud estate labour force was very high (Table 4.5). At the end of the village where land had been lost, the Bud work was sought as a partial recompense; at the other end, farmers hoped to add wages to their existing farming incomes. This differentiates Bud work from the previous wage work done by the villagers, which had all been migratory labour seen as a (possibly temporary) alternative to settled farming.

Among the men, it was the millet farmers or other active married farmers, that is those with the strongest commitment to farming and supporting a household, who were the most likely to work at Bud (Table 4.6). (Furthermore, two of the millet farmers not working at Bud had done so, but had lost their jobs.) Elderly household heads, and other married non-farmers, did not work at Bud. Single men tended to do both or neither. No one worked at Bud who did not also farm.

Bud was therefore providing wage work for the married men who no longer wished to migrate in search of it. The interview data show that single men over fifteen, to whom the migration option was still open, tended to work irregularly if at all at Bud. Of the eighteen single men in the sample, six worked at Bud in 1975/6. Six were in Coranic or Arabic school, either in the village or elsewhere, one was studying in Koweit, and one in Lycée in town.[7] The remaining four were in apprenticeships in Dakar. Only 3 per cent of school age children in Kirene were undertaking education in French, but there had been in Kirene a tradition of putting the boys through some form of religious education and apprenticeship training, and Bud did not see · greatly to have eroded this in the three years of its presence. Furthermore, any immediate effect in discouraging migration by single men may have been wearing off by 1975/6. Several younger people in the village said to us in 1976 that young men in their compound had gone back to Dakar that year for the season, after a couple of seasons' work at Bud: a mixture, it seems, of disillusion stemming from the high hopes of permanent employment at Bud which some villagers had had at the start, and unwillingness to exchange the environment of the town for the exceedingly hard agricultural work at Bud.

Women's participation in the Bud labour force was also associated with their participation in farming, although the association was not as close as for the men. Married women who farmed were more likely to work at Bud than those who did not, and the association becomes even closer if we remove from the figures those married women who said that they were prevented from farming by lack of land.

Among the women, farming, in the sense of taking responsibility for a farm plot, was generally undertaken only by older married women. The determinants of both farming and estate work by women were not simply a function of age, however, and if household position was important, so were the problems of organizing domestic work. Given the physical stress of domestic work, a woman could not do the cooking and washing for a household single-handed, and work at Bud, without risking physical exhaustion. As the discussion of domestic work in Chapter 3 showed, it was women with married sons, and women not living in the household as wives, who did not have domestic work obligations, and it was they who were the most likely both to farm and to work at Bud. One young woman, the first of her generation to marry into her household, described her Bud work history.

> When I was first married I lived with my mother, and I often went to Bud looking for work, but I never found any. Then when I joined my husband I was already pregnant and could not work. This year I have not been there: I am the only person who does the housework . . . She [her husband's mother] would not agree to stay in the house while I went to the field [Bud].

For married women Bud work, in other words, had been fitted into the existing social relations within the household determining their access to income. No combining of households developed, in the manner of the wet season farming, to make estate work easier for women. Many married women with household responsibilities did manage to do wage work, however, though less easily than others. Some shared both housework and Bud work with unmarried daughters. In some cases co-wives in the same household[8] co-operated in organizing the housework around Bud, sometimes doing different shifts so there was always someone in the house. In the worst position were women with no help in the household: in the Bud season the working day of one such woman ran frequently from 4 a.m. to 11 p.m. with little break during the day. There was furthermore no flexibility at all in the sexual division of labour in domestic work (unlike that in farming). Men and boys never helped. As one woman with the working day just described explained: 'I have only sons, so there is no one to help me.' And in Kirene there was no tendency for women to take on young girls as paid maids in these circumstances: for the villagers this was something which happened in town, not among themselves.

Opposition by men to women working at Bud was rare. The only two women in the sample who said that their husbands were opposed to their working at Bud because the work was 'too hard' were both married to men working outside the village. Women denied the existence of such opposition by men present in the village:

> All the women here are workers: that is why the men do not want to prevent their wives from going to work.

> I did not have to ask. Everyone was going off to work there.

> The first time, you must say to your husband 'I am going'. That is all.

Despite the similar determinants of Bud work and farming, more women worked at Bud than had previously had their own fields. Married women generally went to Bud if they could. Furthermore, girls began to work there much younger than boys: as young as twelve, despite the efforts of management (who found them unproductive) to prevent it. Of eleven girls aged twelve and over in the sample, eight worked at Bud for some part of the season, two were maids in Dakar, and one was in Coranic school. Girls, it appeared, were generally seen by their parents as available for wage work at a much younger age than the boys, and in some households Bud was seen as a preferable alternative to letting young girls go off alone to Dakar.

Conflict between Estate Work and the Farm Labour Calendar

The view propounded by the Bud management was that Bud, being a dry season enterprise employing seasonal labour, should have no effect on villagers' farming of their own crops in the wet season (loss of land apart, presumably). Some villagers appeared to concur in this. As they put it, Bud would be an excellent thing were it somewhere else (nearby) on someone else's land.

In 1975/6 there was some seasonal overlap between farm and estate work (Figure 4.1). The Bud seasonal work began just as the groundnut lifting was ending, and overlapped with beating and winnowing the groundnuts for sale. The vegetable picking ran well into the Bud season, though it was largely over by the time the Bud harvests were ready in late February. At the end of the Bud season, the work ran well into the clearing of land for the village crops.

Clearly, the 1975/6 farm calendar may itself have been compressed by the demands of Bud work. The vegetable season in particular was shorter than it would have been had this still been a major village crop, and the groundnut lifting may have been hurried. In the two previous Bud seasons, the overlap with village farming had been greater. The 1975/6 picking season was short on both Bud farms: in 1973, the work had gone on well into the wet season, so that some farmers had missed planting their fields, or had done it badly. The 1974/5 season had gone on right up to the rains, holding up the land clearance and the planting of the millet, which is seeded before the first rains. As one man described it: 'I was clearing my groundnut fields, with people coming behind me planting, I was so late.'

Furthermore, the Bud work did not fit so neatly into the agricultural cycle that the Bud *land* could be used for wet season crops. The Bud management were not willing to relinquish control over the land for any period of the year, since the villagers would not clear the land soon enough for Bud's preparation for planting in October/November.

Bud had not changed the sexual division of labour on the village farms, and the chief conflict between Bud and farm work therefore arose for the men. As Table 4.7 shows, the greatest intensity of work was in July, before and after the first rains, followed by the hoeing in August and the harvests in October. The October figures, furthermore, are an underestimate since they do not include

Figure 4.1
Kirene: First and last dates recorded for agricultural
tasks and for Bud work 1975/6

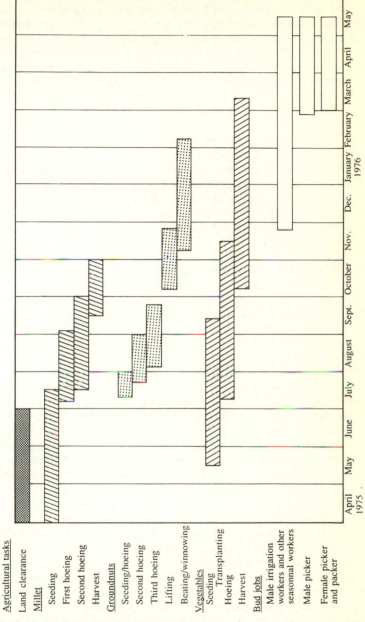

Agricultural tasks		April 1975	May	June	July	August	Sept.	October	Nov.	Dec.	January February 1976	March	April	May

Land clearance

Millet
Seeding
First hoeing
Second hoeing
Harvest

Groundnuts
Seeding/hoeing
Second hoeing
Third hoeing
Lifting
Beating/winnowing

Vegetables
Seeding
Transplanting
Hoeing
Harvest

Bud jobs
Male irrigation
workers and other
seasonnal workers
Male picker
Female picker
and packer

communal labour parties. The work of those men who were not millet farmers for a household went on for longer than the millet farmers, since their fields did not have priority, and they did more of the threshing and winnowing. From these figures it is clear that in years when the Bud season went through May–June, or began in late October, it conflicted with the wet season crops.

For the women, the figures in Table 4.7 are less reliable, since the men tended to underestimate or forget the women's work, and the women tended to be vague since they would fit in tasks such as shifting the crops from the fields, or winnowing, when domestic work permitted. Since the women virtually never worked the long season at Bud which was worked by the irrigation workers and tractor drivers (Figure 4.1), the clash between estate labour and farm work on the millet and groundnut crops was small for women.

The conflict with the vegetable crop has already been discussed. This arose particularly for women, who had a majority of the remaining vegetable plots (Table 4.3), but a few men had found market gardening land. In some cases, people lost their vegetables through neglect of fencing and picking once Bud had started. But the impact of this conflict by 1975/6 was small because by then vegetables had been largely abandoned as a cash crop.

The Effects of Bud on Collective Millet Fields and Communal Labour

Like the principles governing land allocation, the principles by which a farmer could call upon the labour of others in the village remained the same in Kirene after the arrival of Bud, but were put under increasing strain, and were no longer producing the same economic results. The most marked effect of Bud on the forms of collective labour was in its effects on the collective millet fields.

The institutions of the household grouping and of the collective millet field were, as Chapter 3 showed, closely related, many members of the associated households working collaboratively on the field and all eating its products during the following year's work. Already by the time of Bud, land pressure was putting some strain on the collective field institution. The collective fields were generally on land held by the head of the household grouping, and as land holding became progressively fragmented among households in the manner described in Chapter 3, it became harder to assemble land for the field.

Nevertheless, all the sample households which belonged to a household grouping (that is, all but the one-household compound) had shared the cultivation of a collective millet field of some size up to 1972. Of these six collective fields, one had ended by 1975, and two had split, with one household in the grouping ceasing to work on the field.

The field which had ended had been farmed by members of a grouping consisting of the households headed by a compound head, two brothers, two sons and the son of a sister: six dry season households. Before the arrival of Bud the sons and nephew had tended to drop out of farming the collective field, and the drought had exacerbated this: 'Times were hard then, and each went off on his own path. In such times it is the youngest who must stay with the old man.'

Bud had taken some of the men in the 1973 wet season and this had completed the disintegration process: those still farming the collective field abandoned it, and it had not been re-formed.

In another sample compound, the collective field, though continuing, was under pressure: 'The collective field still continues in the compound, but it is like a man who limps.' In a third, while two brothers continued to have their collective field, the rationale for it had gone, since they no longer had enough land for millet.

> The millet from the collective field used to be kept for the rainy season. Now we just eat the millet until it is finished, and then we buy.

In this way Bud, through taking land and introducing sporadic competition for labour, had contributed to the disintegration of these fields.

Once the collective fields disintegrated, part of the rationale for the household groupings went. The grouping which had abandoned their field entirely continued to share equipment, but acknowledged that the strains within the grouping had increased. When exchange labour of this sort is based on no strict accounting of obligations, then it depends on both a sense of fairness and a concept of reciprocal obligation: people contribute when they can and benefit when they must. If people began dropping out of the work of the collectivity for their own material benefit as wage workers, then strains quickly arose. A situation of systematically uneven participation by different millet farmers in a collective field because of wage labour obligations was unlikely to continue for many years without destroying the institution, and the effects were already visible in strain and mutual resentment.

Just as the dropping out of individuals undermined collective fields, so uneven participation by active household heads in the work of a household grouping would be likely to undermine it. Such strains were particularly evident within the household grouping which had abandoned its collective field. There were no household groupings which had not had a collective field until two years previously, and the two institutions seemed likely to disintegrate together.

There was also another form of labour exchange in millet and groundnuts which Bud potentially threatened. As Table 4.6 shows, within the household groupings men who had their own fields but were not millet farmers put in as much agricultural labour, although they farmed on average smaller areas of cash crops. There was a net transfer of labour, therefore: the millet farmers spent on average 22 per cent of their time on the fields of others; the figure for the non-millet farmers was 73 per cent. Any reduction of the willingness of the young dependent men to farm would therefore affect the areas cultivated by millet farmers. By 1975 there were signs of such unwillingness: some young men made no secret of their lack of interest in cash crops, and one young tractor driver on the Bud estate loudly proclaimed his reluctance to farm by hand in the rains.

The impact of Bud upon the other main form of collective labour in Kirene, the *dahira*, was different from its effect on the collective fields, in part because the *dahira* had been partially monetized before Bud's arrival. Although the money did not go to individuals, the cash payment for the *dahira* meant that only farmers with cash could use it. A *dahira* could cost 2,000–3,000 francs c.f.a. in cash. Before Bud, a tendency had developed for men who worked away from the village, but whose wives were in the village – a tiny proportion of the village population – to give money to assist the farming. This would be partly spent on the *dahira*s. Similarly, there had developed a system of fines for non-participation in the neighbourhood-based *dahira*, the money for which went to the mosque.

The effects of Bud on the *dahira* followed from this situation. First, men doing the longer seasonal jobs at Bud went back to work early, and tended to drop out of the *dahira*s, most of which were in September (10 per cent of the total), October (36 per cent) and November (32 per cent), paying fines in lieu. This they could afford to do, since they were the best-paid workers, but it increased the work of the other men at the busiest point in the farming cycle. Early November was particularly pressured, and men who did not drop out went back to Bud with no break at all (at least one collapsed as a result).

Second, those men with the better Bud jobs tended to use the *dahira* on their fields more than those who had only irregular work at Bud. Table 4.6 demonstrates this income effect: the groups who used the *dahira* most were those men who did not work at Bud (many of whom had other incomes from shopkeeping, trading or traditional healing), and those with seasonal jobs. Those who worked irregularly, many of whom had lost land, could not afford the outlay of the *dahira* on their small cash incomes. Thus the better-off men, with the better Bud jobs, were ceasing to put their share of work into the *dahira*, while continuing to call upon it in the period of the agricultural cycle when time was most pressing. This seemed likely in the longer run to erode the *dahira*s, based as they were on a general, though vague, concept of reciprocity.

On the other hand, there was little evidence that collective labour was being replaced by individual paid labour. Men did not pay individuals for their groundnut lifting although the use of *firdu*s (paid day labourers from outside the village) for threshing, long known, may have been increased by the departure of young men to Bud in November. And the income effect could work both ways. One farmer commented that, some years before, he had worked making bricks and had paid *firdu*s to thresh his groundnuts; having lost his cash crop land and having only irregular Bud work, he could no longer afford to do that.

Bud was thus an agent of disintegration of mutual assistance in farming within Kirene. Through this effect, it was reducing the commitment to food production within the village, despite farmers' attempts to give priority to millet growing, and increasing the vulnerability of any household to economic disaster in any year by reducing the 'safety nets' embodied in the collective labour system. These effects were still only partial three years after the arrival of the estate, but the trends were clearly visible.

The Probability of Future Farming Decline

Like the reconstruction of the more distant past, the future evolution of the Kirene farming system in the presence of Bud had to be a matter for reasoned speculation. Several reasons suggested that the decline in food farming and the individualization of the economy were not likely to stop in 1975. The strains which were pulling apart the collective labour institutions would continue, and were likely further to damage labour co-operation among households. The physical toll of doing two, or in the case of women three, competing or overlapping types of work would continue, and women and young men, in particular, seemed likely progressively to drop out of farming. The withdrawal of dry season work from farming would in the long run reduce the productivity of the system, reducing land preparation, manuring and fencing; faced with a choice, the married men would sacrifice their cash crops to Bud where Bud provided a higher cash income, which was in a majority of cases. The division between men with the better paid seasonal jobs at Bud, and those with only casual work, seemed likely to harden as people gained experience, and to put further strain on the collective labour system.

To the extent that that occurred, the level of food farming would be likely to drop further. This argument, though partly speculative, is one of the most important in this book, and it is elaborated in a later chapter. The decline in the collective labour system in Kirene was being accompanied, as the next chapter shows, by a marginalization of the farming system within the Kirene economy as a whole, and a trend, still in embryo, towards the monetization of internal exchange within the economy. Chapter 7 argues, on the basis of data from the farming area near the other Bud estate, closer to Dakar, that once a farming economy of this type becomes monetized, a process which includes the use of wage labour, millet farming tends to collapse. It becomes uneconomic, for a series of reasons to be explored.

In effect, in Kirene the millet farming was being maintained by the very fact that millet was not treated in the same way as a cash crop. The rare farmer who grew it as a cash crop found it extremely unremunerative. Millet was grown as part of an integrated farming system which sought to provide food for the household. The continuation of millet growing at the expense of cash crops in the households which were short of land was in part the result of the social importance of millet growing as the source of the basic household food. Other factors were the capacity of the household head to enforce that priority on others, and the social exclusion of the cash option: giving up millet for groundnuts, and using the income to purchase millet.

Ironically, however, the household head appeared to be gaining increased power over farming decisions at a moment when the basis for consent to that power by other household members was being weakened. Monetization of the economy, the wider distribution of the burden of food provision among household members as described in the next chapter, and the changing position of the household head: these were processes which potentially challenged the old decision-making patterns. Millet growing in Kirene had continued because of the integrated way in which the village economy and society had evolved and adapted; Bud was finally challenging the whole direction of evolution.

And would it matter if millet growing declined? For Kirene, it would make the villagers more dependent on Bud, and on the market. And the market for millet was thin, localized, partly controlled by the state. The Kirene villagers tended to buy their millet in the surrounding villages and could probably continue to do so on a larger scale. They could also buy rice which was more expensive (and partly imported). But the point, of course, applies more widely than the experience of Kirene alone. If wage labour on plantations in the dry season does tend in the way demonstrated to undermine rather than to complement agricultural systems which include food growing, then that is an important observation given the ambitions with which the Bud experience began – and given the spread of big projects to other areas of the Sahel. Senegal was already in 1975 a country with large food imports, and serious hunger and famine in the drought years. To undermine a rather effective farming system which was still producing substantial quantities of food and replace it with an export crop plantation system was to further weaken the food base of the rural areas.

Notes

1. The detailed farming information in this chapter is based on an intensive study of sixteen sample households in the village. The Appendix gives brief details of the research method; full details are in Mackintosh (1980).

2. A great deal of cross checking was done of these and all other replies. The likely accuracy of the statements about land loss is suggested by the fact that those who had lost no land readily said so. The statements refer to the land over which people had usage rights before 1972.

3. That is, a member of the Rural Council in the nearby village of Diass. The Council had rights to allocate unused land; the interviews suggested that the head of Kirene village also had considerable influence over such allocations.

4. That is, young dependent men.

5. On risk and risk spreading in peasant farming, see Richards (1985), Moscardi and de Janvry (1977), Lipton (1968), Anthony *et al.* (1979). On the social importance of millet growing among the Serer, see Pélissier (1966: 235ff.).

6. Caution is of course needed in interpreting small sample results; see Table 4.2 for a note on the statistical significance of the results.

7. There was a dry season Coranic school in the village, taught in Arabic, for children of both sexes. Total numbers in French language secondary schools in Senegal were very low: only 59,000, or about 14 per cent of the 12–17 age group in 1975/6 (*Le Sénégal en Chiffres*, 1976: 51).

8. 'Co-wives': the term includes wives of brothers sharing a household, as well as two or more wives of the same man.

Table 4.1
Kirene: Effects of Land Loss on Estimated Cropping Areas

	Households having lost no land	Households having lost some land	Households having lost a great deal of land
Average millet area farmed (ha.)	3.9	2.50	2.53
Average groundnut area farmed (ha.)	3.6	3.21	1.7
*Average ratio $\dfrac{\text{ha. millet}}{\text{ha. groundnuts}}$	1.25	1.06	1.98
Average area farmed (ha.) (millet plus groundnuts)	7.49	5.71	4.21
No. of households	7	3	6

* This figure is calculated by averaging the ratios for each household, thereby giving the decisions of each household equal weight irrespective of size.

Table 4.2
Kirene: Correlation Coefficients for Determinants of Areas Farmed

Correlation	Whole sample	Households having lost little or no land	Households having lost a great deal of land
Millet area and adjusted total of persons in household	0.68	0.58	−0.07
Groundnut area and adjusted total of persons in household	0.91	0.92	0.63
Millet area and male adults in household engaged in farming	0.55	0.60	0.17
Groundnut area and male adults in household engaged in farming	0.68	0.71	−0.13
Number of households	16	10	6

Notes
'Adjusted total' implies children under 15 counted as one half.
All correlations in the first two columns are significant at the 95 per cent level.
None of the correlations in the last column are significant at this level.

Table 4.3
Kirene: Distribution of Farm Plots by Crop in Sample Households 1975/6

	Total number of plots planted in:						Total adult individuals in sample	Total number of individuals farming
	Millet	Groundnuts	Vegetables	Cassava	Mangoes			
Household heads and other millet farmers	33	21	4	9	4		20	17
Other married men		2					5	2
Single men	2	10	1	1			18	9
Married women		17	8		1		37	21
Single women							6	
Total	35	50	13	10	5		86	49

Table 4.4
Senegal: Output of Millet and Groundnuts in Thiès Region

Year	Millet output (tons)	Groundnut output (tons)
1965/6	53,000	n.a.
1966/7	42,000	85.4
1967/8	68,000	158.2
1968/9	45,000	112.8
1969/70	77,000	114.5
1970/1	53,000	72.4
1971/2	81,013	172.7
1972/3	13,200	18.8
1973/4	103,300	138.3
1974/5	87,525	144.4
1975/6	98,100	191.3

Source: *Le Sénégal en Chiffres* (1976, 1982/3).

Table 4.5
Kirene: Participation in the Bud Labour Force According to Age

Age group	Women No. of Bud workers	Women % of age group	Men No. of Bud workers	Men % of age group
15–19	28	50	14	22
20–29	58	66	48	49
30–39	55	86	30	68
40–49	29	69	30	64
50–59	13	45	17	55
60–64	1	1	2	11
Total	184	63	141	47

Table 4.6
Kirene: Farming Practices According to Participation in Wage Work — Sample Households

Farm practices	Men who did not work at Bud	Men who worked irregularly at Bud	Male irrigators or other seasonal Bud workers	Women who worked at Bud	Women who did not work at Bud
Total in sample who farm of whom:	10	8	10	16	5
farm millet*	4	6	6		
farm cash crops only	6	2	4	16	5
Number of paid tasks on millet fields	2		1		
Number of *dahiras* on millet fields	6	3	4		
Number of paid tasks on groundnut	16	2	5	7	3
Number of *dahiras* on groundnuts	9	1	10	10	5
Area farmed in millet (ha.) (average for millet farmers)	2.75	2.45	3.05		
Area farmed in groundnuts (ha.) (average all farmers)	1.36	0.95	1.25	0.5	0.62

* That is. farm millet for household use. The two young men who grew millet as a cash crop are included in row 4 'farm cash crops only'.

Table 4.7
Kirene: Number of Days Spent in Farming* — Averages per Person, by Gender and Position in Farming Structure

Month (1975/6)	Married males growing millet	Other men having own fields	Single men and boys without fields	Married women having own fields	Married women not having own fields	Single women and girls
March and April	0.5					
May	10	5.5	4			
June	12	9	6	1		
July	18	16	13	3	1	
August	13	13	11	6		5
September	8	12	3	4		
October	15	14	6	6	6	3
November	8	10.5	1	2	2	
December	3	7		5	2	
January	2	1		1	1	
Total days/person	89.5	88	44	28	13	8
No. in sample	16	12	16	21	17	6

* Millet, groundnuts, beans, cassava.

5. Wage Work, Individualization and Solidarity in Kirene

The argument made at the end of the last chapter concerning trends in the development of Kirene farming depends in part on an understanding of changes in the position of farming within the village economy as a whole after the arrival of Bud. This chapter demonstrates that farming was being marginalized. Not only did it provide a lower cash income than Bud work, but the destruction of the vegetable crop had rigidified the farming system and removed both its investible surplus and the incentive to invest. In such circumstances farming could not continue to provide, as it had done in the past, the material basis for social organization and the dynamic for change within the economy as a whole.

This role of stimulus for change had instead been taken on by the institution of wage labour, that is, a set of economic relations entirely different from the non-monetized production relations in farming which we have been analysing up to now. Wage incomes from the estate were an individual form of income; what one earned depended little on the assistance of others, and brought few implicit obligations. Furthermore, the distribution of wage incomes was very different from the distribution of cash incomes from farming. Such a situation created new social divisions and processes of social and economic change. Kirene was caught between two different principles of economic organization: the farming system, based on unchanging if threatened principles, and the new processes introduced by wage work. This contradiction – source of the contradictory perceptions that everything and nothing had changed – implies that the Bud estate disaggregated the village economy, replacing a rather integrated set of economic processes with a highly contradictory set destined to produce considerable further change.

The villagers initially reacted to the new cash incomes from wage work by attempting to integrate them into the existing pattern of cash use within the village. But this attempt was doomed to failure: because the cash was distributed in different ways, because there was no longer an incentive for agricultural investment, and because the organization of people's lives was changing. The result was, as this chapter shows, the development of new patterns of spending among household members, some small moves towards internal monetization of the economy, and new divisions and patterns of differentiation based on differential access to wage incomes.

The Kirene villagers reacted strongly against what they saw as new estate-created divisions among themselves. They developed, in particular, a strong demand for control of hiring for the Bud estate, control which they saw as partial recompense for the loss of their land, and which they defended with a strike. As a result, the resistance and self-organization of the Kirene villagers – becoming semi-proletarianized, balanced uneasily between land which was slipping through their fingers but still largely the basis of their social organization, and the new pressures of wage work – was more effective than that of the far more proletarianized workers at the big Baobab estate nearer the city. The strength of this solidarity reflected the villagers' contradictory economic position: on the one hand, it was based in the existing social integration of the village; on the other, the new forms of organization it involved, especially the increasing influence of younger people, were in contradiction with the older hierarchies which had in the past maintained and reproduced the farming system.

Changes in Village Cash Incomes

Bud somewhat increased the cash incomes of Kirene villagers relative to their incomes from cash cropping. Subtracting the cash required to replace the basic food no longer produced because of the loss of land, Bud distributed an estimated 53,000f. c.f.a. additional cash on average per household in 1975/6, (about £125 at the exchange rate of the time) as compared to farming incomes in the absence of Bud. By 'farming incomes in the absence of Bud' is meant the estimated marketed agricultural production (for the households studied) in the last reasonable farming year before Bud (1971/2) valued at 1976 prices. The additional cash income per year can be compared with an estimated average cash income per household in the absence of Bud of about 230,000f. c.f.a. (or about £540) per year.

These averages of course conceal considerable differentiation within the village and a complex pattern of gains and losses from the presence of Bud. The net cash gain also needs to be set against the argument made in the previous chapter, concerning the probable long-term decline of the farming system if Bud's presence in the village continued. The net gains arose partly from the fact that the agricultural system at one end of the village was still largely intact in 1975, a situation already increasingly under strain. They arose partly from a net cash gain going to the women, whose income from cash cropping had been even lower than their (low) Bud wages. The pattern of distribution of gains had implications for the resultant changes in the use of cash in the village, and thus for the long-term effect of the wages on the village economy.

The Distribution and Scale of Income Losses Attributable to Bud

Farming was the basis of the Kirene economy up to the arrival of Bud; incomes from the small list of trades practised in the village (see Chapter 3) were marginal to a farm-based living standard, and in any case the incomes of a few of these part-time traders or artisans, notably the shopkeepers, had been raised by the arrival of Bud. Abstracting for a moment from the wages distributed, the absolute losses attributable to Bud all concerned the drop in income from farming. These losses were experienced chiefly by the heads of the households at the end of the village where land loss had been severe, and to a lesser extent in the centre of the village, because of the loss of the valuable vegetable land. Dependent household members in these households also lost income, particularly, again, from the loss of the vegetable crop.

Vegetables had been a lucrative crop, and the higher incomes gained had been concentrated in a few hands (Table 5.1). In the households studied, three men had been large gardeners and also *banabanas* (traders). Of the other 21 adult males in these households who were farming in 1971/2, four at the far end of the village had never tried market gardening for lack of suitable land, and three others had given up because of the drought. The others had all grown some vegetables. In 1975/6, only five men gardened: all from the households in the centre of the village, and all on a smaller scale than their previous gardens (Table 5.2). One of the big gardeners, however, had returned to gardening part time while working at Bud, growing vegetables on a smaller scale on remaining land on Bud's borders; he made 296,000f. in 1975/6 (£700). These earnings give plausibility to the estimate of a total loss to the 17 male gardeners in the sample households of just over one million francs c.f.a. (about £140 per gardener); the losses are more likely to be under- than over-estimated.

The women gardeners lost less because their returns had been much lower, they had always fed many of their vegetables to their households, and more women continued to garden on a small scale (Table 5.2), although some were finding it increasingly difficult:

> I farmed vegetables before Bud . . . When you work for the whole season you are very tired, your whole body is tired. Groundnuts are easier, you only hoe them twice. Even those I grow less than before, I am too tired.

The total estimated loss to women gardeners in the sample households was only 120,000f. (or about £15 per gardener), but concentrated in a few households.

The groundnut losses represented less in cash terms because the crop was less lucrative and because some people had returned to groundnut growing when vegetables collapsed. In the households which had lost most or all of their land, the land constraint was the chief determinant of income: comparison of the returns of married male groundnut farmers in these as against other households suggests an average loss of 13–15,000f. per farmer (about £30), relative to the incomes of the other growers of about 32,000f. (rather less than £75 per year) (Table 5.3). Single men in these households who continued to farm suffered a similar scale of loss on a smaller 'without Bud' income, and three single men found no land to farm at all. In the area where land was sufficient, the income effect already referred to emerges in higher incomes: those Bud workers with reasonable incomes (the seasonal workers) spent more on growing groundnuts, and gained higher net incomes, than irregular workers with smaller wage incomes (Table 5.3). Women had previously earned sums similar to the earnings of single men from their groundnuts, and more continued to farm them on a small scale: the hierarchy of land rights put their claims ahead of the single men. The estimated loss to women groundnut farmers in the households which had lost land was about 3,000f. per farmer (about £7 per year).

Finally, the sample households had lost six producing mango trees (value about 30,000f. income per year, or about £70) and about 40 young trees of which the owner said that, if they had matured, 'it would have been enough to take me to Mecca'. The sample under-represents the losses of fruit trees to the village: nearly 800 trees were lost in all, more than 10 trees per household at the end of the village where they had been owned. To these cash losses, the scale of which illustrates both the poverty of the village and the importance of the vegetable revenues relative to those from previous crops, have to be added the implicit losses from cash needed to replace lost millet. As shown in Chapter 4, although houschold heads gave priority to millet growing, the link was broken between the size of the household and the food grown. Among the households which had lost most land were some which had seen their food crop drop sharply. Of the six households, two had lost almost all the land they possessed, and they planted only an estimated 1.7 hectares of millet each, the lowest of all the sample households; one had millet for only one month in 1975/6. Three others said their total crop had dropped because they had been pushed from good to poor land. These households appear to have lost an average of four months' food supply, which at 1975 prices cost 17,000f. (or about £40) per household to replace.

This last calculation should be seen in the context of the existing level of food supply in Kirene. By 1972, most Kirene households were not regularly growing their entire year's food requirements, although some households might have a year's supply in a good year.[1] 1975/6 was a year of average rainfall following several disastrous years: in that year, in the areas of the village which had lost no land and whose residents said they had not reduced their planted area, the millet ran out between February and April, after which they were buying; in addition, Bud had weakened the practice of retaining a separate store of millet to eat during the farming season.

Distribution of Net Income Losses by Social Group

When these income losses from farming are set against the wages paid by Bud, it is clear that the net gains and losses were very unequally distributed according to gender and according to position within the household.

For active men as a group, Bud reduced farming to a secondary source of cash income after wage work (Table 5.4). Total Bud wages paid to men in the sample totalled about 2 million francs; farming provided about 1.3 million. And Bud wages outweighed estimates of farming incomes lost by 250,000 francs.[2] Bud wages were generally higher than the lowest returns from farming: fourteen men made less than 20,000 francs from farming whereas those who worked at Bud generally earned more than 20,000 in a season.

However among the men the gains and losses were unevenly distributed. As a group those providing food for households lost out to single men with fewer responsibilities. The worst losers, as the villagers frequently pointed out, were the older household heads in the households which had lost land. Furthermore taking all the household heads and millet farmers together (some households had both an elderly head and a young millet farmer) the command over cash of this group dropped absolutely as a result of Bud. Although the group of millet farmers included the highest cash earners both before and after Bud's arrival, the number of millet farmers earning less than 50,000f. (about £120) per year increased by three in a sample of sixteen. Allied to the drop in millet production, Bud brought worsening poverty at one end of the village, since there was no priority in hiring for the better jobs those who lost most. And the absolute losses were not outweighed for the millet farmers by the gains at the other end of the village.

Agricultural wage work, more than other wage work, favours the young and strong. Single men gained absolutely from Bud, and in all areas of the village. The gap between their incomes and those of millet farmers lessened considerably, and they were more dependent on Bud wages than the millet farmers.

Women's cash incomes also increased, though for different reasons. Bud increased considerably the number of women with access to cash (Table 5.5): though their average wages were lower than men's, the gains still outweighed their cash losses from farming, and their total access to cash roughly doubled in the households studied. The income distribution among women narrowed. However, while women's incomes from farming before Bud were not markedly lower than those of single men, the single men gained far more from Bud: Bud widened the gap in income by gender among 'dependent' household members. Finally, the gains were again rather unevenly distributed: older women, in areas where the vegetable land had been lost, lost all their incomes.

In summary, Bud reduced the share in total village cash incomes of those who headed households, and increased the share of dependent household members (Table 5.6). The effect was strongest for the women in the households which had lost most land. This result had a considerable impact on expenditure patterns, as explored below.

Incomes and Income Distribution by Household

> Bud can never replace what we had before.
> Bud has brought prosperity.

These two quotations come, predictably, from people living at opposite ends of Kirene, one from a household which had lost almost all its land, and the other from one which had lost none. Just as individuals lost less or benefited more from Bud at the far end of the village, so this was also true of households treated as a unit.

The problem is that, while one can add up a notional total income per sample household in Kirene, this has no particular economic meaning. All income, in cash or kind, was not, any more than in Britain,[3] a common fund to which all members of the household had equal access. Only income which went directly into collective consumption – food especially – was collectively available in this way, and the proportion of any person's income made available to others was dependent on internal economic relations within the household. Nevertheless, despite these problems, it was clear to an observer in Kirene that individual living standards were related to total household income, and the expenditure data bear this out. Changes in income distribution by household are therefore relevant data if treated cautiously.

Bud increased the dispersion of household incomes in the village, increasing the number of lower income households (less than 100,000f. a year), and of higher income households (over 200,000f. a year) (see Figure 5.1). This result is rather striking, given that vegetables had already introduced considerable dispersion of current cash incomes, and that wage incomes are often assumed to have a levelling effect in such situations.

The changes in the ranking of households within the sample emerge most sharply in the terms of household income per adult member. In these terms the better-off among the households which had lost land became considerably poorer, especially three with middle-aged to elderly household heads. By contrast, one land-loss household actually improved its relative position in these terms: a house with two young men and a young woman with seasonal jobs at Bud (the young woman as a supervisor).

On the other hand two households which lost no land moved up sharply because they each contained three people with relatively good jobs at Bud and had done little vegetable growing. The arrival of Bud had tied current household income much more closely than before to the number of young adults in the households,[4] heavily discounting the influence of older household heads. For any household, the larger the decline in farming income, the greater the dependence on Bud, and therefore the more strongly this statement held. By weakening the influence of farming on total household income, Bud had weakened redistributive mechanisms towards older household heads, and made household income more dependent on the position of a household in the 'household cycle'. 'Demographic differentiation'[5] had been a relatively weak determinant of income distribution in Kirene before Bud: the wage incomes made it a much more important determinant of household income.

Finally, while these statements hold in general, there are always exceptions. Two household heads who had not lost land had kept their households in the top half of the per adult income distribution by a mixture of market gardening and commerce, without help from Bud. And one man, the largest vegetable farmer before Bud, who had lost all his vegetable land, had got himself a supervisor's job at Bud, found some land for gardening as well, and was *still* the single highest earner in the sample in 1976.

Figure 5.1
Kirene: Income distribution between households:actual 1975/6
and estimated in the absence of Bud

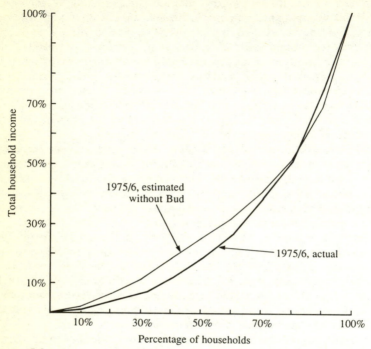

Figure 5.2
Kirene: Scattergram:Income of household head, and
proportion spent on millet and rice (sample households)

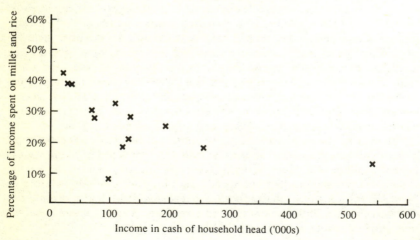

The Effect of Bud on Spending Patterns

Just as participation in estate work was closely related to farming, so the principles governing the expenditure of cash income from Bud by household members were the same as those which had long determined the use of income from cash cropping. But, as the relative weight of the cash income of different groups changed, so the implications of these principles altered. In particular, in the poorer households, the declining share of household income of the household head had implications for the expenditure patterns of other household members.

Just as the household head or millet farmer supplied the basic food grain from the farm, so, if there was a deficit, it was in principle he who purchased sacks of millet or rice. All the household heads in the sample had to buy some millet in 1975/6, and this ate sharply into the cash income of the poorer household heads (Figure 5.2). The absolute cash expenditure on food grains, however, was positively related to the income of the household, given the number of months of food required, since the better-off household heads provided larger quantities, and also purchased more rice (the more expensive grain). Furthermore, in poorer households, others in fact contributed to the purchase of food grains.

In addition, household heads had some necessary expenditure on ceremonies, taxes, and their own clothes. For other categories of household expenditure – including other food items (oil, fish, vegetables, and occasionally milk, bread or coffee), clothing for household members, construction and house repair, medical costs – other household members might contribute. Expenditure on ceremonies[6] was relatively low in Kirene – relative, for example, to the village where I lived 30 kilometres nearer Dakar – and while the absolute level of expenditure was clearly related to income, no villagers thought that Bud had greatly raised the costs of weddings or baptisms.

Cash in the hands of different household members served different functions within the Kirene household. The married men living in a household headed by another effectively contributed to the food grain supply. They worked, of course, on the millet fields (or assisted the farming with cash if they were not present), and they also bought millet, and gave cash to their wives for the additional ingredients of meals. They undertook this expenditure themselves, rather than giving cash to the household head. Of the three men in this position in the sample, one had a permanent job at Bud and estimated that he was putting about a third of his income into household food; of the others, working more irregularly at Bud, one was spending the major part of his wage on food (living with an elderly household head), and the other rather less because his household head was more active, and he had recently been saving for his marriage costs.

Single men had in principle quite different obligations. Income which they earned from cash crops was their own, and if they went to Dakar to work they did not generally send much of their income home. Similarly, they were not bound in principle to contribute to the household from their higher Bud wages, and some in 1975/6 virtually did not. In the better-off households this group could and did save, and the savings were spent on marriage costs, on construction of cement block houses, and, in one case, on the re-stocking of the village shop. Bud had increased the funds available to young men, and one of the most common positive comments about Bud was, 'It has permitted some of the young men to build.'

However, the ability of the young men to save depended on the relative poverty of their household heads. Among the households which had lost land, only one contained a young unmarried man. This man effectively shared responsibility for the household food with his brother, and bought most of the millet when their own ran out so that his (married) brother could complete a house. This situation throws some light on a comment made by two villagers on the migration of young men: they said that the young men had 'hoped for a great deal' from Bud, and that after two seasons, disillusioned, some returned to migration to Dakar. This was not evident in the sample, but the area cited for this renewed migration was that which had lost most land. It seems plausible that these renewed departures were as much the result of the financial demands made upon the young men in that area of the village (as compared to the lesser demands if they were in Dakar) as because of disappointment at the level of rewards at Bud.

There was visibly little building in the areas which had lost most land, while 180,000f. was spent by unmarried men in the sample on housing elsewhere in the village. In general a young man in a poor household spent more on food than those in better-off households, often by giving cash for food to the household head, and sometimes by their own purchases.

Women rarely transferred cash to the household head. As with their cash from crops, they retained control of their wage incomes. However, Bud, by increasing women's incomes, had increased their expenditure on food, especially the additions to meals which they had long provided by vegetable farming and gathering. The men tended to underestimate women's contributions to food; furthermore, often only millet or rice (or only millet) was called 'food'. Women, however, sometimes challenged this: when one husband said his wife 'did not buy food', she retorted indignantly, 'I buy fish, I buy vegetables, aren't those food? If my husband told me to buy a sack of millet I could not do that, but I buy lots of other things.'

Other women, however, bought even millet (especially millet flour) and rice in small lots from the village shop. The poorer the household head, the more married women undertook of essential household expenditure, and Bud incomes seemed to have led to a more open recognition of this. The women were matter-of-fact: 'When your husband has no money, it is you who buys food.' 'Whoever has money buys food.' The women bought directly any food purchasable in small lots. It was not that these purchases by women were new; indeed one of the older women argued: 'When in the household the man and the woman are the same' as regards expenditure. But Bud, by reducing the millet and cash incomes of household heads at one end of the village, had increased the scale of purchase of food by women. Furthermore, Bud had increased the needs for such purchases in other ways: the decline in vegetable growing meant far fewer vegetables available in the household, and millet flour and rice were time and effort savers in food preparation by over-worked women estate workers.

Apart from food, women's major expenditures were on clothes for themselves and their children. A man remarked that an effect of Bud had been that more women bought their own clothes, 'to help their husbands'. These expenditure patterns only changed when women ceased to have regular cooking responsibilities. Then, if still active, they had more time to earn cash, and made larger purchases. Several older women did buy sacks of millet in 1975/6, and one 'lent' a sack to a household head in distress. They also spent cash on daughters' marriages and medical expenses for children. They saw themselves as having to provide for their own needs where possible, and also sought to aid their children. Some gave cash for food to the women who were cooking, as the men did. The ability of older women thus to take on some of the financial role of men had been weakened by Bud, however, because access to cash had been shifted from older to younger women.

In this way Bud had tilted the burden of household subsistence provision towards the women: a shift that was absolute at one end of the village, and relative at the other. Food provision shifted from growing, or planned purchase, towards a hand-to-mouth pattern in the poorer households, and from the men towards the women. One implication of this was that women did not spend their somewhat increased incomes on durable goods: these remained the preserve of (some) men.

Changes in the Use of Cash within the Village

Thus Bud had increased current expenditure in Kirene and some of this new expenditure occurred between village members. Bud increased the turnover of the existing village shop, and encouraged the opening of others. It increased the trading of vegetables and fish from outside, generally undertaken by villagers, although these vegetables did not replace fully the vegetables which previously had been consumed from the village gardens. And there were some indications that Bud was tending to break down general resistance to the use of cash among villagers, especially in payment for services. One way in which this occurred was through the creation of new activities paid for in cash within the village, but this was difficult to research since people were reluctant to discuss the commoditization of goods not previously bought and sold. Despite questioning, I only discovered by accident that in 1975/6 for the first time people had begun to fetch containers of water from the Bud-installed tap[7] and sell them in the areas of the village furthest from the tap. The main buyers seem to have been women, tired from Bud work and without the time to wait at the well or the energy to carry the water long distances. This was the comment of one woman:

If you work, and they pay you, and then you use your money to buy water, your wage is no use to you, you have no *bénéfice*[8] from your work . . . It only started this year because this year the work is *forcé*,[8] you don't have time to fetch water . . . So to help people, people who have a cart give that and a barrel to their son who goes to fetch water and then sells it.

The water cost 100f. a barrel, which can be compared with the women's weekly wage during the harvests of 1,000–2,000f., or 2,000–5,000f. during the short season in the packing shed.

Bud had also encouraged the buying of prepared or semi-prepared foods by women. I have already commented on the relative lack of such trading in Kirene. At the Baobab estate, in a far more monetized rural area, there were many women selling prepared foods at the estate or in the surrounding villages, while in Kirene the single doughnut seller encountered was something of a straw in the wind. It seems probable that one way in which a village economy of this kind becomes monetized internally is through the development of petty exchange among women – in cooked foods, semi-prepared millet, small lots of vegetables, small bundles of wood – and Bud, by increasing women's cash income and putting very considerable pressure on the time of the younger married women (while leaving some of the older women with little other income), seemed likely to produce this result.

Such a development of internal monetization of the economy, along with the decline in the communal labour patterns already described, would threaten the non-commodity circulation of cash within the village and reduce the economic importance of the older villagers. Kirene up to the arrival of Bud had been a village characterized by the mutual dependence of the villagers within production, by the investment of a small surplus in expanding agricultural production, and by consumption patterns which included joint consumption of part of the food produced and of part of individual expenditures made especially by the household head. Bud was opposing to this a different principle: individual dependence on the outside for income, absence of opportunities for investment within the village, joint consumption of part of individual wage incomes (especially those of the younger people), and mutual commodity exchange relations within the village. By 1975 the conflict between these two sets of economic principles had already moved Kirene a short distance towards the kind of economic organization described in the next three chapters.

The Disappearance of Investment

In this process the virtual disappearance within Kirene of any incentive or field for investment was one of the most important steps. By destroying the vegetable crop, and taking away the most valuable farm land along with the investment in fruit trees, Bud cut off the direction of evolution of the Kirene economy, described in Chapter 3, towards a market gardening village with a food growing system that could lay some claim to continuing productivity. It thereby removed all incentive to accumulate for the purpose of improving farming, and hence reduced the economic importance of the goods which could be passed on between generations. At the same time it offered an alternative source of current income earned on an individual basis. The developing differentiation within the farming economy was thereby cut off, and the farming system reduced to a lesser and more static role in the village economy. 'Investment' in durable goods became limited to non-productive assets such as housing.

In effect, Bud had raised current cash incomes while reducing the invested surplus in the economy; in that sense as in others it began a process of proletarianization. Stratification in Kirene became, with Bud, more a question of current wage differentials, no longer a progressive or fluctuating differentiation of farms. At the same time Bud increased pressure for individualization – of property and farming activity – and for monetization. Households were becoming more an aggregation of wage-earning individuals, less a centre of productive activity. The effects of this were likely to be disastrous for what remained of the Kirene farming system; and if farming decayed, the net increase in cash incomes represented by Bud wages would turn out to be temporary. In the long run farming would decline for lack of investment and the dependence on wage incomes would increase. The next three chapters examine the economics of survival on insecure and seasonal Bud incomes, with a decayed wet season agriculture, in an area where the process had gone much further.

But in 1976 the Kirene villagers were far from fully proletarianized, a fact which coloured their response to wage work. While economic change pushed the villagers towards individualization, older forms of solidarity were re-focused on attempts to control the impact of wage work through social organization. On the one hand, the shift in work and income towards younger people was reflected in new forms of organization led by those younger villagers; on the other, the demands put forward by the estate workers emerged from their continuing position as farmers, as did their solidarity in disputes with Bud.

Perceptions of Wage Work: Land and Job Rights

Most Kirene villagers who worked at Bud did not see themselves as, and were not part of a wider wage labour market, because they did not see themselves as having alternative wage work possibilities. They had long considered themselves chiefly as farmers, and had not chosen to migrate once married. They therefore saw the estate work, not as a job among others, but as a partial recompense for the loss of their land; the aim of their self-organization was to retain the jobs by priority for Kirene villagers, that is, to control the hiring process in their own interests.

It is relevant here that there had been no major resistance to the loss of the land. The villagers argued they could not have resisted, and had consciously accepted the *fait accompli*. Their opinion had not been asked before the first 50 hectares had been cleared, and before the second section was taken they had proposed in the Rural Council only a number of minor conditions which they knew they had no power to enforce. Thus the minutes of the Rural Council meetings[9] register demands for more taps, a public path across Bud land, the sale of village market garden produce to Bud, and use of Bud lands for millet in the wet season: Bud implemented none of these.

As a result, the deeply felt grievance over the loss of the land was transferred to disputes over the hiring question. 'The work' at Bud, the Kirene villagers said, 'belongs to us.' They claimed they had been promised priority, a claim the management sometimes denied.[10] The emotions ran deep: on one occasion, angry exchanges centred on a letter containing the phrase: 'our land, work or death'. This transferred anger was expressed clearly by the contradictory role of the man who was both Kirene representative on the Rural Council, and the village representative of the governing party in Senegal.[11] This man, who also occupied an important position in the village through birth, played an important role *both* in reconciling the villagers to the land loss (since the decision, as he said, 'came from the government'), *and* in expressing their demands to the management for priority in hiring.

'It is not that we want to be alone here. All we want is priority.' Many workers came to the Kirene estate from Diass and other nearby villages, and skilled workers from further afield, and resentment chiefly arose when it was felt that too many Kirene workers were unemployed. But it was clear from the incidents of conflict that the Kirene villagers genuinely sought, not just priority, but some measure of control over hiring. This is illustrated by an incident shortly before the strike discussed below. As the story was told by a Kirene woman, two Diass women were added to a harvesting team by a supervisor, without any explanation. The Kirene women refused to work with them. The comments of the woman telling the story were illuminating: 'If he (the supervisor) had talked to us, had told us that they were friends of his who needed work, then we would have accepted it. But he said nothing, just put them to work.' One of the women was sent home, but the other was allowed to work after a Senegalese skilled worker, living in Diass, had interceded: 'He said that she was an orphan, that she had no one, and that she prepared his meals for him, so we accepted her to work with us.'

This stress on the difference between unknown outsiders, and those who were accepted through the conscious development of personal ties, reflects attempts to establish some form of control, in a situation where the Kirene villagers as a whole had experienced a sharp decline in their control over their own society. It can be related, I suggest, to the grievance that was expressed nearly as often on this estate: the sense of not being treated with respect, or being 'hassled'[12] while working, or being subject to arbitrary orders. In contrast, during these earlier years on the Kirene estate, the level of wages was never a source of dispute. The Kirene villagers had no alternative jobs and therefore nothing with which to compare their wages but their previous farming incomes.

The Bud management understood that the villagers sought to control the hiring process, and reacted sharply. Though at first they had requested influential villagers to assemble work teams, in 1976 the Managing Director said, 'I have told [a village spokesman] that I will not permit him to influence our personnel officer . . . We *must* have control over hiring. We will hire whom we like, from wherever we like, that is the only way to run an enterprise.' The management had also brought workers from other villages, including nearby Safen villages, in an attempt to break resistance to piece rates, thereby almost causing a fight. The management thus played upon divisions between villages, and it was this issue which finally caused a walkout.

Resistance to Division: the Kirene Stoppage

In addition to job rights, the second major aim of the Kirene villagers in relation to Bud was the prevention of estate-created divisions among themselves. Because of the strength of the sentiment of solidarity, the position of Kirene supervisors was often difficult. They tended to absent themselves when a dispute arose, where an outside supervisor might have chosen sides, and one of the strongest objections in Kirene when the Bud management attempted to introduce piece rates for hoeing was that piece rates put the team leader in the uncomfortable position of policing the quality of work done under pressure, and hence introduced new tensions within the teams.

The Kirene work stoppage which I witnessed in 1976 demonstrated the capacity of the villagers for mutual solidarity and self organization in the face of threatened internal division within their society. The dispute arose over the issue of hiring for a newly installed packing shed in Kirene. Previously, Kirene produce had been packed in Baobab, but in 1976 an open-sided shed was installed with a conveyor and mechanized grading equipment. Initially, the shed was staffed with women from the Kirene harvesting team, plus a few men to load produce and handle the boxes. The women preferred this work to the harvesting, because it was easier work and in the shade: the Kirene women therefore felt that they should have priority in these jobs over women who had not previously been harvesters, and especially over new women from outside Kirene.

The dispute began when the farm manager tried to put into the packing shed teams of women from the nearby Safen village of Bandia, in preference to Kirene women. The latter objected violently – indeed threatened violence – when the Bandia women arrived, and prevented them from working so that they were eventually sent home. Precisely why the management acted in this way is not my concern here, since the origins of the decision became lost in mutual recriminations which rapidly descended to personalities. What is of interest here is that the Kirene workforce saw the whole incident as an unnecessary challenge to their rights, and one which they could not countenance.

The precise order of events then becomes somewhat unclear in the accounts of both management and workers. But it is agreed that an 'ultimatum' (the management's word), or 'complaint' was sent to the Managing Director, asking him to come to Kirene, and listing a series of grievances, including the hiring question and perceived ill-treatment and harassment of workers on the farm. The letter was sent by elected delegates of the workers, and when the Director did not arrive by a deadline proposed, a walk-out occurred. On his arrival later the same day, he found the whole labour force, *Kirenois* and others, male and female, sitting at the side of the field. 'Well', said one of the women to me, 'here we are on our strike', using the French word for strike.[13]

Confusion followed during that day and the next, with the management first sacking the delegates, and then backing down.[14] Finally, the villagers returned to work, having gained only the original demand of priority for Kirene women in the shed. Discussions with the villagers during the stoppage showed that they construed the events as an attempt by the Bud management to divide the Kirene workers among themselves, and to cause trouble between them and kin in nearby villages, while they, Kirene villagers and others, were attempting to prevent this.

The women put this interpretation particularly strongly. These are the words of one Kirene woman with a sister married in Bandia:

> Women have more solidarity than the men . . . women are together like the beads on a rosary. If we had fought with the women of Bandia, there would have been women here who would have beaten their mother's child[15] . . . and the children might fight without knowing they were related through their mothers.

The theme of control of the hiring process also recurs. The same woman added:

> There have been women from Bandia who picked on the harvests . . . we did not forbid them to come, we could not . . . it was the method of doing it that caused the trouble. They should have asked us, and we would have said, go and get certain people . . .

These comments point to some of the reasons for the solidarity of the Kirene strike, in a situation which initially involved only the women. Bud's very existence was necessarily a source of upheaval and conflict within the village. In a society which put a high value on agreement and consensus, and on mutual assistance between kin, the act of publicly closing ranks had the effect of denying the importance of such conflict, and blaming dissension upon specific machinations of the Bud management. The villagers were in effect asserting that the wage work experience could be inserted into the older social structure of the village, and need not conflict with existing obligations, if only they were allowed what they saw as reasonable control over hiring. This interpretation is reinforced by the fact that all the skilled workers and team leaders joined the strike.

New Forms of Social Organization: Women, Young People, Trade Unions

The Kirene villagers did not, of course, begin work at Bud with the view that if they could control the hiring process they could reduce the unpleasant impact of the work on their lives. They developed this view while at the same time developing new organizational responses to the problems and possibilities raised by wage work. Both women, and young people in general, developed new organizational roles within the society.

The effect of Bud on the position of women in Kirene was complex. On the one hand, the shift from farming to wage work weakened the position of older women, some of whom had tended to emerge, in Kirene more than in the other villages studied, as individuals with considerable economic and social strength, and strength of opinion, in their own right. Similarly, the wage work had reinforced the weak economic position of women relative to men while increasing the burden of expenditure on women. Women's work was paid less at Bud than men's (an issue discussed further in Chapter 8) and in Kirene both men and women tended to accept this differential. The women sometimes said they should be paid 'more', but did not use men's wages as a standard, and a Kirene man, commenting on his wife's low wages, said not that she should earn more, but that 'the day they pay that to the irrigators (all men) the fields will be dry'. On the other hand, the men supported the women in their dispute over the hiring of outsiders, while at Baobab, as will be seen, male solidarity with a women's dispute was not forthcoming.

Furthermore, Bud had given access to cash income to younger women in a society where young women occupied a very subordinate role and were generally unwilling to discuss any events outside their immediate experience (a reticence not shared by young men). Some of these young women, especially those with a little formal education in French, were beginning to play a role in workforce organization. This was part of a general increase in the influence of young people within the village as a result of the activities of the 'personnel delegates'.

These delegates, who played the role of spokesmen and spokeswomen in the Kirene stoppage, had been elected a couple of years previously with the encouragement of a Senegalese member of the Bud personnel staff. The delegates, who included two from the village of Diass, and two women, had visited the offices of the food industries' trade union[16] in Dakar, and learned some labour law. Though it was unusual for young *Kirenois* to have authority (most were in their twenties and thirties), they were well respected and played an important role in forming opinion among the Kirene workers, who referred to them as 'our delegates'. When the Bud management sacked these delegates as trouble makers early in the stoppage, they thereby solidified the strike.

This crisis consolidated the influence of the delegates in Kirene. Because of the small size of the labour force and the close-knit community they came from, the stoppage involved a great deal of on the spot debate and negotiation. Many of the workers heard these discussions, involving management, representatives of local state administration, the delegates, supervisors and workers, and including an argument between the delegates and the *Sous-Prefet*[17] about the latter's attitude to events at Kirene, and some very open discussion about the position of supervisors, caught between management and workers. In a village which already put a high value on discussion and negotiation, the delegates emerged as personalities.

To some extent the delegates, though young, emerged from existing patterns of influence. One was a young woman who had attained the highest level of education in French (to *brevet*) of any Kirene villager on the estate, and was the daughter of a woman who many said had been a 'leader' among the Kirene women. Another was the Imam of one of the small village mosques, and a son of the village head, and another the brother of a very influential older man. Nevertheless, their influence in their own right was a sign of the changing times. It was the woman who expressed this most clearly.

> In a way it is easier for a woman like me, of 21, to do this job than a woman of 25 or more; I have less work, more time. But it is difficult . . . I have had a lot of trouble in having the women listen to me. But they listen now. After all, it is the women of Kirene who elected me for this job.
>
> There are always old men who oppose us – for example, who were opposed to the strike. But then they did not state their opinion. They just have no idea what a union is. So in the end they are quiet, and the village supports us. And another thing – the sons of those old men are part of the *masse*. So in the end you can calm them.

While there was a tendency for the older men to argue that Bud had changed nothing in the social life of the village, this woman felt the transformation had been enormous, especially in the attitudes of the young people. She cited a new interest in education in French, and a 'greater assurance and influence' of younger people.

> These young people had never been grouped together for work before. They had never had to choose delegates for anything. The meetings give them new ideas. There are young people here who were asleep, who have now woken up.

The young women in her village area had that year organized a fête for the first time, with religious singing. 'Before we just had *sabars*.[18] We chose to do religious songs to attract the attention of the old women, so that they would take us seriously.'

For one middle-aged man, Bud had continued a widening process in the forms of village solidarity, a shift from the power of a few elders, to wider groups and age classes.[19] He saw this as associated with a shift in time horizon. In his words, 'those old men had thoughts which were too long', thinking always who would replace them when they were gone. Now the time scale was shorter, the sense of continuity slipping away, and younger people had to participate in new forms of solidarity in the new situation.

Conclusion: Economic Division and Social Cohesion

The arrival of the Bud estate had cut off one direction of development in the Kirene economy, and imposed another of its own. It had cut off a pattern of development of mixed farming and market gardening involving increasing current differentiation of farms, and an increasing emphasis on inheritance from father to son, but not associated with internal sale of labour within the village. It put in its place a development based on unstable differentiation through differences in current wage income, and a shift in income away from those who had previously organized the farming economy. Given the fact that individuals within the households retained, as is usual in West Africa, control of the expenditure of their income – except for very young girls, not handing it over to the household head to spend – this implied a shift in household expenditure towards subordinate household members, a drop in cash invested in durable goods, and some moves towards internal monetization of the economy. The economy was in a process of change, and would not function in the same way in the next generation. Bud, in other words, had begun a new process of economic transition in Kirene.

This transition was associated with a series of social changes in response to the incursion of Bud into the villagers' lives, in particular the growing social influence of those who now contributed more to the village incomes, and also understood best the nature of the estate work. In saying this, I am not arguing that a given change in the economy produces necessarily a given set of social changes. On the contrary, the response of the villagers to Bud in Kirene was coloured very strongly by the pre-existing social and economic organization of the village, as these three chapters have sought to show. The ironic result of the pre-existing social organization of Kirene, and of the continuing influence of this complex solidarity based in farming, was that the villagers produced a response to the policies of the estate management which was considerably more coherent and well organized than that of the workers on the Baobab estate. One result was that when management or government officials in Dakar discussed the dangers posed by rural proletarianization as a result of Bud, it was particularly to Kirene that they would refer.

Notes

1. The variability of yields from year to year in this kind of rainfed agriculture is enormous.

2. This figure excludes a proportion (two thirds) of the wage incomes of the two permanent Bud workers in the village, who both happened to be in the sample: this was done on the basis, first, that they were absent from Kirene most of the year, and second, to allow for the absence of permanent workers in the other village households.

3. In Britain, as elsewhere, money brought to a household is treated differently according to the social position of the person who brought it; see Whitehead (1981).

4. The correlation coefficient of number of active adults (aged 20–49) with current household income in 1975/6 was 0.455; in the estimated situation without Bud it was 0.33; only the first figure is significantly different from zero at the 95 per cent confidence level.

5. 'Demographic differentiation' is discussed in Chayanov, ed. Thorner (1966), and applied to Africa in Hunt (1979). Essentially, the theory proposed that household total incomes and farming patterns are dominated by a household's position in a demographic cycle of growth and fission.

6. Ceremonies which required expenditure included funerals, baptisms, weddings and the main Islamic festivals.

7. Bud had put a water tap in the central village area at the request of the villagers. The villagers argued that Bud's deep well was lowering the water table in their own village wells, but I could not find evidence for or against this.

8. Both of these words were in French, during a discussion in Wolof. *Bénéfice* means 'profit, income, benefit' in several local languages; *forcé* means 'pressured'.

9. The minutes of the Rural Council at Diass for 6 December 1973, kindly shown to me by a member, contain a discussion of the proposed extension by Bud of 75 hectares.

10. On another occasion, they agreed that a commitment had been made, but attributed it to a Senegalese manager who had since left the farm.

11. At the time of this study, the governing (and only) party in Senegal was the *Union Progressiste Sénégalaise*.

12. Several workers used the French word *dérangé*.

13. We were speaking in Wolof, apart from the word *grève*.

14. My interpretation; the management later denied backing down, but I can see no other interpretation of events.

15. *Dom u ndeye* in Wolof: a close kinswoman of your own clan, such as the daughter of your mother's sister.

16. In 1975/6, Senegal had a formal, industry-based trade union structure, rather closely tied to the governing party, but still providing a focus for worker organization. See Chapter 8 for a discussion of the agricultural workers' union. See Mackintosh (1975), Davies (1966), and Meynaud and Salah-Bey (1963) for a discussion of the role of the unions, and for the history of the links of the unions with political party formation at Independence in West Africa.

17. The Sub-Prefect, the local administrative officer appointed, on the French model, by central government, and having considerable administrative power.

18. A *sabar* is a drumming and dancing party.

19. The old institution of age classes, linked to initiation ceremonies, had taken new form in the Youth Organization in the village.

Table 5.1
Kirene: Estimated Incomes from Vegetable Farming without Bud

Income (f. c.f.a.)	*Number of farmers*	
	Men	*Women*
>500,000	1	
100–200,000	3	
50–99,000	4	1
30–49,000	5	3
15–29,000	3	1
5–14,000	1	7
<5,000		5
	17	17

Note: These are gross incomes without deduction of costs; see Appendix for method of construction of estimates.

Table 5.2
Kirene: Net Cash Income from Vegetable Growing 1975/6 (f. c.f.a.)

	Households which lost a lot of land		*Other households*	
	Number of persons	*Net cash income (average)*	*Number of persons*	*Net cash income (average)*
Married men			4	104,100
Single men			1	20,100
Women	3	1,583	7	16,059
Total net income		4,750		548,915

Table 5.3
Kirene: Costs and Returns of Groundnut Farming: Male Farmers (f. c.f.a.)

	Households which lost a lot of land			Other households		
	No. of men	Cash cost of groundnut farming (average)	Net return (average)	No. of men	Cash cost of groundnut farming (average)	Net return (average)
*Married men**						
Seasonal Bud workers	1	1,000	19,000	4	6,462	43,900
Irregular Bud workers	4	743	11,250	3	1,450	26,640
Do not work at Bud	1	6,450	48,550	4	6,504	32,569
*Single men***						
Seasonal Bud workers	1	8,750	7,250	4	2,143	21,511
Irregular Bud workers						
Do not work at Bud	1	375	5,625	1	5,075	20,925

* Excluding the two permanent Bud workers.

** These totals exclude two young men who grew millet as a cash crop.

Table 5.4
Kirene: Cash Income from Bud and from Farming, by Position in the Farming Structure (Men Aged 15 and Over) (f. c.f.a.)

	Number in sample	No. who work at Bud		Net cash income from farming (average)	Cash income from Bud wages (average)
Household heads who do not farm millet	3			26,512	
Millet farmers	16	12	(75%)	62,847	96,052
Other married farmers	2	2	(100%)	11,450	235,690
Married non-farmers	3				
Single men who farm	9	6	(66%)	16,712	70,520
Single non-farmers	9				
Total	42	20			

Table 5.5
Kirene: Cash Income from Bud and from Farming, by Position in the Household and Farming Structure (Women Aged 15 and Over) (f. c.f.a.)

	Number in sample	No. who work at Bud		Average net cash income of farmers from farming	Average cash income from Bud of Bud workers
Wives who farm	19	14	(74%)	15,393	16,009
Wives not farming	12	8	(66%)		19,214
Other married women farmers	2	2	(100%)	19,450	20,670
Other married women not farming	4	2	(50%)		75,092
Single women (no farmers)	6	3	(50%)		28,453
Total	43	29			

Table 5.6
**Kirene: Proportion of Total Household Cash Income Held by Different Groups:
Actual, 1975/6, and Estimated without Bud**

	Proportion of income held by: (%)		
	Millet farmers and household heads	*Other men*	*Women*
Households which lost a lot of land			
Actual, 1975/6	49	10	41
Estimated, without Bud	73	5	22
All sample households			
Actual, 1975/6	48	28	24
Estimated, without Bud	71	15	14

6. Migrant Labour on the Baobab Estate: Labour Market Formation

The wage workers in Kirene were a long way from being fully proletarianized; theirs was a particular form of that 'semi-proletarianization' discussed in Chapter 2. They retained very strong connections with their land, and their farming organization formed a strong basis for solidarity in their new role of wage workers faced with employers. Nevertheless, they were unable to insulate their farming system from the economic pressures produced by wage work at Bud in the way that they *had* been able to restrict the impact of previous migrant labour. Bud had brought them a step closer to the point where farming would compete with wage work as an employment for individuals throughout their working lives.

The class position of the Baobab estate workers, on the much larger Bud estate in the Cap Vert Region close to Dakar, was rather different from that of the villagers in Kirene, since the Baobab estate drew heavily on migrant labour. It is the central purpose of this chapter to demonstrate that, despite its proclaimed intention to provide dry season work for Senegalese farmers, Bud in fact drew the bulk of its labour force for its big estate from a large, highly geographically mobile, and only partly seasonal migrant labour force; and that, in doing so, it contributed to promoting longer-term migration within Senegal, and to enlarging the scope of the wage labour market. To demonstrate through this case study the scale and importance of this labour market, formed by large numbers of people moving frequently in search of work, is a secondary purpose of the chapter.

By its employment methods, Bud provided incentives for migrants to settle in the area of the estate; it paid higher than average wages for agricultural labour; and it drew women into agricultural wage labour on a previously unknown scale. As a result Bud encouraged the further detachment of the migrant workers from independent farming: while many migrants settled in the area of the estate, they did not form productive farming communities in their new area of residence. The Baobab workers were therefore considerably more proletarianized than the Kirene villagers.

They were also – and as a result – much more divided amongst themselves. This chapter traces the patterns of migration to the areas from which the Bud workers were drawn, the determinants of the participation of different groups of established workers and newcomers in the Bud labour force, the alternatives open to them, and their ideas about Bud work as opposed to other types of work. The interviews show a complex gradation of attitudes towards Bud, depending on length of time in the area, work experience, age and gender. The work experience of women was very different from that of men, and their position in the labour market and their ideas depended in part on the enconomic status of the households within which they lived, and particularly that of their husbands.

The pattern of differentiation, division and conflict among Baobab workers and in the organization of their village lives was much greater than in Kirene. This was partly because of the divergent experiences and ideas discussed here, and partly because as Chapter 7 shows, farming played a quite different role in the local economy around Baobab: here it was not the basis of the economy, but one option among many for individuals attempting to earn a living. The migration and settlement processes discussed in this chapter form the basis for the discussion in the chapters which follow of two specific aspects of the process of proletarianization in the Cap Vert to which Bud added its characteristic contribution: the decline of farming, and the reorganization of the household, and more generally of the economic relations between men and women, in the face of dependence on cash incomes from wage work.

The three chapters are based on two village studies, undertaken using similar methods to those applied in the study of Kirene (see Appendix), of villages supplying labour to the Baobab estate. The villages do not, however, lend themselves to an examination of the before-and-after type, as undertaken for Kirene. In one case, the village of Ponty had scarcely existed before Bud, being largely the creation of the Bud migrants: while the other, Bambilor, had in the years of Bud been subjected also to a considerable range of other influences. Rather than examine the evolution of the two villages as such, therefore, I have used the material in the village studies, along with interviewing on the estate itself, to examine my themes of migrant labour, farming, and the nature of the economic relations within wage labour households and between men and women.

Recent Male Migrants at Bud: Migratory Lives

I came to this village by chance on the way to France.

The village in question was Ponty: a village with a curious, indeed unique, history. It had been the site of the famous William Ponty school, which had trained so many of the élite of Francophone West Africa. The school had been moved there from the island of Gorée in the 1930s by the French colonial administration, and the village had grown up around it to house the gardeners, cooks, caretakers, and other non-professional staff. The two-roomed concrete houses inhabited by agricultural workers in 1975 had been built for this purpose. When in 1965 the school had left Ponty for the town of Thiès, the village had lost its *raison d'être*. By common consent in the area,[1] the village had been 'dying' until Bud's arrival revived it. Within (strenuous) walking distance of the Baobab estate, long an ethnically diverse migrant community and therefore welcoming to new migrants, Ponty was a popular place to settle for people who came to the area to seek work at Bud. The village grew rapidly after 1972, and was economically completely dependent upon the Bud work.

The quotation above is just one version of a common story. Many of the men living in Ponty in 1975 had originally come to the village almost by chance, in the course of a life spent wandering in search of work. Bud-Baobab had created in Ponty just one more (temporary) stopping place for many of these men, fitting into an existing flow of constant (as opposed to permanent) migration within Senegal. It is not always appreciated that the better-studied migration to France (see, for example, Adams, 1979) often forms only an aspect of a more extensive migratory history within West Africa.

The pattern of these migratory wanderings can only be conveyed by describing a few of the work histories of the men. Here are five of the men from Ponty households. The speaker quoted at the head of the chapter was a Mauritanian. In Ponty there was a village shop run by Mauritanians and this man had stayed with the shopkeepers in 1974, on his way from Kaolack, where he himself had run a shop, to Dakar, from where he had hoped to go to France. He had heard of Bud, found a seasonal job there, and been in Ponty ever since.

A second man was much older, about seventy, born in the Casamance. In the early 1920s he had worked as a seasonal labourer in The Gambia, returning home with the rains to farm. From the mid-1920s to the early 1930s he had worked as a navvy, first in Rufisque, then in Dakar, hired irregularly by the day, and no longer returning to farm. One year he worked as a servant for six months in Dakar, and in 1936 he was labouring in the docks. 'Work had become very hard to find by then.' In that year he heard about the new Ponty school from a labourer in the firm building the school, and came to work on the site. When the school was completed he was kept on as a labourer, then as a foreman. By 1975 he was retired, still living in the same house with a small pension.

A third man was around fifty, born in the Sine Saloum. From 1949 (that is, his mid-twenties) he had done irregular labouring in Kaolack, Fatick, Bambey and in The Gambia, frequently returning home to farm in the wet season. In 1956 and 1957 he did two seasons' labouring at Mbacké in the Diourbel region of Senegal, and in 1958 he was in Dakar working irregularly in various factories and in the Shell depot. At this point his wife was living in Thiès. At some time in his career he learned to sew, but never managed to save the price of a machine. In the mid-1960s he was offered a job in a market garden in Sangalkam (near the Baobab site), and later he found himself some land and gardened on his own account for two years. Then, since the land was really too small, he moved with his wife to Ponty, hoping for more land, especially for millet. But, 'the millet never grew well', and he worked as a casual labourer for a nearby villager. In 1971 Bud began to clear land, and he found a job there. He had worked sporadically at Bud between then, and 1975, with one season in a Dakar factory. He continued to farm a little in the wet season in Ponty.

The last two men were younger. One was from Mali or Sénégal Oriental, and had travelled seasonally for some years between Mali and Senegal. On the break-up of the Mali Federation in 1960 he settled in Kaolack as an agricultural labourer. In 1963 he and his brother went to Dakar, intending to go to Europe, but instead ran a shop. By 1975 he had split up with his brother, and came to Ponty looking for the work he had heard was available. He rented a room in the village, married a village woman and moved into her household.

The last man was thirty-three, and had come to Ponty when only five with his family. His father was from a nearby village and worked at Ponty school. From 1962–66 he had learned accounting in Kaolack, and had then not been able to find a job. For several years he worked unpaid in Kaolack, hoping to be hired, and then gave up and joined his brother in Ponty. He was unemployed until Bud arrived, then worked on the hoeing teams for two years. Then he had a work accident which permanently harmed his arm, and since then Bud had employed him seasonally as a janitor.

These are not isolated case histories. All the men over 26 in the sample households, resident in Ponty, had had another wage job besides Bud, with the exception of an elderly household head who had never been a seasonal wage worker, though his brother had, and who in 1975 was supported by his son, a primary school teacher. Ponty contained migrants of very diverse origins and ethnicity (Table 6.1), and their histories make evident the extent to which Bud-Baobab, unlike the Kirene farm, was drawing on a labour market of long distance migrants travelling in search of all kinds of wage work, rather than providing off-season employment for men who were essentially farmers. The scale of these only partly circular migrations in West Africa is still poorly documented,[2] which partly accounts for the common misunderstanding of the nature of the Bud-Baobab labour force.

All of the men whose migration patterns have just been described were settled in Ponty in the sense that they did not leave in the wet season when Bud was closed; all the villagers in Table 6.1 were similarly resident, since our census was taken in the wet season. But there was no clear line between seasonal and permanent residents: people might remain one rainy season, and leave the next. And the seasonal residents during the Bud season had similar work histories to the permanent workers. Of twelve seasonal residents interviewed, four had no previous wage work before Bud, though two of these had been to Ponty several seasons running. The other eight had all had previous jobs, or apprenticeships, or both, ranging from work as a servant to various seasonal labouring jobs in the towns, or in the Cap Vert market gardens. One man had served an apprenticeship as a painter, another as a tailor, another as a bricklayer. The seasonal migrants were therefore half-way at least to the kind of semi-permanent wandering described above for the older[3] men.

Baobab was therefore drawing to Ponty men who would otherwise have been seeking work elsewhere. The flow of migrants of this type was probably dominated by events in the areas of origin: the drought, the low real price of groundnuts, the lack of new jobs in the towns. One quarter of all Ponty migrants from beyond the Cap Vert were from the Fleuve Region in the north where the drought was worst; but 17 per cent of all villagers were from elsewhere in the Cap Vert including Dakar (Table 6.1). No doubt Bud had helped to increase the flow of migrants, as any substanial new offer of jobs for migrant workers was bound to do. A number of the team leaders, for example, were migrants who had been to Baobab several years running; they had powers over hiring, and some tended to give preference to men from their home areas. One migrant from the Casamance had found jobs for a number of fellow villagers the following year.

Agricultural Labouring in the Cap Vert

Bud seems to have drawn its male labour force from two distinct groups of existing migrants in the Cap Vert area: those who had done a very wide range of urban and rural work, who often had some skills, and those who had worked chiefly in agricultural labouring jobs of different types. While Ponty, on the main road into Dakar, in an area where there was very little farming apart from Bud, tended to attract the former group of migrants, those specifically seeking agricultural labouring work were more likely to go to the village of Bambilor, on the other side of the Baobab estate, which was in an area offering a variety of such work.

Bambilor, like Ponty, was an ethnically diverse village with a high rate of recent immigration, but there the similarities end. Bambilor lies on a paved road which runs north through the main market gardening areas of the Cap Vert, and contained at the time of our census over 100 commercial market gardeners selling to the Dakar market. These gardeners, discussed in detail in the next chapter, gardened with the aid of paid labour. They hired workers by the season, migrant labourers called *surga*s who came to work in the market gardens once the groundnut harvest was in, and had done so for many years.[4] These *surga*s had earlier been 'paid' by being given land to garden themselves; by 1975 a cash payment was more usual in this area. In addition to the *surga*s, the gardeners hired casual labour on a piece rate basis ('*tâcherons*').

In addition to the gardening jobs, there was a range of other wage jobs within reach of Bambilor, and these had expanded considerably in the 1970s. A study of Bambilor in 1968[5] shows 53 wage workers, including a few gardeners' *surga*s: this is an underestimate of the number of such workers since the study was done in the low season for gardening, that is, the wet season. In 1975 however, a census done at the same time of year nevertheless showed over 320 wage workers. The number of gardens employing labour appears to be about the same at the two dates; the expansion had come in other areas. There had been an expansion in the area of villas and orchards owned by the Dakar élite as weekend retreats, which employed gardeners/caretakers. Furthermore, a cattle ranch had opened in 1970 on the land of an old sisal plantation near the village, and by 1975 was employing 60 villagers in permanent jobs, and 39 in casual labouring work. Bud had opened in 1972, and 133 villagers said they worked there seasonally or casually – also an underestimate. And finally,

Bambilor was only ten kilometres on a paved road from the industrial town of Rufisque, and public transport was reasonable, so that some villagers commuted to work in the town.

In addition to all this, the economic expansion of Bambilor had attracted the self-employed to the village, and encouraged existing villagers to take up trading or artisanal work. In 1968, the census registers 72 people with some form of self employment, including cowherds (herding for a number of different owners, and having rights to sell the milk), and religious teachers and healers. In 1975 the total was 163, and that was certainly also an underestimate.

The work available in the gardens and orchards, and earlier on the sisal plantation, had been drawing people to the Bambilor area long before Bud. Of adults in Bambilor in 1975, 60 per cent of men and 53 per cent of women were born outside the village; of all migrants present in 1975 (including children), 50 per cent of men and 54 per cent of women had arrived before 1970. Of the earliest male migrants, before 1956, one third said they came looking for land to farm, 17 per cent that they were looking for wage work. By the 1960s, over half were looking for wage work or work as a *surga*. The sample work histories and the censuses together show a pattern of migration – generally of men alone – to the market gardening area on the Cap Vert coast, in search of work or land; and a pattern of work in different villages in the area. Sometimes they worked seasonally, sometimes remained through the wet season, depending on the work found. People would settle in a place for a few years, perhaps remaining, perhaps moving on.

In the Bambilor households studied, several of the settled immigrants had come first to the village for seasons as a *surga*, then found a permanent job, in the orchards or on the ranch, and settled down. Some of them brought wives from their home areas, others married into the Bambilor area. One man, for example, had married a local woman while continuing to live in the household of the gardener who had employed him as a *surga*; when we met him, he was building his own house nearby. Other immigrants had worked for some years in the Bambilor area, as cattle herders or orchard labourers, before coming to Bambilor.

Within Bambilor, this migratory pattern had produced a village containing a nucleus of long-established compounds, including all the most successful market gardeners and most of those with permanent town jobs, and containing a disproportionate number of the better cement block houses in the village. Alongside these compounds (which however varied in size as people came and went) there was a fluctuating group of impermanent residents: smaller compounds, with fewer assets, poorer housing, insecure access to land and work. The compounds which were present in 1968 but had left by 1975 were small in size – an average size of 3.6 people as against 8.4 for the compounds which stayed – and 70 per cent were headed by people who had arrived in Bambilor in the previous twelve years. Compounds could shift, of course, from one group to the other, but the social division in the village was a real one based on differential access to economic resources.

After 1970, the process of immigration to Bambilor had speeded up: people were drawn by the work opportunities, but also propelled by the drought in the north. Fully 25 per cent of all adult male migrants who had arrived in Bambilor between 1971 and 1975 were from the Fleuve Region where the drought was worst (Table 6.2). The Peuhl migrants among them (many of whom were cattle herders) were particularly attracted to Bambilor by the possibility of work on the cattle ranch. The resident population of the village grew from 1082 in 1968 to 1674 in 1975, a rate of increase of 6.4 per cent, three times the population growth rate for the country as a whole and almost as fast as Dakar itself.[6]

Female Migrants and Wage Work

The above material makes it clear that Bud Baobab was drawing its male labour from an established labour market – one which was well informed on alternative job possibilities, as will be shown below. Women, on the other hand, never formed part of a labour market in this way. In the Baobab area – in this it was unlike Kirene – the relation of women to the hiring process was fundamentally different from that of the men, a fact which would have consequences for the nature of labour organization and conflict.

The reason for the difference is that women did not migrate independently in search of wage work, although they were almost as willing to undertake wage work as the women of Kirene. Over the longer distances, men had usually migrated independently in search of work, women interviewed almost all said that they had moved to marry or join kin. While this may be in part a set of conventional responses, and 'joining kin' could mean looking for work, nevertheless the sample work histories of women in both villages bear out the rarity of independent migration by women. Men who settled in the area either brought a wife from their home areas, or married nearer at hand. In Bambilor, the recent adult female migrants had moved on average a shorter distance than the men (Table 6.2). And very few of the women interviewed had wage work experience before coming to Bambilor. Migration had been imposed upon them, in one form or another, and they said that they simply sought means of earning money wherever they found themselves.

A similar pattern emerged in Ponty. Of the women who had been in Ponty before Bud, three had worked as maids in Ponty or Rufisque; none of the others had been wage workers previously. Those who migrated had generally come as girls with families, to join husbands, or to marry. As one woman from the Fleuve Region put it, 'My husband was here on his own, he had no one to cook for him, so he sent me the money for the ticket.'

The Ponty data show that there were just two broad exceptions to the rule that women did not migrate independently, and neither typically involved more than short distance migration. In the sample households there were five young unmarried women present for the Bud season, staying in the household of (in some cases rather distant) kin in order to look for work. None of these had come from further afield than Thiès. On the other hand four women were working full time away from the village, returning only at weekends. All were older women, with no young children. Those who lived in a household as a wife had a daughter-in-law to do the housework; one was a sister of the household head who returned once a week and provided food and cash to help support the household. The existence of both these two groups was more marked in Ponty than Bambilor, reflecting Ponty's more complete orientation to wage work.

The fact that women did not migrate independently meant that their choice of work was limited to what was available near their homes. In Ponty this meant Bud and little else: in Bambilor, Bud work or various types of trading. The women were therefore a captive labour force for Bud in the way that men were not.

Bud and the Market for Male Labour

Bud-Baobab never suffered from a shortage of labour, either male or female. There might be days when some workers on a particular team did not arrive, or when there were too few people to supply a sudden increase in the need for labour, but queues at the gate rather than shortages were the rule. Hiring practices varied in Baobab, but in general, whether officially or unofficially, the Senegalese supervisors and team leaders had considerable influence over who was hired. Length of time in the area, and contacts, therefore influenced the chance of being hired, and of being rehired regularly each year. Since there was some, sporadically enforced, management pressure to rehire the same, experienced workers for the teams each year where possible, and since the starting dates of the different tasks varied and people were only hired if on hand, there was a considerable incentive to remain in the area of the estate during the wet season, waiting for the rehiring to start.

Bud was drawing in effect on two groups of male workers, those who saw themselves as seasonal migrants, and who intended to return to farm in their areas of origin in the wet season, or who had not decided; and those who were settled in the area while Bud or some other employer was there to hire them. By the seasonal migrants, and recent migrants still unsure of their strategy, Bud was regarded as a reasonable employer, better than the other options. In particular in Bambilor, Bud competed for workers with the village gardeners, and the workers greatly preferred Bud since it paid much better. Bud paid men about the minimum legal hourly wage for agricultural labour, which was the equivalent of 5,1338f. for a 48 hour week, or 21,410f. for a 25 day month. In the Bambilor sample a hoeing worker in fact made an average of 19,750f. per month from January to mid-May, and a skilled mechanic 27,000f. per month all season. *Surga*s on the other hand received board and lodging, and a monthly wage which in Bambilor in 1975 was about 3,500f. rising to 4,000f. a month later in the season when labour was harder to find. The *surga* wage furthermore was generally a promise to pay at the end of the season, when the crops were sold. And the payment was not always forthcoming. One gardener in Bambilor gave us a figure for his wages, but did not pay them, later handing over part of his garden to the *surga*s to sell the last crop on their own behalf. Life as a *surga* was precarious; you were assured board and lodging, but worked a whole season before you knew if you would be paid.

In these circumstances, the *surga*s preferred Bud, and the result was a shortage of seasonal migrant labour for the gardens. As the gardeners said:

> They earn more money at Bud so that is where they go. If they work for me it is just so as not to be unemployed while they wait for something better.

> I cannot pay what Bud can pay.

People resident in Bambilor never worked as *surga*s (though they may have done when they first arrived), except for a very few permanent *surga*s living as dependants with gardeners. Residents would only work by the task, or as daily paid labour.

Despite this huge wage gap, Bud's influence had pushed up the wages of *surga*s only a little. Several farmers claimed the *surga*s' wages had doubled over the previous five years. 'Before Bud a *surga* was 2,000f.; now they refuse 4,000f.' Published surveys (Arnaud, 1970; Navez, 1974) give figures for *surga* wages of 2,000–4,000f. for 1969, and 3,000–5,000f. for 1973, the higher wages being generally those closest to Dakar. But these wages, it must be remembered, were taken from the statements of the gardeners, that is, from the employers. Our interviews with seasonal migrants suggested that the chief effect of Bud had been to shift wages in Bambilor, which is in the eastern Cap Vert, up closer to wages paid nearer Dakar, and above those in nearby villages. But the rest of the increase had been general in the market gardening areas, and had also resulted from the sharp rise in the cost of living after 1973 and government-instigated wage increases in the towns. Furthermore, the increase in Bambilor barely, if at all, covered the cost of living increase, and so was not a rise in real wages. Bud, therefore, though it caused a labour shortage in the gardens, had not closed the wage gap. The labour market was highly segmented: the gardeners could not and would not pay more, and simply hired those seasonal migrants who found no work at Bud.

However, while Bud had the choice of the seasonal migrants, the situation was very different once someone decided to settle in the area. A recent migrant to Ponty might say, when asked his opinion of Bud, 'I just pray that I find a job there.' But anyone trying to support a household in Ponty or Bambilor on the basis of Bud work was likely to become bitter at the short seasonal duration and the uncertainty of the work. The lower people's standard of living, and the more they were dependent on a single wage, the more important security of that wage became relative to its level, and people in Ponty always complained about the insecurity and seasonality of Bud before they complained of the wages they earned while working there.

The result was that in Bambilor men often preferred any job with a prospect of lasting all year to a Bud job, and only 7 per cent of male adults resident all year worked there. Everyone preferred the permanent jobs in the public or private sectors in town or on the ranch to the Bud work. The town jobs were the best in terms of income and security: the four men in the sample with such permanent labouring jobs earned an average of 21,700f. per month all year; a skilled worker earned 42,200f. Those working at the ranch (which offered the bulk of private sector wage jobs in Bambilor), or in one comparable cattle ranching operation nearer Dakar, were earning 18,300f. a month unskilled, or 26,800f. skilled. The ranch jobs, even the permanent positions, proved as insecure as Bud was to be, however; in January 1976 the concern went bankrupt and the only further payment its employees received was some money they earned through a scheme they set up themselves to fatten cattle for private owners. Many people were leaving in search of jobs elsewhere at the time we left Bambilor.

Some permanent migrants who were supporting households even preferred the orchard gardening jobs to Bud. They paid far less: the six orchard workers in the sample earned an average of 5,822f. per month and had to find their own board and lodgings. But the work lasted all year and was fairly dependable, whereas the workers complained that the Bud work was insecure from week to week as well as seasonal.

Finally, the permanent migrants had the option of self employment, particularly gardening or cattle keeping. Those exercising other trades in the village tended to do so in addition to wage work if they could find it. Recent migrants, however, could rarely make as much money at gardening as from a Bud seasonal job. The average return to gardeners on a small scale on borrowed land was 25,000f. for the season. Only the established gardeners on their own gardens had a good probability of making more than the 100,000f. necessary to make it worth gardening rather than going to Bud: their average returns were 135,000f. for the 1975/6 season. The result was that one recent migrant who found a job on a hoeing team at Bud sold off the small garden he had planted on borrowed land when he was offered the job, while the established gardeners consistently refused to seek work at Bud, arguing correctly that they could on average do better at gardening. The two herders in the sample, both herding for a number of people, also seemed to be doing well enough not to be tempted by Bud, even if they had not felt, as one put it, that 'herding is all I know'. Our, rather insecure, estimate for their average earnings was 110,000f. a year.

In addition to the divisions between seasonal and permanent migrants, there was also a difference between the position in the labour market of recent and long-established migrants, especially household heads. In both villages few long-established household heads worked at Bud. This was partly because it was this group of men who had access to the best-paid alternative jobs. In Ponty, the long-established household heads who had not found jobs had drifted away before Bud; five men remained who worked at the school in Thiès, having moved with the school; two others were a schoolteacher and a clerk; three others were factory workers in a small roofing tile factory in Sebikotane, a large village nearby. Another five men worked abroad and had families in the village. Similarly, in Bambilor, it was the group of long-established household heads that included both the most successful gardeners and those with the coveted urban labouring jobs.

Indeed several of the most successful gardeners combined gardening with a full-time town job, employing more wage labour than other gardeners, and working evenings and weekends on the garden. Length of time in the village, position in the village society, contacts and patience determined access to the public sector wage jobs. Or, as one man in the village with reason to know and no grudge against the system explained, 'Each year they decide the number of people to be hired in each region, and this number is divided among the politicians' (for patronage purposes). Whatever the precise hiring method, of 17 public sector employees in Bambilor, no less than seven were established gardeners. And in one of the most influential families in Bambilor, three married brothers all combined market gardening with the much-coveted public sector manual and semi-skilled jobs. They had thus used their position to achieve an income above the average for the village.

Furthermore two of the eight permanent Rufisque factory workers in Bambilor were also established gardeners, a majority were born in the village, and none had arrived later than 1966. These factory jobs, too, were only obtained by patience and contacts: one man in the sample households finally landed a permanent job at a Rufisque factory in 1975/6 after many years as a casual labourer there.

Not only did these established household heads not need to work at Bud, they also actively disliked the work provided, as employment either for themselves or their sons. For themselves Bud was a last resort job. Three of the gardeners in the sample had been forced in the past to seek work there when their gardens had dried out in the drought, and had disliked the experience intensely. It was not merely, as several put it, that the work was too 'uncertain' to support a family. One man in his late forties, born in the village, who had always been a market gardener, said of the Bud work, 'It is work for children.' This was a man from one of the old land-holding families of Bambilor, accustomed to employ men himself, who clearly felt the Bud work was beneath him.

However, the established villagers in Bambilor, gardeners and others, all had a strong bias against putting their sons into either farming or casual labouring work. Their aim was for their sons to have a skilled trade. One old man said crossly, speaking of Bud work (in a typical mixture of French and Wolof), '*journalier, du métier*', irregular labouring is not a trade. Of all the established gardeners interviewed, only one had sons who had worked extensively on his garden, and some of these sons had subsequently left to seek jobs in Dakar. Bambilor was the only village of the three studied where substantial numbers of young men had gone into trade apprenticeships in town: 20 per cent of men between fifteen and 29 who had been born in the village were in apprenticeships in town, as compared to 5 per cent of migrants, and two others born in Bambilor were apprenticed in the village. The most popular trades were mechanics, tailoring/dressmaking and bricklaying.

Of the young men who did not go into apprenticeships, most had had a few years of schooling. Of those interviewed in the sample households who had grown up in the village, none had had more than four years in primary school.[7]

Those with more schooling had left the village, as would most of those with trades. Of these pursuing trades in town and returning to the village at weekends, all were born in the village or were early migrants, all were relatively young, and none were household heads. Presumably, once married, men working in town tended to move there to set up a household. We interviewed no young men among those who had been brought up in the village who saw themselves becoming farmers. As one put it:

> For the old men, this will always be a village of farmers. But for the young men, even if they wanted to farm they could not, because they have never learned to farm.

Not only would the young men brought up in the village not farm, they also would not work as agricultural labourers in the village, in farm or orchard. As a last resort only they preferred Bud, which was at least a large enterprise; it was also outside the village, and therefore less humiliating.

In Ponty, farming as a separate option had entirely ceased to exist, as the next chapter explains. As a result, the participation rate in the Bud labour force was much higher: 43 per cent of men over 15 years, or little short of the Kirene participation rate, and 70 per cent of the peak age group of 20–29 years. Given the hiring system, it was easiest for the younger men who had long lived in the village to find jobs, and some new migrants had failed to find work. However the younger men who had grown up in the area, who had no farming experience and needed wage work in order to set up a household, were of all the workers the most critical of conditions of work on the estate. It is significant of their attitudes that when asked what work they did, they would often reply, 'unemployment is my profession', or some such remark. They were the only group who would use the concept of unemployment in this way. Their main complaint against Bud was the uncertainty of the work and its seasonal nature though they also complained more than the migrants about the physical conditions. The long-established migrants, older kin of these young men, shared the aspirations of the younger men *for* the younger men, and indeed had helped to create those aspirations. The following was a typical comment:

> Bud holds no future for the younger men. If they fix their hopes on Bud they learn no trade, and as long as they have no trade they will always be labourers. They only see the money they get, and they are pushed by their parents to go and earn.

The same view was held by a younger man with horticultural training and a full-time job at Bud:

> I don't think Bud is good for the young men. They should be at school or learning a trade. They leave school to work for a few thousand francs a month, then they are unemployed, and a few years later it is too late to catch up and be trained. Bud is a way of holding the young men back.

These comments in part reflect a view of the usefulness of having a trade which was not entirely realistic – as witness the number of men in the Ponty sample who had a trade but had given up trying to make a living with it in favour of work at Bud. But the first speaker is nevertheless correct: having a trade or training of some kind was a necessary, though not sufficient, condition for finding a job other than irregular labouring work.

Despite the hostility to Bud, participation in the Bud labour force by the local young men was high because of the lack of alternative options. In the words of one, who was angry that Bud had first taken him on full-time for training on the experimental site, then sacked him and transferred him to seasonal work: 'If I have nothing else when Bud opens I will go back there.' Most did have nothing else and most went back, but some were willing to accept considerably lower wages for a less insecure life. The trained horticulturalist quoted above had a full-time supervisory job at Bud (at the age of 24), which put him in a much stronger position than most Bud workers, but also in a position to know the precariousness, financially, of the whole Bud enterprise. He commented, 'I would rather work for the State [he had in mind training as a teacher]. They do not pay well there, but one has security.'

Women's Employment at Bud

Bud thus drew its male labour force from an active labour market, where the fluctuating population of the two villages, the low level of participation of Bambilor men in Bud work, and the criticism of the conditions of Bud work all resulted from the high level of dependence on Bud work and the awareness of other options. Women, again, were in a quite different situation. Bud-Baobab hired women for two specific tasks, the packing shed work and picking beans. The first offered regular work during the packing season, on four established teams drawn from four geographical areas, and involved shift and night work; the latter was casual piece work.

To the Bud work most women had exactly one alternative, self-employment as a trader. The option only existed for older women in Bambilor. In Ponty, opportunities for such work were very limited because of a virtual absence of village agricultural production, and low village incomes. In Bambilor, generally only the older women were traders; younger women felt it would be unacceptable for them to sit at a market stall, as one said, 'I should be ashamed to sell.' Women rarely took up selling before thirty years of age (Table 6.3).

The general rise in incomes in Bambilor in the 1970s, along with the continuing viability of gardening, had increased the number of traders, all women except for the shopkeepers. A village market place had been established for the first time, trading in cooked and semi-prepared food had increased greatly, and one woman had opened a restaurant. Trading, especially market trading, was not, however, something of which all women could make a success. It required energy, to transport goods from village to village or into town; it required skill in buying and selling; and, above all, to make the best returns it required capital. One woman, a wife from one of the poorest households in the sample, who said she had tried and failed to find a job at Bud, traded in a range of goods according to the season. She described the difference initial capital could make to her returns.

> I also sell mangoes, but there I cannot make very much because I do not have the money . . . For example, when the mangoes are ripe, you can buy a whole field for, say, 20,000f. You pay a 15,000f. advance. When you have sold all the mangoes you have perhaps 25,000f. You pay the other 5,000f. for the field and the 5,000f. are yours. But to start you need the money for the advance.

Only the wives in the better-off households were likely to be able to raise this kind of working capital. The wife of one of the established gardeners in the sample traded in mangoes in exactly the way described, as well as selling her husband's vegetables in Kayar (a fishing village on the coast), buying fish on the return journey to sell in Bambilor. In the vegetable and fish trading, she made an estimated 22,000f. in a couple of months, but gave up selling in the year of the study before the mango season. Another woman, also the first wife of one of the better-off households heads in the sample, made an estimated 50,000f. in rather less than five months at the same trading. When one compares this with the Bud wages, which rarely exceeded 30,000f. for the three-month season, it is clear that women might reasonably prefer to work as *banabanas* if they did it well, especially as selling was something which could be dropped if necessary for domestic crises, whereas Bud work was much more rigid in its demands and involved shift work including night shifts.

It was therefore the women from the better-off households especially the wives of established market gardeners, who predominated as *banabanas* and chose to sell rather than go to Bud, saying dismissively 'it is the children who work at Bud'. The women from the poorer households, and any young women who needed cash, had no choice but to seek work there. There was not, however, enough work for all the Bambilor women who looked for it. Bud recruited a single packing shed shift from the big village, and as one young woman put it, a second shift could easily have been found. The proportion of women who worked there was high: 21 per cent of adult women, far higher than for Bambilor men, but many women, especially in the pooer areas of the village housing the recent migrants, failed to find a job. The Bud hiring process for women as for men tended to favour the longer-established and those with contacts. Despite the option of market trading, the women Bud workers were significantly more likely to be from the market gardening households, from the longer-established areas of the village, from earlier than more recent migrants. All the women in the sample who complained that they could not find work were from the areas of the village housing the recent migrants.

While the women interviewed from the recent migrant households said the main constraint on their working was finding a job, women in the longer-established and better-off households said that male household heads often strongly opposed their working at Bud. One of the most emphatic – and startling – replies I was given when I asked what changes Bud had brought to the village came from a well-established gardener. 'It has ruined', he said, 'workers, prices and the women.' The women? 'Yes', he elaborated, 'they earn nearly nothing, but once Bud starts they will not stay at home.' In the sample households, it was the heads of the better-off households in terms of asset ownership who tended to express opposition to wage work by their wives (the opposition was particularly to wage work by wives, rather than other female household members). Some men gave distance or lack of time as their reasons for opposition, others offered an unexplained refusal. Such opposition was rarely voiced in the migrant households – at least so the interviews suggest – but the women were less likely to find work, and, furthermore, where households were smaller it might be difficult for a wife to find sufficient help with housework and child care to enable her to do a job involving night shifts.

Similarly, in Ponty men generally did not oppose their wives working. Women in Ponty, of all ages, saw it as natural that they should go out to work, and did not generally expect men to oppose this. An elderly woman approved the younger women's attidues: 'A countrywoman must work.' She had farmed in her youth; now women did wage work: she saw it as little different. Similarly, the women said, 'the men here never refuse'; 'I have never seen the men refuse to let the women work.' The women made it clear that they needed cash and had decided for themselves; only one said the deicision had been her husband's.

Nevertheless, the overall participation rate for women in Ponty, 35 per cent, was far lower than that in Kirene (63 per cent). In part this was the result of difficulties experienced by recent migrants in finding work. Some recent migrants said they had had trouble the first year, partly because of timidity. Thus one young migrant from the north:

> I wanted to work last year, but I was not taken on. I was a stranger here, no one knew me, and they took on the people they knew.

In 1975/6, however, she went to the farm with a group of women from Ponty and was hired. In the high season that year, it should be said, few women in Ponty who wanted work were without it. The village was close to the farm, the women knew the system, and though smaller than Bambilor the village supplied most of a packing shed shift.

One determinant of the lower participation rate than in Kirene was the smaller households, which made domestic work less compatible with wage work, particularly for recent migrants with no other family nearby. As a result, wives had a lower participation rate than women living as kin of a household member (Table 6.4). But a close look at the evidence shows the more subtle influence on women's work decisions of the incomes, and also the attitudes, of the husbands. Among the women in the sample households who did not work at Bud were three who seemed to find the whole idea alarming and unfamiliar, and to prefer not to go. The rest divided into two groups: those who said that they would go out to work just as soon as their daughters were old enough to help with the housework, and those who justified their not working on the principle that a woman once married should stay at home and look after her husband and children. The division coincided precisely with a division on the basis of husband's income. Thus the wives of full-time wage workers (or those retired from such jobs) said:

I cannot leave my husband. My home is my job.

I want to stay with the children. What would happen if they were ill and I was not there?

I would rather stay home than go out to work.

On the other hand, these were the comments of those whose husbands had irregular jobs and uncertain incomes:

I want to work. It is the children who keep me at home.

My husband does not want me to work at Bud because I am pregnant and you have to stand all day. But I want to work.

I want to go on working now I am married. (A recently married woman).

Finally, the woman who had worked long hours the previous year to support children and a household summed up her new husband's attitude: 'Now my husband does not want me to go out to work. Now I have *his* child he would rather I stayed in the house.' The girls from the poorest households were those most likely to say they would go on working after marriage; the other girls were more likely to say they wanted to stay home and 'look after my husband' after marriage.

It was thus not simply pressures of domestic work, but those pressures in relation to the position and attitudes of the husband, which had most effect in determining women's participation in wage work.

Individual Work and Class Formation

Bud-Baobab was therefore fitting into, and developing, a wage labour market around it. But the discussion so far has been written, at least so as the men are concerned, almost entirely from the point of view of individual attitudes and individual decisions about wage work. This reflects the reality to some extent, since wage work, and most of the other income earning activities in Bambilor and Ponty, were from the standpoint of the village economy individual economic activities in the way that farming in Kirene was not. That is, they required little co-operation within the village itself. Clearly, however, this is far from the whole story of the process of class formation: that is, the way in which Bud was creating a labour force in its own image around its estates. To understand fully the impact of the Baobab estate, we have to look at the kind of society which was being created in this part of the Cap Vert, and the impact of Bud upon that. For no village economy is simply an aggregate of wage-earning individuals. If it were, it would have no stability, no dynamic of its own. Bud was creating or helping to create, depending on the area, a new type of village economy based on dependence on wage work, and economic relations within the village premised on such dependence. Once established, such new relations were potentially lasting ones, conditioning the ideas and possibilities of the next generation.

To establish what kind of new village economy Bud was creating, the next two chapters seek to answer two questions. First, if agriculture had become just one more individual activity among others, how had that occurred, and how much of the process can be attributed to Bud? And second, what type of internal economic relations were developing within the villages near Bud-Baobab, especially Ponty village which was so entirely dependent on Bud work?

Notes

1. The village of Sebikotane, where I lived during the fieldwork, was close to Ponty and had many social links to it. I owe a good deal of background for this chapter and the two which follow to friends in Sebikotane.

2. While the extent of migration to Dakar and other main urban areas is documented (Diop, 1965; Elkan, 1975; Lacombe, 1970), and there are a number of collections and individual studies of migration and its impact on the sending areas (for example, from a large literature, Amin, 1974; de Latour Dejean, 1975; Van Binsbergen and Leilink, 1978; Lindsay, 1985; Painter, 1987), there seem to be few studies which assess the overall scale of migration and its socio-economic impact on West African societies, so that quite unrealistic ideas of rather static peasant societies persist for many countries. For a general attack on such misconceptions see Hill (1986). For a further discussion of this literature see Chapter 2.

3. The average age of male seasonal migrants interviewed was 25; those who said their migration was permanent were older on average and had a much wider age spread.

4. This is the group called 'strange farmers' in The Gambia (Haswell, 1963: 9). But in this case, the seasonal migrants left the interior after the wet season, and worked on gardeners' land, and gardened for themselves sometimes, in the dry season.

5. The Ecole Nationale d'Economie Appliquée in Dakar held in its library a number of field reports (*rapports de stage*) by students; the report cited here was written by five students after a stay of five months in Bambilor in 1968. It was used with the kind permission of Mr Pape Kane, then Director of the School.

6. A 1971 estimate put the growth of the Dakar population at 7 per cent per annum; later (1976) estimates suggest a lower growth rate, but may underestimate the effects of the drought (*Le Sénégal en Chiffres* 1976; République du Sénégal, n.d.).

7. There was a primary school in Bambilor which 49 per cent of children aged 7–15 were attending. There was no significant difference between the attendance of boys and girls.

Table 6.1
Ponty: Place of Birth, by Ethnic Group, of All Villagers as Percentages of Total in Each Group

Place of birth*	Ethnic group:					
	Wolof	Lebou	Peuhl	Toucouleur	Serer	Other
Ponty	40	75	45	30	48	28
Nearby village	2	2	3		1	1
Elsewhere in Cap Vert Region	21	18	15	19	5	22
Thiès Region	33	6	4	3	15	9
Diourbel Region (Central Senegal)	2		3	4	4	2
Sine Saloum Region (Central Senegal)			5	1	26	3
Fleuve Region (Northern Senegal)			12	34		2
Sénégal Orientale Region (Eastern Senegal)				6		5
Casamance Region (Southern Senegal)			1			16
Outside Senegal:						
Guinea			10			1
Other	2		1	2		11
Total (100%) individuals in each group	43	106	73	120	73	120

* See Map 1 for the Senegalese Regional divisions.

Table 6.2
Bambilor, 1975: Place of Origin of Recent Migrants (1971-75), by Age at Migration (Adults/Children) and Sex

Place of origin	Percentages of totals in each group			
	Females		Males	
	Age at migration			
	below 15 years	15 years and over	below 15 years	15 years and over
Nearby village	12	9	3	2
Elsewhere in Cap Vert Region	39	17	47	14
Thiès Region	14	33	13	16
Diourbel Region	7	15	5	17
Sine Saloum Region	15	10	9	7
Fleuve Region	11	12	7	25
Sénégal Orientale Region			1	
Casamance Region		3	7	5
Outside Senegal:				
Guinea		2		8
Other	1		7	6
Total (100%) individuals in group	72	102	68	128

Note: Data for one female and three males are missing.

Table 6.3
Bambilor, 1975: Women's Work, by Age and Types of Work

	15-19	20-29	Age group 30-39	40-49	50-59	Total
Total number in age group	101	164	92	53	39	449
Percentages who work at:						
Market trading, milk selling, *banabana*		7	29	30	38	17*
Petty selling		2	8	8	8	4
Bud, seasonal or irregular	19	21	27	25	10	21†

* Seven women older than 59 also declared work as a *banabana* or market trader.

† Eight girls younger than 15 also declared that they worked at Bud.

Table 6.4
Ponty: Women's Participation in the Bud Labour Force, by Age and Household Position. (Total individuals in group, percentage working at Bud in brackets.)

Age group	Household head		Wife of household member		Kin of household member		Total	
15-9			2	(0)	33	(45)	35	(43)
20-29			31	(39)	17	(65)	48	(48)
30-39	2	(0)	18	(33)	5	(60)	25	(36)
40-49	1	(100)	17	(6)	1	(0)	19	(11)
≥50	1	(0)	10	(10)	6	(0)	17	(6)
Total	4	(25)	78	(26)	62	(47)	144	(35)

Note: Data for one person incomplete.

7. Wage Work and the Decline of Farming in the Cap Vert

Wet season farming had largely decayed in the area of the Baobab estate before the arrival of Bud. When the land for the estate was destumped and levelled, there was one long-established Lebu[1] village which was inclined to lay claim to some of the land, but the claim had very little emotional force compared with the feelings of the Kirene villagers. The small Lebu villages around the estate boundary, like Kirene, resisted settlement by migrants and sometimes demanded priority in hiring, but their numbers were small as compared with the totals employed at Baobab, and the issue marginal to conflict on the estate. There was little hostility in the area to migrants, and the inhabitants of the Cap Vert villages had ceased to be farmers by the 1970s except for those, like the Bambilor gardeners, who had access to the valuable low-lying land called the *niayes* suitable for dry season market gardening; nor did they see themselves as agricultural labourers, except as a matter of last resort.

Although the decline in wet season farming predated the Baobab estate by many years, the reasons for the decline are relevant here because they help to explain why the new settled migrants to the area did not farm successfully in the wet season. For the reason was *not* lack of land. The reason for farming decay was the change in the social relations of production associated with the dominance of wage labour and the monetization of economic relations in the rural economy. The same changes turned market gardening into a commercial, wage labour enterprise which was threatened by Bud's impact on the labour market. This effect of wage labour on farming is, in turn, partly the result of the characteristic pre-existing household structure in this part of West Africa, which governed the way in which monetization affected the social relations of farming. This sequence of argument is a necessary basis for understanding why Bud and other similar seasonal plantations could never create around themselves farming communities which treated the seasonal wages incomes as merely an addition to existing farming income, but rather tended to produce company villages impoverished by dependence on seasonal incomes.

The Decay of Wet Season Farming in the Cap Vert

In the 1940s and 1950s, the Cap Vert area of Senegal had contained established wet season farming communities, producing food crops as well as a range of cash crops. In Bambilor in the 1950s there had been a number of much larger compounds than those found in 1975, with farmers producing millet, groundnuts, vegetables and a number of subsidiary crops such as sugar cane in the fertile land of this area. The elderly villagers could remember communal labour parties on the millet and groundnut fields before about 1950. The big compounds seem to have been assembled by compound heads of strong personality, in a way rather reminiscent of Kirene, although in a rather different economic context. One of the largest, for example, had been headed by a man who farmed wet season crops on a large scale, and vegetables for the city market, as well as being a successful trader in groundnuts before the nationalization of the trade. The compound included a number of sons and other kin, and only finally split after his death in 1967.

On the other side of the Bud estate, in the area of Ponty, the story was similar although the land had never been as good. Here, as in the case of Bambilor, many of the original villages had been Lebu. Beside Ponty village was a small, long-established Lebu village which had existed before Ponty, and whose inhabitants had moved a short distance away to found Thien Thiou village (included in our study of Ponty) when the school was founded. The head of one Thien Thiou household, who had grown up in the area, remembered the arrival of groundnuts as a cash crop in the village. He himself had only farmed, never worked for wages, although his brother had done seasonal wage work, 'for money to buy clothes, to buy cattle and to pay the taxes. He stopped when we began to make enough money from the groundnuts.' He had gone with his uncle into the interior to learn the Coran, had farmed for his father, and taken over his father's household. He was married by 1936 when the school took over what had been an army camp. He grew millet and groundnuts, and remembered that the village had grown millet where the Baobab estate was set up. He attributed the abandonment of these lands, well before Bud, to an epidemic of plague in the 1930s which decimated the population and meant that there were not enough people to farm the land, the survivors moving their farms back closer to the village.

Since the 1940s the decline in farming had been sharp. By the 1970s groundnut production was very low in the Cap Vert, and the millet production so small it was rarely registered in the statistics. Only market gardening remained as a viable economic activity (Table 7.1). Why had this decline in farming occurred? The villagers with whom we discussed this all associated it with the increase in availability of wage work to the Cap Vert inhabitants. From their descriptions of the decline of farming, two rather separate arguments emerge about the nature of the link between wgae work and farming decline. Wage work provided an alternative and more lucrative occupation for many men. And this offer of wage work caused the individualization of farming as an occupation, by making younger men unwilling to work unpaid on the farms.

The first argument is exemplified by the story of the Thien Thiou household head just cited. For this man, the decline of farming in the area had been associated with the decline in strength of men of his generation. His eldest son had gone to the primary school established in Ponty after the war, and become a school teacher himself, working in various places and finally returning to teach in Ponty and take over the household. When he began to contribute to the household, they began to eat rice as well as millet, of which they consequently farmed less. Some other household members worked at the school and contributed cash for food. The shift away from reliance on farming was gradual, caused by other sources of cash, by declining groundnut prices in the 1960s, and then finally by the drought in the late 1960s which caused the millet yield to drop almost to nothing. Tastes in food changed to those of the town, with a preference for rice; there was cash coming in; and as the father's strength declined, no one took over the farming. 'I have no strength any longer and the children are no longer willing to work in the fields.' The early decline of agriculture meant that at no point had the people in these villages acquired agricultural equipment other than the hand hoe: by the time animal-drawn equipment became available, the villagers had lost the incentive to acquire it.

In Ponty proper, full-time work at the school meant that people had little time or incentive for farming. 'While the school was here people did not farm much. It was after the school left that they were forced to go back to farming.' The school had had a vegetable garden down near its own small reservoir, but the staff seem to have done little farming, on the evidence of the work histories of the heads of two sample households, a cook and a foreman at the school. The first said he had had little time for farming having just a small kitchen plot. The other grew a few vegetables near the school fields (where there were irrigation channels, later left to decay with the reservoir). In Ponty the 1950s and early 1960s were much like the mid-1970s, people gaining their main income from the school, and farming for a small subsidiary income or to supplement food. But, as people were quick to point out, the level of living provided by the school had been well above the effective purchasing power of Bud wages.

As a result of the counter attractions of wage work and the aspirations of their parents, children who had grown up in the area in the previous thirty years had not become farmers: they had learned little about farming technique, since they had at most helped their parents to plant and harvest small fields of groundnuts, maize and tomatoes. Most of the girls said that they had never been to the fields. The young men did not want to farm, not only because of a dislike of the occupation, and of how the occupation was regarded by others, but also because they lacked the knowledge of how to farm successfully, so that their farming was likely to have been unrewarding had they tried it.

The second argument was put with more force in Bambilor, where farming had been particularly productive. The head of Bambilor village attributed the decline of the collective millet fields and the communal work parties (called *maas* in this area) to the counter-attraction of wage work in the nearby towns and market gardens. People, especially young men, ceased to work collective fields, so they were split up. He dated the final abandonment of millet to the early 1960s, and attributed it to the loss of the big fields, to the children going to school which meant that they were not available for bird-scaring, and to the final blow of the drought.

This man was arguing, in effect, that by the 1970s the economic basis for the large compounds had gone. They had depended upon the large-scale cultivation of wet season crops with dependent labour: labour which did not have to be paid in cash. This in turn depended upon land being available for millet and for those dependants to grow cash crops, on the price of groundnuts, and on the lack of alternative opportunities for dependants. By 1975, all three of these conditions had effectively disappeared. Farming had become by and large an individual occupation.

Individualization and the Unproductiveness of Wet Season Farming

In Sebikotane many people do not have any land and do not miss it. The people whom you now see farming, with their hoes, they are workers (*ouvriers*) who are unemployed.

In order to see the extent of individualization of wet season farming and its effects on the productiveness of agriculture, we can examine the farming which was undertaken in Bambilor and Ponty in the 1975/6 season. The quotation above is from the head of the household in which I lived in Sebikotane, near Ponty, and makes the point clearly: when a male inhabitant of Ponty or Sebikotane found no wage work, he might pick up a hoe. The resultant farming was done poorly, on a small scale, resentfully: an activity in default of any other.

The farming in Ponty in 1975 shows this pattern clearly. Nothing in the Bud and farming calendars prevented Ponty residents from farming. Only the tomatoes overlapped, and the plots were tiny, easily harvested on days off. Nevertheless, few men did both in any one year (Table 7.2) A pattern emerges from sample and census: older household heads tended to farm, but to be too old for Bud jobs or unwilling to go there; younger, recently arrived household heads were the only people who might both work at Bud and farm; dependent men in Ponty households very rarely farmed, but earned what they could from irregular wage work.

Few women farmed. Only four women in the sample households studied grew crops, and the distribution suggests that they tended to live in the poorest households: two of the four were wives of pensioners; the other two were a woman supporting a household virtually alone, and her elderly mother. The interviews show that the decision to farm was an individual one, taken when nothing better presented itself; who farmed varied from year to year.

The small number of farmers and the small scale were not the result of land shortage. The land in and around the village had belonged to the school; it was not in the National Domain and the villagers lacked all rights to it under the law. Nevertheless, they continued to use it from year to year, and a villager who wished to farm could obtain land to clear and use. About 50 per cent of farmers used land which still belonged to the school, with the agreement of the village head; another 40 per cent had cleared land outside the school domain at some distance from the village, and the rest borrowed spare land from Thien Thiou and other nearby villages. Though the farmers lacked tenure, there was little competition for the land.

Farming in Ponty involved almost no intra-household *or* cross-household economic relations. As is clear from the above description, finding land was an individual activity: subordinate household members found their own. Furthermore, all but two of the farmers (both men) did the bulk of the work on their plots themselves: five out of thirteen entirely alone, the other eight with sporadic assistance from some household members.

Two, both elderly, used *surga*s. This had a different meaning from the same word in Bambilor: in Ponty a *surga* was a migrant who stayed in Ponty in the wet season, being given board and lodging only in return for some help with farming. Finally, two men used *tâcherons* (casual day labourers) for some operations, and two sold fields of cassava to *banabana*s (travelling traders) who did the harvesting themselves.

Farming was thus a highly individualized activity, involving no cross-household relations except the occasional day of paid labour. The difference between Ponty and Kirene is enormous. There was no farm equipment in the village to be shared or hired, and in the Ponty area no one remembered any communal labour system. An elderly woman who came to Ponty in the late 1940s said that there had been no such system in Ponty when she had arrived: 'In the Cap Vert no-one helped anyone even then, everyone here is for themselves.' A farmer could call on extra-household labour only in return for cash, and while household members might sometimes help, they felt themselves under no obligation to do so (especially if they were also bringing cash into the household). There were far more people looking for casual labouring work in Ponty in the wet season than there were jobs available.

> The people who worked at Bud are many of them still here [in June 1976] looking for any work they can get. So it is very easy to find *tâcherons*.

The problem was to find the money to pay them.

The returns on this individualized farming make it clear why there were more people willing to labour than willing to hire labourers, despite the availability of land. Without equipment, without access to unpaid labour or any forms of mutual labour co-operation, the farming was too small-scale and unprofitable to allow payment of wages. Apart from a couple of elderly household heads who had 'kitchen gardens', small plots near the house to supplement family food, most farming in Ponty was for cash. This was clear from the choice of crops in 1975, the main criterion being a rapid cash return from a small area. The school teacher in one of the households studied described in detail the changes in crop choice this had meant.

> With falling groundnut prices,[2] especially in the 1960s, people stopped growing so many groundnuts. And then came the drought, which ruined the sorghum which needs a lot of water. We did not get ten kilos of millet from our fields in

those years . . . We had grown cassava for a long time but a few years ago a new variety became known that was much more profitable: from a hectare of that you can earn 1–2 million francs. Over by Diender they almost grow only cassava now . . . We also knew maize long ago, but it has only recently developed for sale . . . The commercial growing of tomatoes began, I think, around 1965: the local variety of small tomatoes.

The cropping pattern in the households studied bears out this analysis. Fifteen farmers farmed 43 plots: 12 tomatoes, 8 maize, 6 groundnuts, 5 cassava, 5 millet or sorghum, 6 other vegetables, 1 rice. The most profitable crops in 1975 were tomatoes (which three women and several men grew) and cassava. In addition, interestingly, the vegetable plots included a few grown for the first time in 1975 on the banks of the small reservoir abandoned by the school. The arrival of Bud had made people aware of the possibilities of earning cash from even small areas of irrigated land, and the land around the only open ground water had therefore been divided up by the heads of the surrounding villages into tiny plots for interested villagers.

Male migrants from the Senegalese interior tended to farm far less in Ponty than they had done before, and to switch crops. Thus a migrant from the North (Podor in the Fleuve Region) paid to have his land farmed at home, while farming only small plots of groundnuts and millet in Ponty. Another, a farmer from the Thiès region, had switched to maize (sold green for consumption as a vegetable) and tomatoes on arrival in Ponty. 'Maize grows quicker and is less work than groundnuts.' Most people gave up millet quite quickly: 'I am going to abandon millet next year: I have planted it for eight years without harvesting anything.'

The switch in crops had a strong basis in returns. Almost all the crops were grown for cash. Analysis of the returns from Ponty farming (Table 7.3) shows that only two farmers made over 30,000f. net from their farming, and these two grew tomatoes and cassava using only their own labour. The two other farmers (both elderly) who appeared to make over 20,000f. only did so if the costs of board and lodging for the *surga*s are not included (farmers A1 and G1, Table 7.3). The other male farmers made an average of 1,600f. each for a wet season's work; the two women who sold any crops made 1,000 and 8,500f. respectively (from tomatoes). In summary, millet and groundnuts in this area were not a paying proposition; there was not the equipment, the assistance nor the motivation to make them pay. Only small fields of higher value cash crops repaid the effort at all, and returns were still low. The results set out in Table 7.3 can be compared, for example, with Kirene farming in the same year: the men in Kirene with enough remaining land made an average net return of 27,500f. from groundnuts alone (Table 5.3), and the women made an average of 15,750f. from their farming after the loss of most of the vegetable crop (Table 5.5). All this was in addition to growing substantial quantities of millet, and after the detrimental effects of Bud were well under way.

The Bambilor farming study provides more information about low returns to groundnuts, since more were planted. The groundnut plots planted by the sample household members earned a negative cash sum in a majority of cases.

Only six out of fourteen made any positive cash return, though all but one said the groundnuts were intended as cash crops. Of the six, only two made more than 10,000f. in all (the price of a 100 kilogramme sack of rice). As Table 7.4 demonstrates, the main reason for this lack of profitability was the cost of labour. Twelve of the farmers used paid labour, and for ten this was the largest component of costs. Two full-time wage workers used *tâcheron* labour for all tasks except some of the hoeing, and both made a cash loss. The one man who made over 40,000f. had huge labour costs and was the only one who bullied several very reluctant sons into assisting with the work. Otherwise seeding was the only operation where other household members helped, in a few cases. Occasionally wives assisted on the plots but this was rare enough for one woman migrant from the inland Diourbel Region to say, 'Here, women do not go to the fields.' The market gardeners differed little from the other farmers in the labour use on their groundnut plots, except that they had some residual access to exchange labour. Three used work parties on their groundnut plots: two of these parties were compensated by meals; the other, a work party of young people, was paid a small cash sum.

The market gardeners did no better financially from groundnuts than other growers, in part because they did not take groundnuts very seriously. They gave priority to the vegetables wherever there was conflict, paying for land clearance for groundnuts, and leaving groundnuts in the ground if the lifting conflicted with planting vegetables.

The vegetables are more profitable . . . people who grow a lot of groundnuts are likely to be late with their vegetables.

And of course it was the early season vegetables which gained the best market prices.

Other growers were equally casual. One reason for the low returns was undoubtedly neglect, particularly at harvest (compounded in 1975 by the effect of rats), and the crop was left to rot if a better income-earning possibility came along. Groundnuts seem to have been planted in Bambilor as part of a strategy of spreading risk by assembling a cash income from as many different sources as possible. Even the better-off households did this. Although the groundnut crop might lose money over all, it did bring in some cash at a difficult moment in the year for all those without permanent wage jobs: that is, at the end of the wet season, before the market gardening season opened. For the same reason, less than a third of the groundnut farmers sold their crop through the *secco* (the stated owned ONCAD[3] store, linked to the co-operatives) in the way prescribed by law. The rest sold privately to traders or neighbours, hoping for a better, or at least quicker, return and to avoid repayment of debts.

Groundnut growing had therefore become an individual and unlucrative activity, useful only for risk spreading. Few women had their own plots: the census shows only 21 women farming groundnuts in their own right, of whom eight were household heads. Male dependents also rarely grew them: only 28 dependent men in the whole village said during the census that they grew them, and the sample confirmed this. Only household heads grew them, as a sideline, and the next generation of men brought up in Bambilor was likely not to know how they were grown.

If the groundnuts were unprofitable, millet was hopeless as a cash crop. Millet growing requires a considerable amount of labour, inlcuding labour in guarding the fields and bird scaring when the crop is close to harvest. An elderly man in Bambilor described how he had 'lived in the fields' at this time when young, to guard the food crops. With the labour of young dependent men no longer available in this way, millet yielded little in Bambilor and Ponty. And prices for millet were too low to make it an attractive cash crop. The two young men in Kirene who grew millet for cash, for lack of groundnut seeds, made only about 2,000f. Thus no farmer, making an individual choice of crops, would grow millet: it made more sense to grow other cash crops and purchase food, especially in areas such as the Cap Vert where rice was increasingly preferred to millet.

Given this comparison of economic returns, it is clear how food farming had ended in the Cap Vert. Millet growing, as in Kirene, continued while food farming was the basis of the social organization of the village economy. Once wage work became available, and the inter-household and intra-household relations monetized, dependents ceased to be willing to work unpaid – including women, who preferred to trade or do wage work, or even to farm on their own behalf like a few young men. And once labour had to be paid, farming became a matter of individual commercial calculation, in which food growing inevitably lost out to cash crops given the relative prices.

The farming system had thus ceased to be the main basis of socio-economic organization, and farming had become one money-making option among others. In Ponty this meant the virtual eclipse of farming: less than 4 per cent of the income of male residents came from farming in 1975/6. In Bambilor commercial gardening for the city markets remained a real, if precarious, option.

The Economic Organization of the Market Gardens

In conditions where farming has become an individual activity, and unapid labour co-operation non-existent, the only farming which survives on any scale is that in which labour productivity is high enough to allow the payment of wage labour. In the Cap Vert villages, only market gardening in the *niaye* land fulfilled these conditions in 1975/6.

The villages of the northern Cap Vert were the main market gardening centres in the country before Bud. Although initially subsidized by the French colonial government to feed Dakar, the gardening had expanded virtually without government assistance, the gardeners buying seeds, experimenting with pesticide powders, and selling to travelling traders. The whole gardening area, which included Bambilor, was called the *niayes*, after the damp, low-lying land where the gardening was done. These damp depressions lie behind the coastal dunes, and have a high water table, only a metre or two below the surface even in drought years, and flooded by rain water in wet years. The gardening thus required little fixed capital: the gardeners dug walk-in wells in which watering cans were filled for irrigating the plants. Only in the area nearest to Dakar did a few larger Senegalese and expatriate farmers use pumps and sprays for irrigation.

The discussion which follows draws on a detailed study of six Bambilor market gardening compounds, containing ten independent gardeners, as well as on other published and unpublished material on Senegalese market gardening.[4] Bambilor is in certain respects untypical of the gardening villages, being more recently established (the village was founded in the 1930s by villagers moving from the nearby village of Sakal which seems to have been dispersed by plague), containing relatively more people who did not garden, and having rather less water than villages near the coast. Nevertheless, the study of Bambilor gardens casts doubt on the characterization by some authors of many *niaye* gardens as 'family farms' (Arnaud, 1970).

The gardens were small. The size of the sample gardens – weighted towards the more successful gardeners – was 3,760 square metres or about a third of a hectare per male gardener. The only woman gardener grew no more than a small area of parsley on her husband's land. These areas, which do not include the large surface areas of the walk-in wells, might be planted with more than one crop over the season. This sample size is close to the overall average for garden areas in the published sources, suggesting that the Bambilor plots were not unusually small; the range was from about one hectare to 425 square metres, the smallest garden being one planted by recent migrants on borrowed land.

The gardens were held on the basis of complex land tenure arrangements, difficult to research because many of the numerous purchases and sales in the *niaye*s area were not within the law. The land is fertile, close to the city, and therefore valuable. Land purchase and sale had been known throughout the area from long before Independence. The father of one gardener interviewed had purchased land in the village in the 1930s, well before the decline of mixed farming. Another gardener had bought land many years before on the basis of a *gage*, that is, as cash deposit as security for a loan of land, later turned into the down payment for a sale. But most of the land sales seem to have been in the 1950s and early 1960s, before the 1964 act, and to have consisted in sales to non-villagers, usually for orchards used also as weekend residences. Table 7.5 shows the extent of such land holding by outsiders in Bambilor: much of this was *niaye* land; some was held under private title registered before the law; some was in the process of being registered; some would not be. The village land was being squeezed sharply by these outsider purchases throughout the areas containing the *niayes* (Table 7.6).

The land purchases for orchards have to be understood, not merely as a result of the desire for weekend residences, but also as speculation with an eye to the resale value of the land. Even before Bud, it was evident that the value of good land close to Dakar would rise as the city expanded. It was an investment in a country with few outlets besides property speculation for private investment. While the orchards were sometimes gardened with hired labour, using pumps for irrigation, few were run as fully commercial enterprises: the Bambilor agricultural extension agent[5] expressed doubts that many orchards paid a return at all over costs of caretaking, gardening and maintenance. Nevertheless, the purchasing power of the Dakar élite owners, called collectively *fonctionnaires* (civil servants) by the villagers,[6] was taking the price of gardening land out of reach of many would-be village gardeners.

Land prices were rising ahead of inflation even in the 1960s. The information is fragmentary and unreliable, since officially these sales did not occur at all. The higher land, not in the *niayes*, was being sold for around 25,000–30,000f. a hectare in the mid 1960s, and 45,000f. a hectare in the early 1970s. Inflation from 1967 to 1973 had been around 30 per cent; after 1973 consumption prices soared, and prices had risen by about 100 per cent by mid-1976.[7] The good land in the *niayes* with some trees, which the villagers were more reluctant to sell, had been selling for about 50,000f. for half a hectare in 1965, and for 200,000–220,000f. for a hectare in the early 1970s. I had no data on very recent sales (1974–76), but villagers said in 1975 that prices were continuing to rise, and sales continued. Two of the sample gardeners with good gardening land had recently been approached, and the drought had increased the villagers' need for cash.

The result of this speculation was that the hold of the villagers on their gardens was becoming increasingly precarious before Bud, and the tenure of the gardeners studied was a curious patchwork. These village gardens were by no means all on inherited land. Four of the gardeners had inherited land from their families and farmed only this land, one other had acquired part of his land in that fashion. One found in Bambilor the last remnants of the matrilineal land inheritance among the Lebu, the dominant ethnic group among the early residents of the village. One sample gardener was one of a group of brothers belonging to an old land-holding family. The head of the family lived in Rufisque and did not farm; the eldest Bambilor brother, his matrilineal descendant, 'looked after' the land. The family had acquired a customary title to some of their land in the colonial period, and had sold a good deal of land for cash before the 1964 law. The father of the brothers had married into the family, and farmed on his wife's land, which his sons took over on his death.

This inherited land now fell in the *Domaine National*; none of the gardeners had private title to the land. The gardeners said, as farmers said in Kirene, 'Now there is no inheritance. The land is for whoever cultivates it.' But the force of this was different in Bambilor, because of the extensive development of an illegal land market, and the (related) failure to set up the institution of the Rural Council in the Cap Vert. The institution, intended to manage the *Domaine National* land at local level, did not exist, the cash transactions were covert, and the chief effect of the 1964 law in this part of the world had been to make it very difficult to know who had effective control of any piece of land. Some land holders lent land or had it cultivated by others. The most accurate statement would be that in Bambilor land was for whoever could lay his – rarely her – hands upon it.

In this situation, even the four gardeners who held inherited *niaye* land knew that they had to garden it in order to retain control of it. One gardener in the sample had had a father who had gardened, during which time the present gardener had been working as a bricklayer in Dakar, where his brother also has a job. On his father's death, the present gardener had realized that if he did not go back to the village to farm (he was the eldest), the family would lose their land once and for all. He returned to garden: he had good land in a *niaye*, and said he had sold none of it.

Apart from the gardeners who had inherited land or purchased it before the 1964, one gardener had borrowed land in the 1950s, and planted mangoes on it; in 1964 he had simply kept it. Since then, borrowing land in the village had become difficult, because of fears of non-return and because of land shortage. Two of the established Lebu gardeners had borrowed land in the village, from kin or neighbours, in 1975. One newcomer had borrowed from a non-resident land holder who allowed the village head to lend out his land on a year to year basis. But there was little land available in this way. The two recent migrants in the gardening sample were therefore gardening further from the village on 'ranch' land. The cattle ranch used part of a piece of land of about 2,500 hectares bordering the village, to which a disputed private title was held by a Frenchman. The owner had sold 100 hectares to a M. Bertin for the cattle ranch; on the rest, villagers from Bambilor (and other villages) cleared land for gardens each year and there were recurrent disputes as to whether the owner could exact rent for such land use. In 1975/6 the Bambilor gardeners said they had paid nothing for the land, though in previous years they had been asked for a small sum and some had paid it.

The effect of land tenure arrangements in Bambilor, therefore, was that the gardeners interviewed did not pay rent for land; some held good gardening land still within the village; generally the others, the relative newcomers, could only garden on precariously held land at a long walking distance from the village. For the gardeners with good village land, both land and labour could constrain the total area gardened, but for all gardeners, the main constraint was labour.

On the evidence of the sample, market gardening in Bambilor was in no sense 'family' or 'household' farming: it was individual commercial gardening where the work was done either by the individual gardener or by paid labour. Unpaid labour by household members was rare, the exception rather than the rule; unpaid assistance exchanged with neighbours was equally uncommon. All this measures the distance between Bambilor gardening and the vegetable growing in Kirene: the latter, cash cropping within a village farming system; the former, a commercial activity, the alternative to which was some other wholly commercial activity.

Bud had not changed the general pattern of labour use on the gardens at all. Hired labour long pre-dated Bud, although the labour contract (the terms of hire) had been changing. The most common hired worker was the *surga*. Labour of *surga*s hired by the season was supplemented by daily-hired piece workers (*tâcherons*). Among the Bambilor sample gardeners one can distinguish a number of different strategies of labour use, associated with other aspects of the gardeners' economic and social situation (see Table 7.7 for a summary of the labour use data).

The first group were two Lebu gardeners (A and B in Table 7.7), born and brought up in the area, sons of market gardeners, farming *niaye* land. Both had a *surga* for three months in high season,[8] paying around 3,500f. a month plus board and lodging. They also used more expensive labour hired 'by the task' in September – October, before they could find *surga*s, at rates of 200f. to 500f. a day[9] and generally towards the upper end of that range. These farmers were full-time gardeners, going to their gardens most days of the week in season. They had little or no assistance from household members (the wife of one occasionally helped with the harvest), and both had sent all their children to school to be educated in French, foreseeing that their sons would not be farmers. Because of their social position in the village, Lebu land holders, long resident in the village, these were the only two gardeners in the sample able to call on assistance of neighbours for occasional urgent tasks (such as digging the gardens in the early season before paid help was available, or preparing seed potatoes for planting). Such work parties could be quite large (eight to ten people), and they were 'thanked' with a meal. The total of this assistance for farmer A is unusually high (Table 7.7) because I have included two people's assistance with a series of harvests where a token payment (described as a 'gift' rather than a payment by the farmer) was more in the nature of thanks to neighbours. This labour was the cheapest assistance available in cash terms.

The second group of farmers (C to F in Table 7.7) had also grown up in the area, but had other jobs in addition to gardening. All Wolof household heads, they included three brothers with inherited land, who had public sector wage jobs in Dakar, and one man with another source of income in addition to gardening, who was quite often away from the village. This last man, unusually, had two sons farming for him. One of the brothers (E) worked a small garden part-time, largely with his own labour, but the others used paid labour heavily, working only occasionally themselves. Some of the *surga*s were paid cash, some given land; one *surga* had become a permanent member of a household and remained all year, farming on his own account. Doing little farming themselves, these farmers could not call on the assistance of neighbours; only one had a work party for a potato harvest, a very small proportion of the total labour on his fields.

Finally, farmers G to J were all first generation immigrants, including the full-time *surga* referred to above (J) working their gardens mainly by their own efforts. One, partially disabled, had had a *surga* the previous year who had stayed for board only in the early season, then left. The farmer had not replaced him, because in his own words, he was 'afraid to take a *surga* in case the crop is bad and I cannot pay at the end of the season'. These gardeners used less casual labour than any of the others, and had no substantial help with the gardens from household members: only one nephew who watered a pepper crop while two gardeners worked briefly elsewhere.

Given the land area available, labour was the main constraint on how intensively it could be worked. Hand watering was very labour intensive, and the first category of farmers argued that they could not manage without *surga*s.

> A garden had to be watered all the time, and the father of a family cannot always be there, he had ceremonies and other obligations, and so if there is a baptism there is no one to do the watering.

The other farmer in the same category offered an example of conflicting labour needs on the garden itself.

> Today I am cutting up the seed potatoes for planting. That means I will not be able to go and water until the day after tomorrow and I have not yet found a *surga* [this was mid December]. The final crop will suffer from that kind of neglect.

He added a similar comment to that of the first farmer.

> A head of compound had ceremonies to go to, baptisms and so on. He needs a *surga* to leave on the fields. Otherwise he is in danger of having to reduce the area he farms, and of not being able to feed his family.

Constraints in the form of social obligations weighed less heavily on the farmers in the third category. This was partly from sheer necessity – they were considerably poorer in land and resources than the first category farmers – but also because they were newcomers to the village and therefore not inserted into the type of social network described by the Lebu farmers above. There seems no doubt that the ability of the Lebu farmers to call upon the assistance of neighbours – as only they could – depended in part on their maintaining just this network of social relationships and social obligations within their neighbourhood in the village. The other farmers, the newcomers, had to fend for themselves.

The gardening season ran from November to June/July, with some planting and preparation in September/October, and some crops such as tomatoes, peppers and aubergines picked through August unless flooded by rainwater. My figures are not detailed enough to calculate total labour hours on the gardens. Another study (Arnaud, 1970) gives figures which approximate six full-time persons per hectare for irrigated crops, with 60 per cent of the time being for watering alone. The sample farmers gardening alone were indeed gardening an average of 1,700 square metres (about a sixth of a hectare) but actual areas varied greatly, the *surga* farming a half hectare alone. The watering is extremely heavy work, for which a farmer needed to be strong and active: an elderly gardener would need paid help for this reason alone. Over the season there were some labour bottlenecks – for example in preparation and planting if the *niaye* had flooded – but planning can reduce these bottlenecks more in gardening than for other crops. Harvesting did not seem to create a bottleneck, some crops being picked as they ripened, others such as potatoes being dug out over a period of days.

The Effect of Bud on Labour and Product Markets

The effects of Bud on these independent commercial smallholders – the only farmers in the study who can properly be described in this way – can be classified in terms of different markets. For established gardeners Bud was not an alternative form of employment – except in unpleasant moments of dire necessity – but a competitor for labour and for markets for products.

Competition for labour represented Bud's most decisive effect on the Bambilor gardeners in 1975. As already shown, Bud pushed up the cost of *surga* labour for the gardeners, but it did not make it prohibitively expensive. The worst effect was on labour availability: Bud created a labour shortage at the busiest times of the year:

> Last year the moment Bud opened, our *surga*s left to work there. There are some who just come here and wait for Bud to open. They say they cannot work for you because once Bud opened they would have to leave.

The season of 1975/6 had been the wettest rainy season in the area for a number of years, and the gardeners in Bambilor said in November that as a result the seasonal workers were slow to arrive that year. That fact plus the existence of Bud meant that in the early season a number of gardeners were in some doubt as to how much labour they were going to be able to find, or indeed afford, and they therefore did not know how large an area they should prepare and plant (some of the seeds or plants requiring a substantial investment of cash, as well as the labour time for preparing the beds). This comment was made in mid-December by a Lebu gardener:

> We need *surga*s from November to June . . . We have started work already for which we really need *surga*s, and it is not certain that we will get them. I have planted aubergines and hot peppers, and they will be ruined if I cannot find workers. At the beginning the land is still damp, but as soon as watering becomes necessary, as soon as the peppers produce shoots, we need workers.

Throughout the season in Bambilor the farmers had problems keeping labour. *Surga*s who left were not quickly replaced. Several farmers did not find a *surga* until mid-January, and some left in March. This labour shortage had an effect on total areas gardened by some farmers.

As for product market competition, there was considerable concern in Dakar in 1975 that Bud, by selling on the local market produce of sub-export quality, would ruin the market for the local gardeners. The evidence from the Bambilor study and from an examination of price trends on the Dakar market was that up to 1975/6 that effect had been small.

The Bambilor gardeners had long been accustomed to spreading their risks by planting a range of crops. In 1975/6, the most popular crops were potatoes, onions and hot peppers, all planted by the majority of the gardeners. Green beans and aubergines were more specialized crops, beans being planted by only one farmer. The average number of crops planted, including double cropping, was 4.3 and the established full-time gardeners planted a range of crops. It was popular to combine potatoes and/or onions, crops which had a guaranteed price, and were seen as easy but less profitable than some, with the more temperamental but highly profitable hot peppers, plus tomatoes or aubergines. People who had problems with labour (for example the disabled farmer) stuck to potatoes and onions; only the two young gardeners on ranch land planted a single crop, hot peppers, hoping for high returns from a small area.

Furthermore, the gardeners readily switched crops in response to selling difficulties and price changes. The farming histories show a move away from green beans and tomatoes over the years 1972–76, and an increase in hot peppers and onions, while potatoes remained a staple crop throughout the period. In 1975/6, four gardeners who had previously grown green beans had given them up, while five farmers took up hot peppers for the first time. The gardeners said 1974/5 had been a very bad year for green beans: prices were low and traders often left the crop in the farmers' hands.

The gardeners attributed a number of these changes to Bud's impact on the product markets. Several said that Bud had ruined tomato prices in previous years. This seems a plausible contention, since the bulk of Bud's local sales were made up of tomatoes in 1974–76. The estimated capacity of the local market was only 100 metric tons a month,[10] and Bud local sales far exceeded that in some months. Even allowing for part of the sales going to the processing factory, the quantities should have had an impact on Dakar market prices.

That impact is difficult to trace in data on retail prices in Dakar. Tomato prices were lower in the main gardening season in 1971–73, the years before Bud local sales, than in 1974 and 1975, but seemed to be falling back again in 1976. It was in the much narrower markets, such as green peppers and aubergines, that Bud's effect on prices showed up most clearly. These are retail prices, however. It is possible that the main competition was at the level of farm gate prices. Certainly Bud wholesale prices for tomatoes were very low relative to retail prices in 1976. And the prices realized by Bud of around 20f. a kilogramme in January and March are very low beside the farm gate price of 45–50f. a kilogramme that the Bambilor gardeners were getting in December. It seems probable, then, that for tomatoes, the low prices Bud offered to offload the produce did compete at the wholesale stage with the local farmer in nearby Bambilor, both by driving down wholesale prices, and by making it more difficult for the farmers to sell the produce at all.

This last factor seems to have been as important as price in causing gardeners to move away from crops Bud was producing. Gardeners said that while Bud had been growing aubergines (it dropped them in the 1975/6 season, after growing large quantities for several years) the local farmers could only make a profit by growing them late in the season, and many preferred to give them up altogether. One experienced gardener added that the main problem with both crops was that the *banabanas* preferred to buy from Bud rather than from the village gardeners: it was cheaper and quicker. Thus the problem for the farmers was not so much the price as not being able to sell the produce at all.

The *banabanas* just are not there, you can have tomatoes and aubergines that you can sell to no one. Particularly since last year people have abandoned tomatoes, green beans and aubergines for this reason.

We asked what tended to replace these crops:

Potatoes especially. If it had not been for potatoes, we would have lost a lot. But they need watering more than tomatoes, so they are more work . . . and some people have not been able to switch to potatoes for lack of water.

Gardeners had thus been able to mitigate the effects of Bud on their returns by switching crops. Switching had occurred in two directions: towards potatoes, for which credit was available from the co-operative, and which had a guaranteed price, and towards hot peppers (a crop Bud did not grow), whose price had risen very fast. Finally, cassava was also increasing, though some of the fields were destroyed by rats in 1975/6.

Bud and the Future of Market Gardening

Up to 1976 one must conclude that Bud had affected local market gardeners considerably less than many people had feared. It had taken none of their land; they had successfully switched from crops Bud dumped on the local market; and even the Bambilor gardeners, closest to Bud, had largely survived the shortage of labour created by competition from Bud. This does not mean that the potential destructiveness of Bud relative to local gardening was not great, as will be evident if we look more closely at the economics of the gardens. Table 7.8 gives the costs and revenues for the gardens of the ten male gardeners studied. Of these, A and B were established Lebu gardeners working inherited land, gardeners C to F had other occupations and effectively managed farms worked by others, G was the disabled gardener, H and I the recent immigrants working borrowed land on the ranch, and J the *surga* who also had his own garden.

From the data and the interviews one can identify a number of preconditions for making a reasonable income from gardening: say, over 100,000f. a season, the sort of income which would imply no temptation to give up gardening and go to work at Bud. Four gardeners managed this level of income, A, B, C and J, the permanent *surga*. To do this, a gardener needed sufficient land: no gardener with under 3,000 square metres (about a third of a hectare) managed to produce such a revenue. And, second, one either needed access to a substantial sum in cash before the harvest (gardeners A, B and E to I incurred 60–100 per cent of their costs before the harvest), or one needed to do all the work oneself and choose the crops very carefully so that the inputs (such as seed potatoes) could be bought on credit, as did the *surga* gardener J. One also needed substantial experience. The four gardeners who did well were all very experienced; F, who farmed a larger area than the others, had less experience, was over ambitious, and failed to manage the farm successfully or to sell the crops for a good price.

The costs incurred before the harvest included seeds, fertiliser and insecticide, cost of board of *surga*s and wages of *tâcherons*. Only the following costs could be deferred until after the harvest: *surga* wages, seed potatoes, onion seed and fertiliser from the co-operative; green bean seed from private buyers of the beans; and some transport costs. The cash for the non-deferred costs came, in the case of the successful gardeners, either from previous gardening (A and B) or from wage work or other income-earning activity (C). While labour costs were the major expense for most gardeners, the other costs were substantial.

The gardeners depended on the *banabana*s for selling the crops. Only one farmer's wife sold his crops. Not even in this respect was farming a household activity. Little produce was sold to the state through the co-operative: only one farmer sold his potatoes this way, reimbursing his seeds in kind. The other potato growers preferred the price on the open market, reimbursing their debts in cash or not at all. (Not at all was, in fact, a real option in Bambilor where there were constant arguments about debts to the co-operative.) Costs and returns in Table 7.8 are calculated, no doubt naively, on the assumption of debt payment.

Few gardeners tried to improve their returns by taking their crop to market themselves, to sell wholesale in Dakar or Kaolak, the biggest inland town. A big gardener with time and resources might improve his returns in this way. But, as one of the smaller gardeners put it:

> If you do not know the market well you can't sell in Dakar. The *banabana*s see you coming, and they know you refused to sell in Bambilor, and they get together on the price. Once you take out your fare to Dakar, it is not worth your while.

This man added that he had no regular buyer among the *banabana*s; as a small grower you took your chances. 'Any *banabana* will leave the produce on your hands if he does not want to buy it.'

The effect of this pattern of costs and revenues was that it was difficult for a newcomer without capital and with no inherited land to set up as a successful gardener. It would be difficult to find the capital to buy land – land purchase being in any case a process which required contacts and influence as well as money – and to raise the working capital. The *surga* in the sample who was an independent and successful market gardener was something of an anomaly, having had a history it would be difficult for another *surga* to repeat: he had previously, as a young man, been a *surga* to a successful farmer in Bambilor with a lot of land, the father of the present head of his household. The *surga*'s land came from the old man, so that he held it securely, and his position in his old employer's household (without having responsibilities for its upkeep) was also secure, in return for some help on the son's gardens. Newcomers in 1975, coming to the village initially as *surga*s or casual agricultural labourers, might manage to borrow some land, or plant some land on the ranch, but it was difficult to achieve security of tenure on a sufficient area of land, and to build up sufficient cash, to move into the ranks of the reasonably successful market gardeners. The shortage, and cost, of land had cut off this option in the 1970s.

The prices of the good *niaye* land were in fact not unreasonably high, given the returns on gardening shown here. A good gardener with full-time wage work, working evenings and weekends and managing the garden, could make over 100,000f. on rather more than half a hectare, so long as he could find around 100,000f. in working capital. The land prices of around 200,000f. per hectare quoted above can be regarded as reasonable in relation to the return, even though in practice they were heavily influenced by land speculation.

There was, however, no functioning capital market. The Bambilor growers were fully commercial gardeners, but they had no access to a capital market; they raised their funds from their own resources, and this was why having a wage job could be an aid to successful gardening. A newcomer was unlikely to be able to raise the cash to garden, and very likely to be outbid by outsiders seeking the land for speculative reasons. The capacity of the outside buyers to raise cash was greater, even if they in the short run produced far less income from the land.

Bud had increased the likelihood of market gardening land passing out of the hands of village gardeners in the next generation, by considerably increasing the speculative demand for land in the area. As a result of Bud, Senegalese private capital had become considerably more interested in market gardening as a field for investment. The government, having originally given Bud a monopoly, later permitted the private firm of SAAF to set up an estate close to Baobab. And there was also another small estate, CSA, which according to a Ministry official was a 'mixed' company with state and local private capital. Some of the Senegalese skilled and supervisory staff at Bud were thinking in terms of private Senegalese enterprise, and there were persistent rumours of speculative buying of suitable land around the rural Cap Vert.

In these circumstances, it seemed increasingly likely that the *niaye* land still in the hands of villagers would be lost to them in the next generation. As already shown, the gardeners' sons had not been brought up to garden, and half the gardeners on their own land were over 50. Their sons, they said, would not refuse to sell the land. It seemed likely, therefore, that the market would intervene between the current generation of gardeners and the future users of the land. If this occurred, Bud had increased the already high probability that non-gardeners would outbid those wishing to use the land for village-based commercial gardening.

Notes

1. The Lebu are an ethnic group with a long association with the Cap Vert area of Senegal. See Angrand (1947).
2. Vanhaeverbeke (1970) traces the evolution of groundnut producer prices before and after Independence.
3. The Office Nationale de la Commercialisation et de l'Action pour le Développement (ONCAD) was until 1980 the monopoly state buying agency for

groundnuts, and the organization which ran the 'co-operative' system for buying groundnuts and providing seeds and equipment on credit. ONCAD was abolished in 1980 as part of a plan to increase the private sector role in marketing and to change the role of the co-operatives.

4. Background material for this section is taken from Arnaud (1970), Dia (n.d.), Sow (1975), Navez (1974) and from unpublished studies by the local Centre d'Expansion Rurale (Extension Centre) and by the Ecole Nationale d'Economie Appliquée (Applied Economics School) students from Dakar, used with permission.

5. The extension agent attached to the Bambilor CER; I owe a great deal of information to the generous assistance and support of this man.

6. Not all were civil servants, by any means (see Table 7.5), but the designation reflected a common perception of the relative privilege of those who worked for the government.

7. Figures based on the 'African' consumption price index compiled by the Direction de la Statistique, Dakar.

8. Both would have chosen to have a *surga* for longer, had they been able to hire one.

9. The payment was negotiated by the task; I have translated this into rates per day.

10. I owe this market information to a 1976 report researched and written by Leah Jordan Humpal; I am grateful for her permission to draw on her work.

Table 7.1
The Cap Vert and Thiès Regions: Production of Main Crops 1973/4 in Thousands of Tons

	Cap Vert Region	*Thiès Region*
Millet	n.a.*	103.3
Groundnuts	1.0	138.8
Vegetables (excluding Bud)	38.8	4.2
(including Bud)	46.1	

* Not assessed.
Source: Le Sénégal en Chiffres (1976).

Table 7.2
Ponty: Intersection between Farming and Bud Work, by Sex (Sample Data)

	Women	*Men*
Number of adults who:		
Worked at Bud only	9	11
Farmed only	3	9
Both worked at Bud and farmed	1	2
Neither	16	4
Total	29	26

Note: Numbers give full-time residents only, excluding those with non-Bud jobs.

Table 7.3
Ponty: Costs and Returns to Wet Season Farming, by Farmer

Household Code	Farmer	Sex	Total costs (f. c.f.a.)	Of which labour (f. c.f.a.)	Total returns (f. c.f.a.)	Net returns (f. c.f.a.)
A	1	M	(including surga) 38,750	30,400	41,580	2,830
			(excluding surga) 14,750	6,400	41,580	26,830
	2	M	2,000		36,850	34,850
	1	M	3,850			-3,850
C	2	F	100	1,500	1,150	1,050
D	1	M	2,405			-2,405
E	1	M	10,100		16,000	5,900
F	1	M	700		11,800	11,100
	2	F	500		8,950	8,450
G	1	M	(including surga) 14,225	12,000	30,010	15,785
			(excluding surga) 2,225		30,010	27,785
I	1	M	250			-250
J	1	M			47,350	47,350
	2	M	3,150		4,000	850

Note: Two women and one male farmer, with no costs or cash revenues, are excluded.

Table 7.4
Bambilor, 1975/6: Breakdown of Cash Costs and Returns to Wet Season Farming, by Crop and Individual Farmer (f. c.f.a.)

Household	Farmer	Crop*	Costs: Labour	Costs: Other	Costs: Total	Returns: Gross	Returns: Net
1	1	G	7,000	800	7,800	10,500	2,700
	2	G	8,750	2,000	10,750	2,500	-8,250
2		G	5,900	4,250	10,150		-10,150
3	1	G	37,500	1,500	39,000	16,700	-22,300
	2	G		6,250	6,250	16,000	9,750
4		G	800	2,575	3,375	12,000	8,625
6		G**	98,000	12,900	110,900	155,000	44,100
7		G	4,500	550	5,050		-5,050
8		G	4,000	2,650	6,650	11,000	4,350
9		G		400	400		-400
	1	Man	4,000	1,000	5,000		-5,000
10	2	G	1,500	5,250	6,750	4,400	-2,350
		G	36,355	21,000	57,355	24,150	-33,205
11		G	3,000	2,300	5,300		-5,300
12		G	26,500	300	26,800	49,000	22,200

* Where a farmer had more than one harvest of the same crop, these are combined. The numbers refer to farmers. G = Groundnuts. Man = cassava.

** This farmer planted a number of adjacent plots for wives and sons; since the costs cannot be separated, however, I have amalgamated costs and revenues from these plots.

Table 7.5
Land holding by Non-Villagers on Bambilor Village Land, 1975, by Occupation of Owner

	Number of orchards	Area of orchards total (ha.)	Area of orchards average/person (ha.)	% of total area held by category
Politician	4	38.0	9.5	9
Civil servant	31	120.3	3.9	29
Police, military	8	26.4	3.3	6
Teacher	5	11.8	2.4	3
Other public employee	11	62.5	5.7	15
Lawyer, doctor, engineer	9	42.5	4.7	10
Tradesman	7	22.3	3.2	5
Artisan, other self employed	5	48.0	9.6	12
Private sector employee	12	43.7	3.6	11
Total	92	415.5	4.5	100

Source: Figures collected by the CER in Bambilor, 1975.

Table 7.6
Cap Vert: Land Tenure and Land Use in the Bambilor/Sangalkam Areas, 1975

Land ownership/use	Area (ha.)	% of total area
Land titles created prior to the Law on the National Domain, or in the process of creation at that date (private)	3,460	19.44
Land titles held by the state	945	5.31
Land titles (private) created after the Law	164	0.93
Requisitioned land	170	0.96
Land whose title is likely to be registered (private)	330	1.86
Forestry reserves	1,516	8.52
Various uses (housing, roads)	890	5.00
Uncultivated area (lakes, dunes, swamps)	1,500	8.43
Area farmed by villages	1,179	6.62
Land in the National Domain, held by 'those who do not farm it in person'.*	7,638	49.93
Total	17,792	100.00

Source: Sow (1975).

* Includes non-registered orchards and Bud-Baobab.

Table 7.7
Bambilor: Labour Use on Market Gardens in Sample, by Garden, 1975/6 Season

Code	Size of garden (m²)	Piece-rate days	Surga months	Days aid by villagers	Work by gardener	Substantial assistance by household members
A	3,000	36	3	96	full time	
B	4,850	51	3	15	full time	
C	6,550	34	24		evg. & w/e	
D	3,575	30	9		evg. & w/e	
E	2,375	18			evg. & w/e	
F	10,225	28	28	15	occasional	two sons, full time
G	850	18	3		full time	
H	425	5			full time	
I	1,000				full time	
J	4,700				full time	

Table 7.8
Bambilor: Cash Costs and Cash Returns from Market Gardening, by Gardener, 1975/6

		Gardener code:									
		A	B	C	D	E	F	G	H	I	J
1	Current cash costs (f.)	112,900	71,395	219,600	137,950	21,050	226,650	25,600	11,975	18,650	18,900
2	Additions to equipment 1975/6 (f.)		1,450							2,500	
3	Cash returns to mid-June 1976 (f.)	188,510	187,000	259,500	134,000	33,000	235,860	19,000	15,350	24,000	167,500
4	Estimated additional revenue to mid-Aug. 76 (f.)	50,000	30,000	100,000	20,000	35,000	60,000		10,000	15,000	30,000
5	Net returns to mid-June 1976 (f.)	75,610	114,155	39,900	–3,950	11,950	9,210	–6,600	3,375	2,850	148,600
6	Estimated total net returns to mid-Aug. 76 (f.)	125,610	144,155	139,900	16,050	46,950	69,210	–6,600	13,375	17,850	178,600
7	Size of garden (m²)	3,000	4,850	6,550	3,575	2,375	10,225	850	425	1,000	4,700
8	Estimated total net returns per 1000m² to mid-Aug. 76 (f.)	41,870	38,051	21,359	4,490	19,768	6,769	–7,765	31,471	17,850	38,000
9	Estimated total net return when board of *surga* subtracted from cost (f.)	134,610	153,155	211,900	43,050	46,950	153,210	2,400	13,375	17,850	178,600

8. Wage Labour and the Household: Gender Division and Class Formation

> In many ways an ideal solution would be that a new village should grow up outside our gates.

These were the words of a Senegalese manager of Bud, reflecting on the problems of creating a stable seasonal labour supply for Bud-Baobab, from which workers would return each year to their jobs in the manner of the Kirene villagers. To the extent that Bud-Baobab succeeded in creating such a company village, that village was Ponty: a settlement of migrant wage labourers, where farming was a marginal and unproductive activity and the community was almost entirely dependent upon Bud wages for its continuing existence.

Because of the seasonal and unpredictable nature of the work offered by Bud, however, Ponty could never become a stable company village. The turnover in village membership was considerable from year to year. Furthermore, unlike Bambilor, where market gardening alongside wage work produced a differentiated village economy, containing trading and artisanal self-employment, and allowing some intra-village accumulation, Ponty remained in economic terms an obstinately homogeneous village of wage workers. The income levels provided by Bud work were not sufficient to support profitable trading within the village except on a very small scale; the farming produced little surplus for trade and the lack of village tenure on land allowed no investment in housing for occupation or rental of the sort that occurred in Bambilor. A study of Ponty therefore throws into relief the evolution of the economic organization of village and household in a situation where such organization had become detached from any basis in agriculture, and livelihood had become precariously dependent upon seasonal wage work.

Household membership and headship in Ponty conveyed no privileged access to productive resources, nor to the labour of others, with one important exception. For men in particular, and for some women, it provided access to the products of the domestic work of other women. Cash income possibilities, including farming, had become highly individualized, and determined largely from outside the village economic system. Many village members had long been committed, as already shown, to an unstable existence as migratory wage workers; the women like the men would work for wages when the opportunity offered, and wives might or might not leave when their husbands moved on. In these economic circumstances, though households continued to exist as the unit of domestic life, their structure and economic organization were different in systematic ways from those of a stable farming village.

The one immutable element within household organization was the fact that domestic work remained the sole responsibility of women (though not all women). Since this domestic work was the only production which was household-based, and since the household boundaries were coterminous with the unit of consumption of the products of that work, the needs of the domestic labour unit influenced household structure and organization in a number of ways. At the same time the individualized access to cash income introduced new contradictions within the households concerning the level of mutual obligations among members; these strains were evident both between older and younger household members, and between men and women.

This renegotiation of economic relations which was occurring between individuals, and especially between men and women, could be traced not only at the level of the household, but also within the organization of the labour force on the estate and in the labour process itself. A familiar process was occurring whereby women's work within the household constrained their participation in the Bud labour force, thus reinforcing the women's subordinate place within both institutions. This sexual division of labour, allied to the different position of women within the wider labour market, produced a division of interests between men and women which was much sharper than on the Kirene farm, a division which became evident at the time of the packing shed strike described below.

It is the argument of this chapter that the establishment of these new types of hierarchy, especially new forms of gender division, is an integral part of the process of class formation. Bud, by its presence, was contributing to the formation of a working class within Senegal, and a crucial part of that process of formation was the creation of new forms of household adapted to the economic pressures of dependence upon insecure wage incomes. These adaptations spelled the end, for the people involved, of older household forms adapted to the needs of a farming society, and the gradual stabilization of a new social organization with new sets of assumptions. And, in a manner all too familiar, this involved the creation of a new, transformed yet still subordinate position for women within the new class structure.

Propertyless Households

The analysis of the structure and organization of Ponty households poses problems because of the rapid growth of the village. While seven out of eight households in nearby Thien Thiou were headed by people born in the village, 58 out of 59 Ponty households were headed by first generation migrants. Most households in Ponty had therefore gone through no cycle of establishment, growth and division, and one cannot interpret the structure of existing households as exemplifying different stages of an existing household cycle.

A further contrast with Kirene was that household membership in Ponty conveyed no rights to land, nor to participation in a production system; no rights of access to means of production or knowledge. Even those people who came with farming skills did not pass them on within Ponty households. Nor did household membership bring inheritance rights over property, since the villagers were virtually propertyless. Land in or near the village was not in the *Domaine National* and, though the villagers lived upon it and many farmed on it, they had no rights to continue to use it from year to year, and therefore no usage rights to pass on to others. In the small concrete houses occupied by 64 per cent of the villagers, the occupants had no security of tenure, nor were the villagers of Ponty proper permitted to build in concrete within the village boundaries. As a result the concrete houses which existed were falling into disrepair, and only in Thien Thiou was any of the cash from Bud being invested in bricks and mortar. In the two villages, there was no agricultural equipment and just one donkey to be passed on to heirs. Since household membership conveyed no continuing rights of access to property, many reasons for drawing people into households, or conversely of excluding them, were weakened. As a result, existing principles of household composition – virilocality, for example – were coming under pressure. The next section argues that a major influence in determining household composition had come to be the demands of women's domestic work, in a context where women needed a cash income.

The Organization of Domestic Work

In Ponty, as in other proletarianized societies, just one type of work remained household-based: domestic labour or housework, by which I mean the characteristically female tasks of cooking, cleaning, child care, care of the sick and aged. This work was crucial to everyone's standard of living, male and female, and men depended on women to do it for them. The tasks were household-based in the sense that the responsibility for them was determined by position within the household, or relation to the household head. In effect, the social rules which placed the burden of domestic work upon certain women were also the rules constitutive of the household as a social unit. The household was characterized, in Ponty as in Kirene, by consumption from a common pot, and the preparation of meals therefore involved a division of labour between some (not all) adult women within the household.

The work which produced this common pot, though less heavy than in Kirene because of the reduced need to pound grain (because of mechanical millet grinding or consumption of rice), was still burdensome and time-consuming: not only shopping[1] and food preparation, but also the fetching of water from the one village tap, hand washing for the whole household, and the fetching of wood or charcoal, as well as care of young children. And, as in Kirene, there was a strict ordering of responsibilities for the work within the household, a division of labour far from egalitarian, and one which held despite the other work responsibilities of particular women.

The principles on which responsibility for domestic labour was allocated are familiar also from the study of Kirene: gender, age, affinal relation to the household head or other man taking a part in supporting the household. Wives thus took full responsibility for domestic work, unless (quite rare in Ponty) a daughter-in-law joined the household and took on the mother-in-law's work. Daughters and by extension other younger female kin of the wives would have an obligation to help with the work, but not full responsibility for it. Women who were themselves household heads would do the work unless daughters were available to help, or married daughters to take it on. The sexual division of labour was rigid, boys still virtually never aiding their mothers.

The comparison with Kirene is not meant, of course, to imply that the Kirene social structure was typical of the ethnically and regionally diverse societies from which the migrants came. It is meant to illustrate the narrower point that the rules governing the division of domestic work emerged from societies which had intergenerational stability and a rule of virilocality, with women moving from daughter in one household, to daughter-in-law and wife and then mother-in-law in another. These rules had largely continued in the very different context of Ponty, where the stability, and most of the non-domestic economic tasks assigned in Kirene through household position, had vanished.

As in Kirene, women living in households by virtue of some relation other than wife or daughter tended to evade the main burden of domestic labour (though they would do their own personal washing, only men had this done for them). But the implications of this were different in Ponty. Thus female relatives of the male household head – and there were five in the households studied – who came to spend the season in the household in order to work at Bud felt no obligation to take part in the domestic work, though the wives doing the work might also be Bud workers. This added very considerably to the work of the wives. On the other hand, younger female relatives of the *wives* tended to become assimilated to the role of daughters, and therefore to take over a part of the wives' work while in the household.

There was, it should be noted, little cross-household co-operation among women for domestic tasks in Ponty, especially for women who were themselves migrants. Only the women who had grown up in the village, with kinswomen present, might sometimes find such assistance. Otherwise, illness or absence could cause serious problems.

Domestic Work and Household Structure

The presence of at least one woman able to undertake the domestic work was, in terms of economic viability, central to the continuation of any particular Ponty household. From a woman's point of view, to be alone in having responsibility for this work, especially with small children in addition, was a serious burden, and especially if she wished also to do wage work, so that a household with several adult women, or at least young girls to help, was more viable. This was especially true if there were kin, male or female, staying in the household over the Bud season, or if the household head was supplementing his or her income by taking in paid lodgers. The ability of the household head to take lodgers depended upon the presence within the household of women able to take on the additional domestic work, since the men did none of the work involved.

This importance of the domestic work unit, plus the fact that it was men rather than women who took the initiative in migrating in search of work, had had a discernible influence on the household structure in Ponty. This factor can be illustrated by the only major exception in the sample households to the above rules for the performance of domestic work. This was a household headed by a widower; the domestic work was done by his sister, herself a widow, who had come with her children to keep house for her brother. One might have expected that this situation would be temporary, in a society where women were expected to remarry on widowhood, and unless elderly to join their husbands. In fact this sister had remarried the previous year and her husband, a stranger to the village, had joined his brother-in-law's household, where his wife continued to do the domestic work as before.

When men became relatively permanent migrants to Ponty, they had several options. They could remain as a dependent male, without a wife present, in a Ponty household. Or, if they wished to establish their own household, they could bring a wife from their place of origin. Women who came to Ponty in this way were clear about the importance of domestic work to this decision. As a woman from the Fleuve Region put it, 'My husband was here on his own, he had no one to cook for him, so he sent me the money for the ticket.' Finally, they could marry locally, either establishing their own household, or joining their wife's household.

It had become quite common in Ponty for migrant men to move into their wife's household. Of 73 married men in Ponty living in the same household as their wives, nine (12 per cent) had married into their wife's household. If one compares Ponty to Kirene, significantly more men in Ponty than in Kirene lived as the spouse of a household member, and a significantly higher proportion of women in Ponty remained, once married, in a household headed by a relative. (Women also married later, so that a lower proportion of women lived as wives, and the polygyny rate was lower in Ponty.)

It appears that one can identify in Ponty, not so much a tendency towards female-headed households – though there are rather more of these in Ponty – as a move towards what the literature on urban households has uneasily identified as female-centredness.[2] There was, in Ponty for example, a household consisting of a widow, several of her children, the child of one of these daughters (her husband being a migrant worker outside Senegal), and the child of another (unmarried) daughter. There were several households where a fairly recent migrant had married a widow with children who had lived much longer in the village, thereby in effect moving into her household. And women appeared sometimes to prefer remaining in a household with kin, rather than finding themselves on their own with household work.

One can see a number of reasons why such a shift might occur, in addition to the desire of women to share domestic work. The households in the village were under constraints more familiar in the literature as those of an urban environment, since generated by dependence on ill-paid and unstable wage work. Any development of a household cycle had been cut short, constantly over the last thirty years, by out-migration. Children, sons especially, had tended to move away in search of work elsewhere; there were few joint households between married brothers, or fathers and married sons, and joint households were as rare among the longer-established households as among those recently arrived. In these circumstances, there was little security for the elderly, and the departure of daughters could leave parents stranded. Their lives would be greatly improved if a son-in-law moved in, rather than all their daughters marrying out.

A male migrant, coming on his own to Ponty, would have to join an existing household. If he did so as a lodger or as the distant kinsman of a household member, he would have to pay for board and lodging, and many Ponty men lived in this way. Many lodgers were seasonal residents, but some stayed on through the wet season, contributing some cash when they had any. By marrying, a man would cease to pay for lodging, whether he established his own household or remained in his wife's.

Control and Disposition of Cash Income within the Household

The move towards female-centredness in household composition was the result, not only of the importance of domestic work to the household unit, but also of the relative economic autonomy of women as regards the disposition of cash income. This relative autonomy, implying that women generally dispose of their own cash income, rather than handing it over to a male household head, implies in turn considerable female responsibility for household expenditure, and appears to be common throughout Senegal, and indeed much of West Africa. As already shown, women in Kirene expended their own cash income on both their own and their households' needs, and in more commercialized Wolof areas the economic autonomy of women led to explicit relations of market exchange within households.[3] This principle of relative economic autonomy – although not, as will be shown, undisputed by household heads – had important implications once household income became dominated by wage payments.

In 1975/6, 80 per cent of the income of male full-time residents in Ponty was made up of wage income, 4 per cent being farm income, and the rest coming from trading, income from lodgers, and pensions. For women, the predominance of wage income was even greater: 94 per cent of cash income of full-time women residents came from Bud work. Every household in the Ponty sample contained someone who worked that year at Bud, and from that work the men earned considerably more than the women. Average Bud earnings of male residents over the season were 167,000f., or 96,000f. not counting the two permanent employees. For the women the average was 29,000f. Only part of this differential was the result of different lengths of time worked: the average season for the women was 2.8 months; for the men 4.6 months. Nor was it the outcome of skill differentials. A man working as an unskilled loader in the packing shed was earning 19,500f. a month, while the women's average on the packing lines in the same shed was 9,600f. for much the same shifts. The effect of this was that the proportion of cash income of full-time household residents brought in by women was low despite the long work hours: never above 16 per cent for married women, only above 20 per cent in two households where the incomes of the household head and his wife were particularly low, so that the earnings of an unmarried girl formed an important part of cash income.

On the other hand, the nature of this agricultural labouring work – benefiting disproportionately the young strong males – meant that a substantial proportion of cash income went to men other than the household head: 45 per cent on average for full-time residents. In addition, seasonal male residents in the sample households earned wages equivalent to 26 per cent of those of resident men; for women the figure was 48 per cent.

The proportion of total cash income of household members over the season which accrued to the household heads was therefore quite small in many households. In two cases it was below 10 per cent of the income of even full-time residents; the average was just below half. Since in Ponty households food was consumed in common, and since virtually all food had to be bought with cash, the questions of control over cash income, and relative responsibilities for the provision of food, become important ones for an understanding of the economic relations within the household.

Within households, there were few transfers of cash between individuals: on the whole, people disposed of their income themselves (though not, of course, necessarily *for* themselves), although there were a few trends towards greater internal cash transfer as charted below. Table 8.1 gives estimates of the extent of cash transfer to the household head from full-time and seasonal residents. The total cash transfers to the household head form 10 per cent or more of total income of full-time residents in only two households; the average was 8 per cent. This was not a society where dependent household members handed their pay packets to either the household head or his wife.

The result of this failure to transfer cash was that the question of intra-household economic relations centred on who paid for what. The principles, not always put into practice, are recognizable from Kirene. Most of the food grains were purchased by the household head, and by any married men who had wives within the household. Thus if there was more than one man in a household. and their wives shared the cooking, then the men would each contribute food grains, dividing the grain among the wives. The married men also said that they gave cash to their wives for the other cooking expenses, though as shown below the women frequently contributed to this. Poorer household heads spent most of their income on food or basic consumption goods; those somewhat better off, or who were sharing the support of a household with other married men, could spend more on clothing, ceremonies and travel.

In practice, as in Kirene, the women also took responsibility for the support of the household from their cash incomes, and there is evidence of some conflict over the issue. Married women who cooked tended to put their own money towards the food, sometimes purchasing food grains in small lots. Similarly, young married women, not living with their husbands but cooking for their mothers, would also buy food in this way. The distinction is illustrated by a household where two daughters had effectively taken over cooking responsibilities from the elderly wife of the household head. One was married, her husband working abroad: in the eyes of the household head her husband 'looked after' her, so that he expected her to do more for the household. She estimated that she spent at least a third of her earnings on cooking expenses; she also gave money to the wife and bought clothes for the elderly in the household, as well as providing for herself. The other daughter, said the household head, was expected to do much less because she was not yet married. The wife had a tiny income from selling, most of which went on food.

The poorer the household, the more likely it was that all the wife's income went on food. 'What I earn, we eat.' But only older women who had ceased to cook, or were not living as wives, would admit to buying food grains. Women were aware that there were conflicting principles at work concerning the use of women's income. On the one hand, one woman, when asked her opinion, said, 'A woman should not contribute to the food; her money is for herself.' But she went on to make it clear that in fact she spent much of her Bud wages on food. Some women, older women in particular, expressed strong resentment that the change in employment patterns in Ponty had brought a situation where a woman might find herself supporting, or partially supporting a household. This was the strongest statement.

It is the men who should work to bring money to the house. When they don't work nothing can be good. Before girls give anything, they must take money for their own needs . . . Women do not buy food, it is their husbands who buy food.

Other, especially younger women, took the situation more calmly, drawing on the different principle that a married woman must work to help her husband and children. One woman in her thirties said, 'A woman's money is for herself, but it is also for everyone: for example, if someone is ill, then the person who is working must pay.' Several younger women, however, suggested that the new situation had brought with it a greater tendency for husbands to try to exert control over their wives' incomes. Thus I asked the woman quoted above whether it was the husband who decided what a wife did with her money. She replied, 'In my mother's time that never happened, a woman decided what to do with her money. Now a husband may decide.' This is further supported by the observation that, while the older married women all said they did not give cash to the household head, two younger wives said they gave some of their money to their husbands 'to keep for them', and both husbands said they told their wives how to spend it, or spent it for them.

In effect, women who were household members took a considerable responsibility for seeing that the household was fed. Young unmarried girls, in this context, gave more of their money for this than unmarried boys and men. Most of the cash transfers summarized in Table 8.1 were from unmarried people to household heads. In one household, for example, with three young people working, sums were given equivalent to 6 per cent of the pay packet for the man, and 10 per cent for the two girls. This was all the young man gave to the household, but the girls also gave cash to their mothers for cooking, or spent it when they cooked. Older women, who no longer cooked, gave nothing to the household head, but helped the young women with cooking expenses, especially their married daughters; as an older woman put it,

> A woman who is married needs money. I tell her whenever she needs money she must ask me. She is all I have.

The unmarried men, therefore, largely escaped responsibility for supporting the household, and would argue that they had to save if they hoped to marry. Younger married men all said that they had paid their own marriage costs, though some older men said that they had helped their sons. When asked about the level of bridewealth, one recently married young man commented that the problem was not so much cost as the fact that, as this became a wage labour area, it became more difficult for a young man to marry unless he had a job, whereas before that had not been true.

Finally, the contribution of the seasonal residents to household consumption depended upon the extent to which the household head saw himself as in the business of taking in lodgers. One sample household, with four lodgers, in additional rooms added within the compound, charged each the same for room and board. Another, with two relatives and a stranger sharing his household, asked nothing for the roof, and a flat sum for food from the stranger; the other two gave smaller sums to the women towards food, and one, a woman, helped her aunt with the cooking. Close relatives could not be charged anything for seasonal lodgings, and many gave little or nothing, constituting a considerable additional burden in the dry season. Distant kin could perhaps be asked for a fixed sum for food. But in both cases, the boundary between kin and lodger could be crossed fairly easily. For example, one stranger, living as a lodger, stayed on after Bud closed, finding casual labour where he could, and during this period the household continued to provide for him, asking no regular cash contributions.

This pattern of disposition of cash meant that women full-time residents in Ponty were valuable household members, a fact of which male household heads were well aware. Women did the domestic work, thus allowing household heads to take in lodgers and charge for lodgings (the money going to the household head). Though their earning power was lower than men, they spent a higher proportion of their wages than did dependent men on support of the household. Young women who had grown up in the area tended to marry later than recent migrants, to stay in their own households longer, and to accept more obligations to the household than the young men. Since they were not free to migrate independently, they were less likely to leave their relatives without support. As a result of all these factors, households were becoming increasingly organized around the women. The social effects were contradictory. On the one hand there was an awareness among the women of the importance of their work and incomes, and a resulting confidence especially among some younger women. On the other hand there was also the contradictory trend, emerging out of the same set of circumstances, of husbands seeking to assert more control than had previously been acceptable over the incomes of their wives.

The obverse of the increasingly female-centred household was the considerable instability of the men, and especially the younger men. The unpredictability of Bud incomes, the difficulty of surviving the wet season, the absence of possibilities in the area for diversification of sources of income, the work conditions on the estate, the frustration with unskilled work or that work classified as unskilled, and the habit of migration in search of work, all this increased the probability of leaving the village, and created strains and tensions within the household. The young men saw themselves as faced with the rather unprepossessing choice of long years of dependent status in a household, or marriage (increasingly difficult) and the heavy commitments that entailed. Male household heads, on the other hand, who had taken on those commitments, found themselves faced with a rather open-ended responsibility to provide for young kinsmen (men especially, that is) who grew up in or moved into the household, but whose future commitment to support older household members had become at best ill-defined, and whose current contribution to household expenses might well be minimal, depending to a considerable extent on the individual's good will. In the general situation of economic insecurity, the relations between the generations were thus potentially fraught with tensions.

The household in Ponty, therefore, cannot be seen as a social unit with a common strategy towards income or consumption. It was only an economic unit in being formed of a group of people within common walls who ate together. But there was no commonly agreed consumption fund, and the contributions of different household members were constantly being renegotiated, explicitly or in practice. Household members had different strategies towards their lives, and household membership fluctuated. The image which the personnel officer appeared to be putting forward, in the quotation which began this chapter, of a stable 'company village' at Bud's gates, where the Bud labour force would live and reproduce itself, does not square with Ponty as it has been analysed here. Such a stable community would never be likely, I suggest, to emerge out of the insecure seasonal work offered by Bud. What emerged instead was an unstable society, painfully riven by the contradiction between open-ended obligations and limited and unpredictable resources, and marked by the tension between the expressed desire of younger men and (sometimes) women to establish 'their own' households, and the constant adaptations forced upon people by circumstances and the needs of kin.

Domestic Work and Sexual Hierarchy at Bud

The sexual division of labour just described within Ponty households – that is, the situation where women did almost all the work – interacted with and reinforced the rapidly emerging hierarchy on the Bud estates. The Bud estates, and Baobab in particular, provide an excellent case study of the speed with which sexual divisons are created within a newly created labour process. It has already been shown that women earned far less than men from their work at the Baobab estate. That fact was the result of an all too familiar process: within three years, that familiar category of 'women's work' had been created on the estate. That is, certain jobs, classified as women's jobs, had come to have attached to them lower pay and worse conditions than the jobs predominantly done by men.

Detailed figures for the Baobab estate in April 1976 show the men concentrated in the more skilled and longer-term jobs. All of the permanent workers were men, as were all but three of the regularly employed non-farming seasonal workers (clerks, transport workers, local sales people, bricklayers, watchmen). Among the farming jobs, all those recognized by the management as skilled or semi-skilled and requiring training were done by men: tractor driving, plant protection, mechanics. All of these jobs were stabilized, with seasonal contracts and pay on an hourly basis, frequently above the legal minimum.

Of the jobs classified as unskilled,[4] certain were done exclusively by men: irrigation work, hand hoeing, melon and pepper harvesting. The others, packing produce and bean harvesting, were done mainly, but *not* exclusively, by women. The men's teams specifically excluded women; the jobs 'where the women are' were sometimes done reluctantly by young men who could find no other work.

Hiring conditions for women were rather different from those for men. All labouring teams were subject to unpredicted fluctuations in work over the season. All the teams were taken on only when work was available and paid only for work done, whether by the hour or on a piece rate basis, so that earnings varied from week to week. However, the male labourers on irrigation and picking were organized into stable groups: teams were small, the men generally known by name to the supervisor, and, except in the case of a corrupt team leader or a conflict between a man and a supervisor, the job of an individual tended to last all season. The conditions were less stable on the hoeing team, with longer breaks in the work.

> The trouble is that they do not do what they say and recall people [after a break]. It is just up to you to go and see what is happening. Otherwise one day they discover they need more *bineurs* [hoeing labourers] and they just hire the first people they see at the gate.

However, even this jaundiced worker allowed that stability had been improving.

The women's packing shed teams were generally much larger than the men's teams, averaging 125 on each of four shifts, and their composition and size on any day were much less stable. These differences derived from the actions of both management and workers. On the management side, the hiring practices concerning the women were from the beginning less scrupulous than for the men. There was more laying off of workers at the whim of a team leader, and the hiring had a number of the corrupt features one might expect when young male team leaders are responsible for the hiring of women. Sporadic attempts by Senegalese personnel managers to stablize team membership had been ineffective. Team leaders were changed from year to year; sometimes women were appointed team leaders, and sometimes they were replaced by men. Older women would work a season, then find themselves not chosen. All this was exacerbated by the fact that the shifts were too large for the supervisors to know all the women personally.

There was, however, another set of causes of this instability in the women's teams, rooted in the conditions of women's lives. Women in Ponty, as already shown, found it very difficult to combine domestic work responsibilities with a wage job requiring long and regular absences from home. If anything, this was more difficult than in Kirene, because of the lower level of support from female kin and co-wives. Women with young children, and no older daughters to help with them, often found it impossible to work at Bud, especially as they could not take babies on their backs to the packing shed, and would need time off to nurse children through illness. Just how difficult the combination of domestic work and child care with wage work could be for women forced to attempt it is illustrated by a woman in a Ponty household who, the year before, had been a widow supporting a household. She worked on the Bud harvests, taking the smallest child to the fields, doing all the housework in the early morning or late evening, and taking a day off when the washing piled up. 'When you have no help and no money, then you have to tire yourself out.' The physical burden of this double day was enormous, and women who did it were aware of the toll it took on their own health and that of their families if they were away all day. And rural Ponty was unlike some urban areas in that it was impossible to find a girl to work as a maid, since any girl old enough to take on this work would make more money at Bud.

The women who worked at Bud sought to resolve the conflict between wage and domestic work responsibilities by using the instability and anonymity of the Bud women's teams for their own purposes. They swapped places with female relatives and friends when they were unable to go themselves, collecting the pay and giving some of it to their substitutes. This sort of job control was essential to many of the married women if they were to work at all. As a result the women fought any attempt to stabilize the teams which was unaccompanied by special concessions to women's needs. In particular, they resented the introduction of identification cards, which made swapping more difficult, and the short-lived tactic of sacking and replacing any absentee.

One older Senegalese male supervisor commented on this latter tactic as follows:

> I firmly believe that this is the wrong way to work with women . . . On a woman's team you are going to have absences. I did not understand that at first. And you are going to have people late. The way I see it is that the line is 150. I can start the line with 120. Those who are late are added as they arrive. I only sack the perpetually absent. That way you have a fairly constant team.

That level of understanding of the situation seemed to be unique. The personnel office declared itself unable to deal with 'the problem of the women', indeed it described the women as uncontrollable. It therefore tended to treat the women workers as a mass of labour, unskilled and anarchic. And when the European management sought examples of the difficulty of controlling the workers on the farm, they generally came up with the example of a woman's team.

These differences between work conditions of men and women were associated with established wage differentials which dated from the first year of full operation of the estate, 1973, when the women bean harvesters were already receiving less than the legal minimum wage, while men were generally paid the minimum wage. The women packers at Baobab worked night shifts, for which they received no additional premiums, and before the stoppage described below they too had been receiving less than the minimum wage for the hours they worked. Until the stoppage, the women generally accepted these wage differentials: they said they should be paid 'more' but did not use men's wages as standard. There had in effect been a rapid and cumulative establishment of differentiation between men and women within the Bud labour force, a process which had its roots both in the material conditions of women's lives – the conflicts between domestic and wage work – and in the preconceptions of management and workers as to the abilities and correct conduct of women. Senegalese culture is as full of derogation of the abilities of women as is European culture, and women occupy a subordinate place in terms of power and prestige. The management at Bud relied on this to establish a gender hierarchy in the estate labour force as one more expression and reinforcement of that social inequality.

Female Militancy: the Baobab Stoppage

In Kirene, as in Baobab, there were divisions of interest on the estate between men and women, but in Kirene these tended to be overridden by economic and social solidarity within the village. In the Baobab area, the disaggregation of the village economy and society, visible in embryo in Kirene, had gone much further, and the conflicts of interest were much sharper. How serious the divisions at Baobab were, including those between men and women, is illustrated by the story of a Baobab walk-out, at much the same time in the season as the Kirene stoppage, and again begun by the women packing shed workers. This walk-out, like that in Kirene, was technically illegal under Senegalese law, where a process of arbitration was required in the case of a dispute. The stoppage was caused by a drop in the wages received by the packing shed workers, following a switch from hourly pay to piece rates. The following description, by a young woman on one of the teams, is similar to many others I heard.

> The strike started when they paid the Den team[5] 1,000f. for a week's work. They paid only two women and those two gave the money back and said they had no need of that. They said they should be paid properly . . . The team refused to work that afternoon.

The strike was spread through the packing shed shifts by messengers sent running round the villages. The other teams refused to work; there was no night shift that night. And the following morning about 500 women were outside the gates of the estate refusing to work until hourly pay was reinstated. There was some shouting and threats directed at a few women and boys who wanted to work: otherwise the packing shed workers were solid. However, neither at the time, nor at any moment during the three-day strike, did other teams (largely consisting of men) come out in sympathy. The progress of this stoppage, and the opinions expressed by the women involved during the three days, illuminate the ways in which the experience of wage work was understood by the women workers, and the ways they felt it had changed them. The difference in perceptions and experience between the men and the women workers also stands out sharply.

The women were well aware of the difference in wages and conditions on the estate between themselves and the men; the wage differential as such was not, however, an issue in the strike. The women went on strike against a decline in wages. When they talked about this grievance however, they did not compare their earnings to the men's, nor to wages elsewhere (since they saw themselves as having no alternatives), nor to the legal minimum wage (of which before the strike they knew nothing). Instead, they concentrated on the relation of the money offered to their needs, and to the effort involved in earning it. They felt strongly that the new lower rates were not worth the effort of going to the estate. They understood the toll their working took on their households, and they needed the money badly. It was their greater sense of dependence on Bud, and the perception of a cost attached to their working, which made them more militant than the men.

There is a parallel here with the situation in Kirene. The Baobab women workers experienced the kind of dependence on Bud felt by all the Kirene villagers, and had a similar sense of solidarity and shared fate. Since they could not go off independently in search of work, even the recent migrants among the women felt more rooted in the area than most of the men. They knew each other better than the men, and saw themselves as better organized and more determined. With this analysis many male workers agreed. The men saw themselves as divided and hard to organize, because there were always more job seekers than jobs available, and because of their history of moving from job to job and the high turnover that resulted. Above all, there were virtually no female seasonal migrants: apart from a few people's relatives from the next village or town, once women arrived they stayed through the year. Many of the men, however, were seasonal residents with no commitment to the area at all, returning to their home areas or going elsewhere in the rains. Hence the men felt solidarity among themselves – or with the women – was almost impossible.

> If you refuse to work there is always someone else willing to . . . it is your *morom* [your equal, your brother, a concept very difficult to translate into English] who will accept your job.

In the villages near Baobab, some of the men tried to persuade the women to return to work. In the ensuing discussion, it was often younger women who took the lead, and many people said later they felt that it was on the younger women in the area that the experience of working at Bud had had the most impact. The phrase used in Kirene recurred: the younger women were 'awake' in ways their elders were not; more aware of themselves, more able to make independent decisions. 'If young girls have money, there are things they cannot be forbidden to do.'

Some conflicts between younger and older women emerged during the Baobab stoppage. Both agreed the strike was necessary, but the older women were afraid to be spokeswomen, afraid of being singled out as troublemakers. One young woman was elected as a delegate to speak for the strikers, and then forbidden by her elder married sister to go with the other delegates. This was one young unmarried woman talking about the divisions.

> There are older women who do not want us, the younger women, to argue against what they do to us at Bud. They are afraid of losing their job . . . Before, those women did not work, they just sold brushes and so on; now they have jobs, and they won't speak up for fear of losing them. But the young women know that we have to argue, that it is in everyone's interest when we do. We are all in the same position, everyone on the team.

Despite the growing confidence of some young women however, the women at Baobab had more contradictory views and aims, and less sense of their own influence, than the women at Kirene. Some unmarried women expressed simultaneously an awareness of the greater scope brought to them by wage work and a desire to give up the hard unpleasant work in order to stay home and 'look after my husband'. The extent of the divisions between men and women in this area limited the women's sense of their own influence as compared to women in Kirene. One young woman said, 'I don't think women can ever change anything. Men can get together and change things, but not women.'

The greater extent of male/female divisions in the Baobab area as compared with Kirene are also in evidence in the role played by the union and the union delegates in the stoppage, and more generally on the Baobab estate. To understand this, a little more background on the role of the union is necessary. Although the situation has now changed considerably, there was at this time in Senegal effectively only one trade union: the *Confédération Nationale des Travailleurs du Sénégal*. This was divided into sections by industrial branch, and integrated into the governing party, the *Union Progressiste Sénégalaise*.[6]

having as its president a government minister. The union had a collaborationist ideology at the national level ('responsible participation' was its slogan), but was of course composed of disparate and conflicting elements further down. Until Bud, this union had had no section for agricultural workers. During Bud's first years, a number of men had tried to organize at Baobab, and in 1974, with the assistance of a sympathetic Senegalese personnel manager, the first union delegates were elected. These delegates – all men at first, but a woman was elected in 1975 – began to go to union meetings in Dakar, and to the food workers' section of the Confederation.

The union was not a body which attempted to negotiate higher wages for its members: such demands were not countenanced by the national leadership. Its chief aims[7] were to see that the labour laws were obeyed, to elicit various concessions (such as loan schemes and protective clothing) from management, and to help organize occasional parades, for example on May Day.

Most workers on the estates were ignorant of and uninvolved in union affairs. The union cards were expensive (1,000f. a year) for someone on a Bud wage, and a low proportion[8] of workers had bought them. The delegates had, however, spread a knowledge of the labour laws: while few people fully comprehended the provisions, they were aware the law gave them some 'rights', for example to paid notice if they had a seasonal contract, to redundancy pay if sacked from a permanent contract, to some protection against sacking if a delegate, and (by the time the Baobab stoppage was settled) to a minimum hourly wage. The Bud management resented both the laws and this awareness, and one manager said that they tried to avoid hiring people from Dakar because these '*évolués*' spent their time trying to manipulate the law in their own interests.

The activities of the union delegates at Baobab, up to the time of the stoppage, had held little relevance to the concerns of the women. They had concentrated on the problems of the more stabilized group of seasonal male workers, discussing the possibility of payment or loans during the wet season, involving the Labour Inspectorate in complex negotiations over the seasonal lay-offs, and taking up individual demands for payment in accordance with skill. They had not taken any position on the issue of the introduction of piece rates, although this was a question which aroused a great deal of opposition on both estates. It was the introduction of piece rates in packing which produced the drop in women's wages in the shed and hence precipitated the strike. It is one of the ironies of the strike that, although the men displayed no solidarity with the women, they were engaged in a parallel argument, which they lost, concerning the introduction of piece rates in hoeing. Although the immediate cause of the strike was a drop in pay, the women rapidly developed a general argument against piece rates, with which many workers on the estate agreed; here is one woman's summary of their views as expressed in a meeting.

They said: sometimes the machines break down. And sometimes the caterpillar which brings the peppers to the sheds breaks down. And we have to clear out the rubbish ourselves. And sometimes the boxes are badly made. And we have to clear up and sweep up afterwards. None of those things are paid for when we are paid piece rates, because you are only paid by the ton.

Despite the widespread opposition to piece rates, the union delegates were taken by surprise by the women's stoppage. The Bud management later argued that the strike had been fomented by union agitators, a complete misperception which can only be attributed to their inability to believe that the women workers could organize themselves or have ideas of their own. In fact, the first reaction of the woman among the union delegates was to urge a return to work, and she was the only person I heard worrying aloud about the crops spoiling. The food workers' union official, when he arrived on the second day of the strike, also urged an immediate return to work pending negotiations. Only when the women remained deaf to these pleas did he begin to argue seriously, for the first time in Bud's history, that the firm should immediately cease to pay any wages below the legal minimum. This was eventually agreed as the basis for a return to work. The women, though largely uninvolved in the union, had succeeded in coercing it into demanding that the Bud management obey the law.

Gender Division and Class Formation

No new class emerges undifferentiated, least of all new elements of the working class under capitalism. There are numerous forms of differentiation which emerge as new firms create a workforce in their own image in different parts of the world: differentiation based on skill, on industrial branch, on age, on race, and on gender. Among these, the differentiation based on gender is a fundamental one because it is closely bound up with the organization of reproduction of the class which is in creation. Furthermore, as illustrated here, the organization of domestic life has its own effect in reinforcing gender divisions within the labour force. These interactions produce a set of new institutions: a changed organization of the household, and changed forms of women's (subordinate) position within the world of wage work. The consolidation of these changes, and the emergence of a new generation brought up within the new preconceptions, signals a rather definitive transition in class terms. It is, one might say, the transformation of the household, that is, of the institution within which the new generation is brought up, which consolidates the transition in class terms.

Thus one saw around the Baobab estate, in ways traced through the last three chapters, the consolidation of a class of Senegalese people increasingly detached from the land, in terms of access to land, farming knowledge and the whole social organization of their lives; seeing their options in terms of the continual search for wage work; characterizing themselves as unemployed when they did not find it; moving on, no doubt, when Bud closed down. From this position, having come through this series of transformations, there was no open road back to a previous farming-based existence based on social relations which had been definitively broken down. Bud had not been responsible for this entire change, far from it; the Baobab estate had drawn its labour force in large part from an existing labour market. But it had nevertheless played an important contributing role in consolidating the migrant working class in creation – not least by drawing women into wage labour, thereby precariously stabilizing its workforce near the farm and accelerating the transformation of household structure and of women's lives and ideas. When Bud closed down, both men and women would protest at their unemployment.

Notes

1. People in Ponty relied on buying food. There was only a tiny food market in the village; otherwise shopping required a lengthy walk or a bus ride and a walk.

2. 'Matrifocality' is sometimes defined to include having a female as household head (Tanner, 1974); female-centredness may be described as a type of living group, usually urban, drawn from a network of largely female kin (see, for example, Stack, 1974).

3. Vercambre (1974) reports a budget study which showed that household income in two Wolof households was not being treated as a common fund. She comments (p. 23, my translation), 'within the compound we do not have a family in the European sense of the term, but rather autonomous individuals who give gifts to each other, who make loans to each other, who sell goods to each other (often at interest)'.

4. That is, paid the minimum hourly rate unless piece workers; many of these jobs, such as melon picking, in fact required considerable skill and experience.

5. That is, the team from nearby villages whose names mainly began 'Deni', e.g. Deni Malick Gueye; the women's packing shed teams were organized by residence to facilitate transport, especially for night shifts.

6. The name of this party has since been changed to Parti Socialiste. Since 1976 additional political parties have been legalized, and the trade union and party structures have changed considerably.

7. The following generalization is drawn from statements made by the union delegates, and from interviews with officials and delegates in 1973; see also Mackintosh (1975).

8. I could obtain no satisfactory figures; a number of workers said they had contributed smaller sums to the union but not purchased a card, and the union delegates said the cards were hard to sell because of their cost.

Table 8.1
Ponty: Extent of Transfer of Cash within the Household to the Household Head,
Sample Households

Household code	Total income of full-time household residents	Income of household head (% of total)	Cash controlled by household head (% of total)	% of total cash transferred
A	511,539	49	53	4
B	241,260	91	96	5
C	84,751	90	97	7
D	396,492	34	34	0
E	88,705	63	63	0
F	161,659	7	17	10
G	98,795	48	55	7
H	60,615	100	100	0
I	1,495,334	6	19	13
J	1,003,386	89	89	0
K	305,659	72	74	2
Total	4,448,195	46	52	8

9. Conclusion: 'Agribusiness', Accumulation and Rural Economic Crisis

Commercial Pressure and Rural Risk

This book began with a survey of the external commercial pressures on Senegalese farmers, and of the changes in agricultural technology and markets which led to a new phase of that pressure, with the arrival of Bud in Dakar. The subsequent chapters have concentrated on the immediate and longer-term implications for the small-scale Senegalese farmers of that new phase. Now it is time to enlarge the frame again.

One of the arguments of the first chapter was that, as the new patterns of vertical integration of fruit and vegetable production emerged, so a conflict developed between European farmers and the users of their produce over the appropriation and control of the benefits of the technological change. European farmers, it was pointed out, did not wholly lose this struggle, but African farmers, facing the same type of pressure, were in a far weaker position. In Senegal, the farmers' bargaining weakness was compounded by the effects of the drought in creating an economic crisis for the farmers, and by the actions of a government seeking to incorporate small farmers into large-scale agricultural projects.

We have now traced the working through of Bud's early history from the point of view of those small farmers. It has been argued that Bud appeared to be catalysing a decline in an existing, small-scale, integrated, semi-commercialized farming system, and to be taking the rural areas towards a more individualized, fully commercial form of economic organization which threatened a sharp decline in food production and greater dependence on wage work. In doing so it was amplifying existing pressures towards individualization of the Senegalese economic system, expressed through the extent of the migrant labour market. This in turn threatened to increase the risks faced by Senegalese rural inhabitants: by reducing the food base of the rural areas, and the patterns of economic solidarity within them, 'the Bud effect' made farmers' livelihoods dependent on Bud's success in bringing in foreign exchange and providing wage work, in order that food be purchasable through the market. The farmers' and workers suspected that Bud was in fact a poor risk for this purpose, and they were proved right: in 1976, Bud Senegal encountered a severe financial crisis, and in 1979 it finally went bankrupt.

It is the purpose of this concluding chapter to explore further this question of risk and profit. Bud Senegal was a risky project from the start, depending heavily on high quality products and therefore good production control, on access to reliable transport and on good marketing against strong and growing competition. But there were sharp differences in the nature of the risks run by different parties to the project. To illustrate this point, we begin by investigating the question of who benefited from Bud Senegal, interpreting this question in the following specific sense: where was the process of accumulation and reinvestment expanded, and where was it choked off as the result of Bud Senegal's presence?

Accumulation in Europe, Deficits in Africa

Among the investors in the company – leaving aside for the moment the farmers – the answer to this question is rather simple. The House of Bud, the European company which set up Bud Senegal, expanded, while all other investors, but especially the Senegalese state, lost substantial sums of money without any offsetting gain. To understand how this occurred – quite legally – despite the financial crises and eventual bankruptcy of Bud Senegal, requires a brief preliminary description of the changing ownership and financial structure of the firm.

Bud Senegal made a financial loss in each year from 1972/3 to 1975/6, and by this last year the accumulated losses exceeded the equity of the firm. Over the same period, the House of Bud S.A. (HOBSA), the European holding company based in Brussels, dropped to a minority shareholding in Bud Senegal while retaining management control as the equity capital increased. Finally in mid-1976 the farm ran into severe financial difficulties, and the Senegalese state took a majority holding, simultaneously taking over management and control of the enterprise from HOBSA. The evolution of ownership is shown in Table 9.1.

The two new inv_ ,.ors in 1973 were overseas institutional shareholders; at no time does there appear to have been any private Senegalese capital in Bud Senegal. The third proposed input of share capital was held up in 1975 through the hesitation of actual and potential investors faced with the scale of losses. Finally, in mid-1976, the existing equity was written down to zero against the losses, and new capital subscribed. At that point a Senegalese managing director was appointed, the contracts of expatriate managers renegotiated or ended, and the monopoly of HOBSA over marketing of the produce removed.

For the four years 1972–1976, it is possible to calculate from information provided by the Bud Senegal management the finance advanced in the form of equity, or advances on equity, to Bud Senegal, and the return cash flow from the enterprise in whatever form, by investor. I have less complete information on loan finance, short and long run, and some information on the provision of infrastructure to the enterprise by the Senegalese state. Fig. 9.1 summarizes the flow of finance in each year over the period by category of investor: the House

Figure 9.1
Bud-Senegal: net cumulative return cash flow less
investments of each investor 1972-76 (current francs cfa)

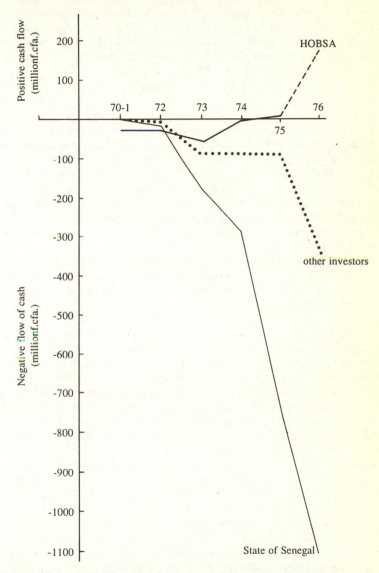

Source: information supplied by Bud-Senegal management
Note: equity and advances only, and estimated gross commission on
sales; loan finance excluded

of Bud, the Senegalese state, and other investors including the IFC (part of the World Bank group) and two private European investment companies. These figures do not include loan finance and infrastructure.

By far the largest financial losses to investors were sustained by the Senegalese state. In 1976, when the existing equity was written down to zero, the Senegalese state lost 180 million f. c.f.a., as against 101 million f. lost by HOBSA, and 41 million f. by the IFC. After 1976, the Senegalese had by far the largest quantity of capital at risk. Up to late 1976, after the financial restructuring, the Senegalese government had put a total of 1,114 million f. (£2.6 million at the 1976 rate of exchange) into Bud Senegal for no financial return. Furthermore, in addition to the capital input, the government had expended a 'considerable' sum (the Bud management's phrase) on constructing a branch pipeline to provide water to the largest of the two estates. And it had stood as guarantor to the foreign-owned commercial banks in Dakar for working capital for the 1975/6 season, thus allowing Bud Senegal to continue to operate despite the losses.

At the same point in late 1976, the external investors other than Bud had put a total of 336 million f. (approximately £790,000 at 1976 exchange rates) into the company in the form of equity, almost two thirds from the IFC. In addition, the two private investment companies had supplied around 100 million f. in long-term loan finance (approx. £235,000), and proposed after 1976 to provide twice as much again. These two investors presumably received interest on their loan finance, but nothing on their equity. However one source states that the two private investors held some proportion of the shares of the House of Bud in Europe (Catala, 1977: 43ff.); from these they may have received a return not included in these calculations.

For the firm of Bud in Europe was the sole investor to receive a return flow of income as a result of its investment in Senegal, a fact resulting from its monopoly of sales of the Bud Senegal produce in Europe. By late 1976, the total capital input into Bud Senegal by HOBSA had been 224 million f. (approx. £525,000 at 1976 exchange rates). HOBSA had steadily reduced its proportional participation in the total equity, had advanced very little additional equity when the company was restructured in 1976, and had provided no loan finance. In return for its minority participation in equity, and provision of management (who received salaries from Bud Senegal) and some expertise, the marketing arm of HOBSA based in Delft in Holland monopolized the sale of Bud Senegal produce and HOBSA received a commission of 10 per cent on sales. It is this *gross* commission which is shown as the return flow of finance to Europe in Fig. 9.1, only part of which constituted profit. To arrive at net profit to HOBSA it would be necessary to subtract marketing costs, data for which are not available.

The figures for the return flow of income to HOBSA are in part estimates: the 1976 figures are based on 10 per cent of estimated total sales. The actual income flow may have been somewhat higher or lower than these figures. On the one hand, HOBSA apparently agreed after 1974 to pay some level of cash refund (*ristourne*) on its commission, while insisting that this did not constitute an admission that its commission had been excessive or had constituted a monopoly rent. On the other hand, HOBSA, by virture of its position *vis-à-vis* Bud Senegal, had had a number of opportunities for increasing the cash flow towards itself, which it may or may not have exploited. HOBSA supplied the management of the project and thereby decided upon the technology and inputs to be used; in addition it had a monopoly of sales. In this situation, as has been emphasized in the literature on the problems of control of multinationals (for example, Vaitsos, 1974), opportunities for abuse are numerous in the pricing of inputs or the costing of sales. I have no information about the existence of such practices between Bud Senegal and HOBSA, though in no situation where a multinational company holds this kind of monopoloy position can they be ruled out. The salary paid to the Bud Senegal's managing director or any other expatriates on HOBSA contracts are nowhere included in the figures on which Fig. 9.1 is based.

On the basis of these estimates, Fig. 9.1 summarizes the major source of acrimony between the Senegalese government and HOBSA in 1976. The Figure shows the cumulative flows of finance between the investors and the company up to 1976. In the words of a Bud Senegal expatriate manager, the Senegalese government 'could not understand' that the marketing company in Europe could make a profit while the Senegalese production company made a loss. In fact, the Senegalese understood very well that they were financing the losses on production which were in turn providing profits on sale in Europe. They also understood that part of this situation arose from the sales monopoly granted to HOBSA, and accordingly in 1976, when the Senegalese state took a majority shareholding in Bud Senegal, the sales monopoly was ended.

From the point of view of the Senegalese, of course, taking the sales monopoly away from HOBSA could do little in the short run to solve their problems, since the main problem for the Senegalese Treasury was the lack of financial viability of the productive activity, even if they were to retain a larger proportion of the sales price. HOBSA always argued that it had operated towards Bud Senegal exactly as would any other marketing company: no marketing organization, they pointed out, would sell the produce without making a profit upon it. There is, of course, truth in this argument, though the Senegalese government still felt, perhaps rightly, that to diversify their sales agents and remove the monopoly was likely to improve the terms of sale. But, unless the state or the local company could act as its own selling agent in Europe (and HOBSA had made no efforts to train any Senegalese to sell in the European market by 1976), there was no way in which the profit on European sales could be captured by a Senegalese agency. A HOBSA manager's reaction to the suggestion, in 1976, that the Senegalese government hoped to build up the competence to sell in the European market was the confident assertion that, if it tried it, it would undoubtedly fall flat on its face.[1] There is no doubt that it is difficult, because of the expertise required, for a new seller to break into the European market: to what extent existing brokers act as a cartel in this market to keep out newcomers, especially state boards with a small volume of produce, is not something on which I have any information.

In fact, by the time the sales monopoly of HOBSA was removed, the European firm had already gained more from the connection with Bud Senegal than appears from the figures just given. Between 1972 and 1976, HOBSA used its supply of Senegalese produce as a basis to build up a new European broking firm. The firm's unprofitable beginnings in the import of US produce to Europe have been recounted in Chapter 1. In 1972, it decided to concentrate on the 'exotic' end of the trade, that is, off season produce, and began to seek other sources of supply besides the Bud Senegal produce. In the two years which followed, HOBSA increased its turnover in Europe while reducing its proportional dependence on Bud Senegal produce. In 1972/3, 43 per cent of its turnover came from Bud Senegal; in 1973/4 the figure was 35 per cent.[2] In 1975 HOBSA became a panel member[3] for Agrexco, the Israeli importer of all Israeli produce except citrus, thereby increasing the reliability of its non Bud Senegal income. When I visited the firm in 1977 it had continued to expand despite problems with Bud Senegal produce after 1976, and then employed 35 people in the selling operation. It was described by people in the trade in Holland as a medium-sized firm, small in relation to the importers specializing in citrus or apples, but large in the 'exotics' field. Clearly between 1971, when they had been making a loss on their US imports, and 1977, the firm had established itself as a European broker of some importance.

The relation of the broking operation to HOBSA had also changed in 1977. At some date between 1975 and 1977, the broking firm in Holland, Bud Holland, was hived off entirely from HOBSA and became a separate company having the same shareholders as HOBSA. These shareholders in HOBSA by then included Heidemaatschappij,[4] a Dutch agricultural engineering firm. The reasons for the split from HOBSA were explained to me by a Bud manager in 1977. HOBSA was to operate as a 'project development company' aiming to set up new growing operations in the fresh produce field for the European market. In doing this, it might wish to go into partnership with other firms or entities, and the new structure allowed it to do this without thereby permitting those new partners to share in the profits of the successful brokerage operation.

The firm of HOBSA was therefore by 1977 looking ahead to new projects, depsite the effective collapse of its relationship with Bud Senegal. The new marketing contract with the now Senegal-owned Bud Senegal had given Bud Holland 75 per cent of the Bud Senegal crop to market, leaving 25 per cent to be sold either directly by someone working for the firm, or through other marketing agents. In fact, according once again to a Bud Holland manager, they had not received the expected percentage of the crop. By mid-1977 there seemed to be little communication continuing between HOBSA and Bud Senegal (though HOBSA were of course still shareholders), and no one on a HOBSA contract (or who had originally gone to Senegal on a HOBSA contract) remained in Senegal.

By 1977, however, HOBSA had a new project in Africa. They had become involved in a project to produce vegetables in Nigeria as part of the Kano River project. Information from a researcher who was working in this area at the time[5] suggested that this was not a successful venture, and it appears to have been abandoned after one year. However, HOBSA, then went on to other export ventures elsewhere (Horton 1986: 192).

HOBSA, then, expanded over the years from 1972 to 1977 from small and doubtfully profitable beginnings, to become an established broking firm, and to find the resources to continue its activities in the agribusiness field in Africa. Since Bud Senegal was its earliest, and captive, source of supply, and never up to 1977 provided less than one third of its turnover, one can conclude from this story that the profits from the Bud Senegal operation greatly assisted the expansion of HOBSA. HOBSA argued, during the discussions of 1975–76, that its commission in Europe was in its eyes a return not only on its selling operation but also on its activities in establishing the Bud Senegal firm (a recompense as it were for the absence of management fees), and there is no doubt that, though HOBSA suffered a loss of equity, it nevertheless grew through the resources provided by the loss-making and state-financed Bud Senegal. In summary, capital accumulation had been expanded within the European broking trade quite legally as a result of the financing, by the World Bank but particularly by an African government, of large losses at the level of production.

State Responses

> Our aim is definitely *not* to create waged agricultural workers, but to organize (*encadrer*) the peasantry. (Civil servant, Ministry of Rural Development, 1976)

The financial losses to the Senegalese state from supporting the Bud Senegal estates were of course only part of the problems and losses created in Senegal by Bud's activities. From the point of view of Senegalese civil servants and politicians (as opposed to the viewpoint of the farmers and workers), the other problem is raised in the quotation above: the labour conflicts on the farms and the involvement of the national trade unions had raised fears of the political and economic consequences of creating an organized agricultural proletariat for the first time in Senegal. By 1976, therefore, debate within the Senegalese state focused on these two problems, rather than on the issues of food supply and rural risk raised in this book. The civil servants were trying to work out how to develop the market gardening sector in such a way as to shift the focus of accumulation partly at least from Europe to Senegal; and simultaneously, how to do this in a way which cut off the growth of an organized rural proletariat.

As Chapter 1 showed, the proposals made by HOBSA in 1971 – a virtual takeover bid for the Senegalese market gardening sector – were in line with the broad rural development strategy in favour with the Senegalese government at the time. Criticism of this strategy soon came from Senegalese private capital, which had begun to display an interest in market gardening largely as a result of Bud's example. From the point of view of local capital, Bud had been given quite unfair preferential treatment, which local growers later began to demand (unsuccessfully) for themselves. The evidence of increasing interest by local capital included the establishment of an estate belonging to the firm of SAAF, involving local private capital, alongside the Bud estates, and also of a smaller estate, CSA, which according to a Ministry official was a 'mixed' company with state and local private capital. Other evidence comes from discussions with Senegalese skilled and supervisory staff at Bud, some of whom had been offered jobs or were thinking of going into business for themselves; there were also persistent rumours about the speculative buying of suitable land.

Over the question of the private appropriation of land there was clearly a conflict between the aims of local capital and the policies of the government. The ability of the state to dispose of non-registered land – that is, land in the *Domaine National* – when it held that its decision was in the national interest, and the partially effective ban on the registration of new private titles, constituted a block on the development of land as a private commodity. The development of a sub-legal land market in certain areas only partly overcame this problem from the point of view of would-be investors. Local private investment in export horticulture created pressure on the government to provide the legal framework for a private market in land, as other African states (for example, Kenya) have done.

Such a development, however, was in contradiction to the approach to market gardening which was being developed in the Ministry of Rural Development by about 1973. In 1973 the previous Minister, M. Habib Thiam, who had negotiated the agreement with Bud, was replaced by M. Adrien Senghor. At this point, as a civil servant in the Ministry confirmed in an interview in 1976, a different rural development strategy came into favour, at least as regards market gardening, one which assigned a smaller role to foreign private capital such as HOBSA and a larger role to the state. The first sign of this change of heart had been a unilateral erosion from the Senegalese side of the terms agreed with HOBSA at the time of the establishment of Bud Senegal. There had been increasing conflict between the government and HOBSA over the non-provision of the promised level of infrastructural investment, some of which the firm eventually undertook itself. There had also been conflict over land title registration to the company: promised, made a condition of several loans, but not implemented. Other issues involved the sale of water to a competitor of Bud, the price of water, the cost of labour, and the question of whether Bud had an obligation to use Air Afrique flights for its exports rather than its own (cheaper) charters.[6]

By 1976, a new government policy towards the sector had been developed. As described to me by Ministry officials at the time of the negotiations in 1976 for the government takeover of Bud, the aim was to set up a National Horticultural Company (Société Nationale Horticole) with a state majority shareholding, plus private shareholders. This was subsequently established (Republic of Senegal, 1977) to act as a buying agency for market garden produce, and to provide technical assistance and credit to co-operatively organized groups of market gardeners: either groups of existing gardeners working their own land, or 'colonization' projects on newly irrigated land. The company, it was proposed, should not necessarily be profit-making, should not hold land or undertake direct production, and should not include Bud Senegal. Bud, under majority government ownership, continued to operate the Baobab farm; the Kirene farm was turned into a small growers project with funding from the European Development Fund (FED). In addition, Bud expanded its purchases of other small growers' production: by 1979, when the firm was finally declared bankrupt, one-third of its turnover was bought in from small producers (Batsch, 1980).

In other words, the government was proposing to increase state control over the market gardening sector by imposing a model based on the state monopoly of the groundnut trade, but associated with much tighter control of production methods. The purpose was to increase the revenue to the government from market gardening, or at least to reduce the drain on state finances and maintain foreign exchange earnings. These plans did not include the extension of private markets in land or produce, but on the contrary sought to organize access to land, and sale, centrally. The existing small market gardeners, who up to this point had largely escaped taxation, and who understood the government's need for new sources of revenue to replace falling groundnut income, viewed the rumours of these proposals with suspicion.

The small gardeners' fears of loss of their independence as well as part of their incomes were well founded. By the mid-1970s there was a consensus in government circles that to develop vegetables and fruit as a successful export crop necessarily required a major change in the social relations of production in the sector, away from individual small growers taking individual production decisions and selling independently, towards a more centrally managed production system. However, this was taken to imply a search for alternatives to the wage labour estate as a means of transforming production. Civil servants interviewed in July 1976 stressed that a political decision had been taken not to encourage the separation of farmers from the land, and M. Bathor Diop, the new managing director of Bud Senegal, emphasized that there had been strong criticism of Bud within the administration on this count.[7]

This decision arose, not from concern of the type discussed in this book about the erosion of the farming system, but rather from fear of the development of self-conscious and organized groups of agricultural wage workers. The governing party in Senegal had always had a difficult relationship with organized labour[8] and its power base had rather been within the established élites in the countryside. In addition, in Senegal the labour laws and the political situation were such that any labour conflict rapidly became a political issue at the level of the national government. Bud had been no exception to this, with the involvement of the local and national administration as well as the Labour Inspectorate in the strikes discussed here, and the increasing involvement of the union federation in Bud's affairs. In 1978 the government used the army to break another Bud strike (Batsch, 1980). Thus the labour troubles at Bud, and the conflict between the union and the foreign management which resulted, increased the persuasiveness of those within the administration who argued that market gardening should be developed, as a matter of state policy, on the basis of small growers rather than wage labour, and under state control.

Such proposals for closely managed small grower schemes involved no less a transformation of the social relations of production in agriculture than did the wage labour estates. Bud had already experimented with small grower schemes which involved central management control of production plans, planting, irrigation, picking schedules and packing and selling; only the labour was done by the grower, and the management of the experimental scheme was based on the assumption that each (male) grower would be assisted by unpaid family labour.[9] Enough has been said about the complexity of social relations within and across households in existing small-scale agriculture for the extent of the proposed change to be evident. The scheme closely resembled the contracting schemes discussed in Chapter 1, which appealed to international capital in the horticulture industry for much the same reason that they now appealed to managers and civil servants in Senegal: they offered to the organizers of the project the advantages of centralized management without the political disadvantage of creating the basis for organized labour, and had the added attraction of shifting the selling risk towards the farmers. For this same reason, they spelled danger for the labour force.

Small Farmers, Capital and the State in Senegal

All of these plans for reorganizing market gardening yet again were scarcely under way when they, and the Senegalese state, were overtaken by a new wave of economic and political problems. On the one hand, all the government's ambitions for the market gardening sector depended upon the conviction, quite unproven in 1976, that large-scale market gardening for export could be made profitable in Senegal (the Bud expatriate management remained convinced that they, and only they, could make it pay – a point which also remained unproven). On the other hand, an increasingly severe food crisis, a renewed drought, and a sweeping change in the development policies demanded by external lending agencies shifted the whole pattern of the government's possibilities and priorities once again.

The late 1970s brought a sharp drop in market gardening exports and rising food imports (Tables 9.2 and 9.3). Exports of fresh produce never exceeded the peak of 1975/6, and fell faster after 1976 (Table 9.2). The other 'industrial' market gardening operations collapsed with Bud (République du Sénégal, 1982: 81), and imports of fruit and vegetables began to rise again. Like cereal production, small-scale fruit and vegetable growing was hit by the new drought which began in 1978 (Tables 9.2 and 9.3). The water table in the *niayes* fell again, and the cost of irrigation water was pushed up by the government's economic reforms. Finally the urban spread of Dakar had compounded the tendency of villa development and land speculation to push the small-scale vegetable gardeners off the *niaye* land (*ibid.*, 1982).

The decline of fresh produce as a new export crop was, however, only a small part of the economic crisis Senegal faced in the early 1980s. 1980, 1981 and 1983 were all poor years for millet production, but 1984 was as bad as 1973 (Table 9.3). Groundnut production, too, was at 1973 levels, and groundnut prices were falling. Senegal's international terms of trade turned sharply against the country in the early 1980s – peanut products were buying decreasing quantities of oil imports and essential food imports (Maxwell, 1986: 33). Food imports rose – and as the crisis worsened, so dependence on food aid rose with it (Figure 9.2). In 1983/4 Senegal received over 200 metric tons of food aid, 28 per cent of total imports and 18 per cent of estimated food available (*ibid.*, 1982: 38). Finally, Senegal's external debt according to World Bank figures (IBRD, 1985) reached over 60 per cent of GNP by 1983: a high figure even by sub-Saharan Africa's standards.

Economic problems on this scale and dependence on emergency aid opened Senegal to pressure from lending agencies to conform to the new fashion in development policies demanded by the big bilateral and multi-lateral agencies (IBRD, 1981, 1986): a move away from large managed projects towards an emphasis on market liberalization, privatization, higher food prices, and support for small farmers through better incentives.

The Senegalese government has adapted itself partly to these new prescriptions. Its Sixth Four Year Plan 1981–85 (République du Sénégal, 1982) proposed a continuing rise in producer prices for groundnuts and food prices, and an attempt to cut 'costs of intervention' (*ibid.*, 1982: 93). Cereals marketing was opened again to private trade. In 1984 the New Agricultural Policy committed the government to reducing the role of agricultural parastatals which had run the big regional agricultural projects from active management to the provision of technical support; it also proposed further liberalization of agricultural markets, plus the use of intervention to support floor prices, especially for millet.

Information on the effects of this new policy on the market gardening sector is still sketchy. In 1979, following the Bud bankruptcy, the government set up Senprim, a parastatal produce contracting and exporting company, to manage the Kirene contracting scheme and a similar scheme set up on part of the Baobab land. The company owns the capital and closely manages the contracting farmers on the model of the Bud experimental scheme (Le Sénégal en Chiffres 1982/3, Horton 1986). The firm buys and exports mainly green beans and peppers; it uses the Bud Senegal packing facility, and has about 650 contracting farmers (Horton 1986: 194). In 1985/6 it exported about 1,000 metric tons of crops (ibid: 174). The company has falling yields and sales and it has made a financial loss in most years since it started. It too would be bankrupt but for government subsidy (ibid: 195–6).

Meanwhile a number of other looser contracting schemes, similar to the pre-Bud export purchasing activities, have expanded in the wake of Bud's demise, and drawing on some of the skills of the ex-Bud workers. The government has supported a project to install young educated growers in the *niayes* (Le Sénégal en Chiffres 1982/3), and a number of other firms have been established, expanded, or have switched to contracting. The government has

Figure 9.2
Senegal: The Continuing Economic Crisis

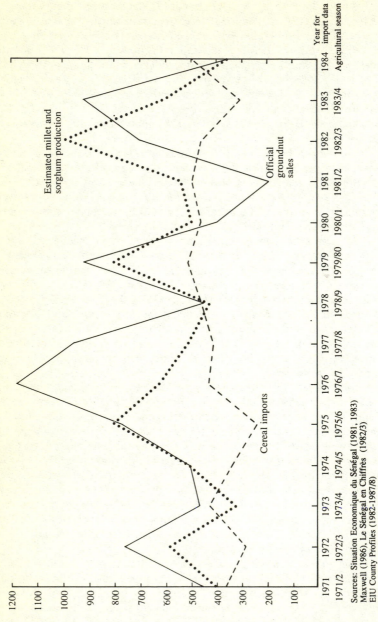

Estimated millet and
sorghum production

Official
groundnut
sales

Cereal imports

Sources: Situation Economique du Sénégal (1981, 1983)
Maxwell (1986), Le Sénégal en Chiffrés (1982/3)
EIU County Profiles (1982-1987/8)

been paying these firms a subsidy of 15 per cent of export turnover, but a number were nevertheless running at a loss in 1985/6 (Horton 1986). These firms, too, mainly contract for green beans or peppers. Total exports rose sharply in the early 1980s (Table 9.2) and then fell back to around 6,000 tons in the mid 1980s (Horton 1986). The number of small producers under contract appears to be larger than before Bud, but the market situation is rather similar, with private trade supplying the local market and a number of firms buying for export. A few Senegalese nationals have now developed expertise in selling in European markets, but their efforts are meeting increased competition from southern European members of the EEC, and from other parts of Africa.

What then have been and are the implications of these gyrations of development policy for the small farmers caught up in them? At the beginning of the 1980s, it seemed to many observers (Adams, 1981; Copans, 1980) that government and private capital were collaborating in an attempt to 'abolish' the independent small farmer at last, turning her or him into a labourer on estates or on managed contracting schemes where all the decisions were taken by others and only the risk, in greater measure, remained to the farmer. In practice few of the contracting schemes in Senegal appear to be this tightly organized (but information from the farmers' point of view is hard to find). Elsewhere in Africa, contracting schemes continue to expand (Watts 1986 Vol. 1). And as the discussion of household and farming organization in this book would lead one to expect, the 'household farming' concept on which these schemes are built have led in West Africa to sharp intra-household struggles, especially between men and women, over the control of land access to unpaid labour (see for example Carney (1988) on a Gambian scheme).

At least in appearance, the New Agricultural Policy and associated economic austerity measures cut across these developments and imply a drop in state and aid-funded support for the contracting schemes. The cut in the public budget and market liberalization proposals imply a reduction in export subsidies which may bankrupt a number of firms. This may finally reverse at great social cost the trend towards the incorporation of the local gardeners, and bring us to a situation predicted by a French journalist in 1980, whereby the Senegalese government has paid a great deal of money to develop a modern high-productivity export activity which has come to look remarkably like the old groundnut schemes (Batsch 1980).

However the new policies of market liberalization and economic adjustment have a characteristic contradiction embedded in them: they generally favour liberalization of product markets, while proposing control of labour and, especially, repression of labour organization and control of wages. In export horticulture, as voices in Senegal are now pointing out, this contradiction becomes acute. Effective export production in this high risk branch *does* involve effective co-operation among farmers, and between farmers and exporters, to manage irrigation water and to ensure high quality and regular deliveries. Given this there are only two possible models. Control by downstream capital, probably in Europe, is one: the Bud model, whether based on estates or on contract farming, shifting the risk to Africa and especially to the African farmers. This might be modified by the successful development of Senegalese selling power – in the way the Israeli state controls the marketing of Israeli produce – and by government investment in production. But the true alternative model represents a more radical shift of focus: projects based on the development of co-operation among local farmers, selling both on the local market and for export, and developing the expertise and organization necessary to retain a somewhat larger share of the return, and to keep control of decisions on investment, technology and project management.

There is some evidence that the shift towards market liberalization and away from state control has opened up a space in Senegal for experiments of the second type. One example of such an initiative is the small-scale irrigated market gardening projects begun in the Thiès Region by groups of farmers with the assistance of RADI (Réseau Africain pour le Développement Intégré), a non-profit, non-governmental organization of African professionals. The produce is initially for the local market and the long-term aim of the project is to use the market gardening revenue to develop a more integrated farming and economic system in the rural area. Ex-Bud workers have been included in the team of technical assistants recruited for the project. Another rather different example may be GIPES, a co-operative exporting company composed of small to medium private farmers (Horton 1986). This is a hopeful approach but any wider and effective shift in this direction involves farmers organizing in their own interests. The desirability of such a development is implied by some academic studies of producer price setting and the new liberalization policies (Bates, 1981; Harvey, 1988), and accepted in principle by the Senegalese government's renewed commitment to the co-operative movement in its New Agricultural Policy. In practice, however, such co-operation may be too close to labour organization truly to recommend itself to external agencies and governments which deplore effective trade unionism.

Meanwhile, the impact of the new liberalization policies on food production remains an open question. I can find no information on the impact of contracting on food production in the wet season, but it would be an important question for research. The central purpose of this book has been to demonstrate that the impact of a large export farming development on surrounding farming organization can be to catalyse a long-term decline in food production. The effect operated in part because of the pre-existing farming and social structure; in part because there were already strong individualizing tendencies operating on and within the Senegalese labouring classes as evidenced by the scale of development of the migrant labour market. The effects fell particularly on food farming because, while productivity and prices were such as to make individualized market gardening on suitable land a viable economic activity, this was simply not the case for food farming. Hence the struggle to expand and appropriate the surplus in market gardening, and the implied danger to food production. The Bud expeience in Senegal provides another African case history in which, as Sara Berry (1984: 79) puts it, not only the fact of monetization, but also and particularly 'the process by which the rural economy was commercialized was . . . important' in determining the effects on food production.

In the last two years (1985/6 and 1986/7) the economic crisis in Senegal has been mitigated by good rains and good harvests, as well as by considerable capital inflow. But world prices for groundnut oil are at an historic low (groundnuts brought in less foreign exchange than fish in 1986) and the external debt continues to rise despite rescheduling (EIU, 1987, 1987/8, 1988). The recovery is extremely fragile, and agricultural transformation depends on investment, the extent and nature of which has been put in question by the economic reforms.

Conclusion: What Kind of Agrarian Transition?

In the light of these arguments, what more general conclusions about agrarian transformation in Senegal might tentatively be drawn? No case study provides definitive answers to questions posed about the wider economy; but only case studies can illuminate the process of change, test models and raise new questions.

At the most general level, the study suggests that there is a contradiction within the Senegalese economy between the development of markets and the production of food. The development of labour markets in particular produces a strong individualizing force within small-scale farming systems, which undermines the viability of low productivity food production. The further development of the labour market undermines food production at the same time as it demands the extension of the food markets. Bud fitted neatly into, and amplified, this basic contradiction.

The contradiction cannot simply be avoided by a policy decision to promote 'peasant farming' or 'smallholders'. This is because the contradiction emerges from some fundamental aspects of the Senegalese rural and national economy. The first of these is the apparent absence of those convenient (for economists) units, household farms based on stable family membership. The evidence suggests instead that it is best, in West African conditions, to regard household membership, and the availability of unpaid labour within the household, as variables responding to outside circumstances. The access of the household head to the unpaid labour of dependent members is best regarded as contingent upon the options open to those dependants, and on the household head's capacity to deliver food and income opportunities to those dependants in return.

In these circumstances, a farming structure more firmly based on households is only likely to emerge if supported by a sharp rise in the productivity of labour in agriculture, and by the restriction of other cash-earning possibilities for dependants, including women. It may also require the availability of cheap casual labour from elsewhere to sustain its flexibility, a point to which we return below. In the absence of a sharp rise in agricultural productivity, the commercialization of the economy may simply undermine the wider cross-household social relations which sustain low productivity food farming, and promote a shift to greater reliance on individual commercial cash cropping. And the prices and productivity of food farming were (and in the near future probably will remain[10]) too low for it to be a viable non-irrigated cash crop in the more densely settled, and the driest, areas of Senegal.

A number of other aspects of the economy suggest that this image of Senegalese rural areas may be more appropriate than that of the kin-based household farm. One is the organization of economic relations between the genders. The economic distance between men and women, the way in which women's partial responsibility for feeding the household is sustained even where their role in food farming declines, the division of labour between men and women which generates women's need for cash, and a certain level of independence in economic decision making from the men: all this is characteristic of West Africa, though it takes many very different specific forms. It implies that the reactions of women to changes in the organization of the economy are as important as those of men, and that women are not inevitably or even usually available within the household as unpaid farming labour. Women's farming labour forms part of a contract by which women gain control of resources in return: otherwise, it will be hotly contested, and simply not undertaken if alternatives are available.

A recognition of these points can emerge only from a more general recognition that economic relations between the genders are problematic, and are a subject which must be investigated if rural transformation and class formation are to be understood. There is still a curious tendency to treat the control of male labour in production as requiring an explanation, while regarding the control of women's domestic and farming work by male household members as unchallengeable and therefore not requiring explanation. But domestic work is not simply an additional element of rural labour which should not be forgotten in farming studies (though not to forget it would still improve many studies). Rather, the social relations within which such work is done – with implications for household structure, women's obligations and responses to pressure – and the interrelations between changes in the organization of domestic work and other elements of the relations between the genders all have to be recognized as central to the farming structure and to the process of class creation. None of these points are now new in the feminist literature, but their implications are still very rarely worked through in studies of agrarian change and the making of working classes.

The other indicator of the appropriateness of this general approach to the Senegalese economy is the scale of development of the migrant labour market. It is increasingly recognized that West Africa has a very substantial labour market not sufficiently described by the concepts of circular and permanent large-scale migratory flow. The extent of casual labour, and of what this study has called wandering in search of work, is an important feature of West African economies, creating what is in effect a landless class: or at least a group whose links to the land are tenuous. Small-scale agriculture and larger employers alike have come to depend on the existence of this labour market. Wage differentials are huge, and the terms of hire likewise vary enormously, but the balance between income levels in this market and income levels in cash cropping nevertheless shifted sufficiently over the last few decades to create this group, and the increasing shortage of land in a number of crucial farming areas such as the Senegalese groundnut basin may be enough to maintain it in the face of the current economic recession. Louise Lennihan (1987: 265) recently made a related point about northern Nigeria: 'There is a category of poor men without farms, often without kin, a hidden proletariat which slips between the interstices of studies where the unit of inquiry is . . . the farm or the household . . . who constitute a modern day "floating population" of casual, transient labour.' We shall not understand economic and agricultural organization in West Africa properly until we know a great deal more about their labour markets.

This image of Senegalese farming, based on the central contradiction outlined above, suggests in turn just how open is the process of transition in the Senegalese agrarian economy. On the one hand there are strong pressures towards individualization and the further development of wage labour; on the other, the economic recession and the difficulties and cost of promoting large productivity increases in agriculture make that road potentially disastrous.

These reflections lead to two further conclusions. First, large-scale development projects should be evaluated, not solely in terms of their own internal viability, or the balance of short-run income effects, but in terms of their longer-term impact on the economic and social organization of the rural economy, within the general framework of questions outlined here. Projects which promote further individualization and commercialization of the agricultural system, with the associated decline in food production and rise in individual risk, are likely to find the long-term detriment outweighing the short-term gain.

Second, *any* agricultural change which is to promote long-term national food security has to promote rural food security as part of its effects. If rural production and access to food drop further, the problem is displaced, not solved, and the longer-term future further undermined. This study suggests that any project which is to promote rural food security cannot be based, at least in the foreseeable future, on individual commercial farming. It must involve some form of co-operation in and division of farming labour if it is to make the system viable, to generate and use investment efficiently, and to use effectively such resources as supplementary irrigation. Wage labour systems, we have seen, create severe second-round problems. Contract farming systems, which imply quite as dramatic a shift in the social relations of farming – perhaps outdoing even wage labour systems in the Senegalese situation – involve intra-household conflict, and tend to remove the surplus for investment, and decision over its use, from the hands of the farmers, hence putting at risk their ability to guard their own security and to make decisions appropriate to their farming situation.

The implied third alternative – leaving more investment surplus and decisions in the hands of the farmers, and trying to promote a social reorganization of farming which builds on existing co-operative and exchange labour systems – has a lot to recommend it as a route: flexibility, appropriate investment decisions, the absence of a sharp break from tested and remarkably adaptive farming systems. While this has been the approach of some extension work, in Senegal as elsewhere, the experiment has been constantly overridden by the large projects seeking fast returns. And it is also undermined by the whole thrust of agricultural economics models which promote commercial 'household' farming.

This argument has taken us a long way from the Bud case study. But that is the purpose of case studies. Bud, it has been argued, fitted into and amplified some tendencies in the Senegalese economic system – such as the extension of the wage labour market and the individualization of farming – while suppressing and destroying others – such as the flexible adaptation of the Kirene farming system to falling groundnut prices and land shortage through co-operative labour organization and new cash crops. Operating in this way, Bud was both a unique case, like all cases, and also an exemplar of a particular approach to African agriculture. There is the constant danger, as the African rural economic crisis continues, that agencies and governments will have recourse to the promotion of high productivity, irrigated 'islands' of the Bud type amid the low productivity, rain-fed surroundings. To demonstrate for one case how detrimental the external effects of such a project can be is to back with further evidence the argument which says that this is the wrong approach to the use of scarce investment funds in a fragile ecological and human environment. Projects are not acceptable or successful when they undermine the livelihood of small-scale farmers, and particularly their food production system, without providing an alternative whereby food will not merely be produced but also made available to those who were previously food farmers, even if their new employer should leave for more profitable production sites.

Notes

1. The phrase is from an interview in Dakar with an expatriate manager of Bud Senegal.

2. Figures provided by a Bud Holland manager in Delft, 1977.

3. That is, a group of sales agents for the importer.

4. Full name, Internationale Maatschappij Voor Landboukundig Onwikkeling. It was a subsidiary of this firm, ILACO, which undertook the original feasibility study for Bud Senegal. Mr Marschall, founder of HOBSA, and General Manager of Bud Senegal until 1976, retained majority control of HOBSA when this new shareholder was added.

5. Personal communication from Cecile Jackson.

6. Bud argued that the Senegalese government failed to provide promised infrastructure, including water supplies, macadamized roads and port and airport facilities, which were to be reimbursed later by the firm. Bud also objected to the supply of irrigation water to a private Senegalese estate, as a violation of undertakings when Bud was established, and protested against the sharp rise in the

minimum legal agricultural wage after the severe inflation of 1973.

7. Information from an interview with M. Bathor Diop, Dakar, July 1976. M. Diop said that even the contract farming experiment discussed below had been criticized within the Senegalese Minstry as turning farmers into effective wage labourers, a charge he rejected.

8. The late 1960s in Senegal saw considerable conflict beween government and unions, which led to the formation of the CNTS under the close supervision of the governing party. Conflict recurred however, especially during the inflation from 1973: Mackintosh (1975) discusses this period. The trade union organization, like the political party system, has changed greatly since the mid-1970s period chiefly discussed in this book.

9. I owe my understanding of this contract farming experiment to the kind assistance of Roger and Brenda Wensel, and to interviews with American and Senegalese staff on the project and with a number of the farmers.

10. Given the current low world food prices, the continuing need to import food, and the lack of prospects for an early increase in productivity, a number of observers regard it as unlikely that producer prices can be kept high enough to make millet an attractive cash crop. See Maxwell (1986).

Table 9.1
Changing Ownership of Bud Senegal

	Total Equity (million francs c.f.a.)	Shareholders (percentage of equity) in brackets
1972	66	HOBSA (51) Government of Senegal (29) IFC* (20)
1973	375	HOBSA (27) Government of Senegal (48) IFC (11) SIFIDA** (7) FMO† (7)
1976	1100	HOBSA (11) Government of Senegal (67) IFC (15) SIFIDA (2) FMO (5)

* International Finance Corporation.

** A Luxembourg investment company: *La Société Internationale Financière pour les Investissements et le Développement en Afrique.*

† The Netherlands Finance Company for Developing Countries.

Source: Information from Bud Senegal management.

Table 9.2
Fresh Produce Production and Exports

| Year | Production ('000 tonnes) | | | Exports* ('000 tonnes) |
	Total	Cap Vert	Thiès	
1973/4	63.7	24.4	16.1	5.2
1974/5	85.5	40.4	19.9	7.7
1975/6	102.7	51.0	19.9	5.5
1976/7	103.4	55.3	20.6	12.8
1977/8	102.2	n.a.	n.a.	7.7
1978/9	85.4	54.4	n.a.	4.3
1979/80	n.a.	n.a.	n.a.	n.a.
1980/1	103.2	37.6	30.8	n.a.
1981/2	n.a.	n.a.	n.a.	10.3
1982/3	n.a.	n.a.	n.a.	9.9

* By calendar year.
Sources: Le Sénégal en Chiffres. 1982/3; *République du Sénégal, Situation Economique,* 1983 and 1985; *République du Sénégal VIe Plan Quadriennal,* 1981-5 (1982).

Table 9.3
Indicators of the Food Situation: Millet and Sorghum Production; Imports of Rice

| Year | Millet and Sorghum Production ('000 t) | | | Rice Imports ('000 t) (Calendar years) |
	Total	Cap Vert	Thiès	
1972/3	322.8		13.2	192.0
1973/4	570.9	1.1	103.3	207.2
1974/5	795.9	1.4	87.5	102.1
1975/6	621.0	0.9	98.1	244.5
1976/7	507.2	0.5	49.4	248.0
1977/8	420.1	0.1	21.5	239.0
1978/9	802.0	0.3	117.7	n.a.
1979/80	496.1	0.2	55.0	275.0
1980/1	531.0	0.8	6.6	319.5
1981/2	985.0	0.7	111.0	255.8
1982/3	590.3	0.6	104.4	127.7
1983/4	352.5		1.6	372.0

Sources: Le Sénégal en Chiffres, 1982/3; *République du Sénégal, Situation Economique,* 1983 and 1985; *République du Sénégal VIe Plan Quadriennal,* 1981-5 (1982).

Appendix: Research Method

This appendix describes briefly the main elements of the research method used for this study in the rural areas near the two estates.

The Choice of Villages for Study

The fieldwork method for this study was that characteristic of 'village studies' within development economics, or of economic anthropology: that is, the detailed study of the operation of individual village economies. The study was done over a period slightly exceeding a single agricultural cycle, beginning early in the wet season of 1975 and ending the middle of the wet season of 1976. During this period, I undertook detailed studies of three villages.

The choice of villages to study was the result of a prior decision concerning the method by which I was to study change. Given that there was little in the way of base line data available for the villages in the area of Bud, in either published or unpublished sources, I had two main options. One was to include in the sample both villages which had been much affected by Bud's presence over the previous three to four years, and also villages, held to be similar in other respects, but outside the orbit of Bud's influence. A comparison of the two would then allow generalizations to be made about processes of change. The second was to study only villages affected by Bud, and to attempt to examine, through the reconstruction of farming and work histories, and an understanding of pressures for change within the village, the impact of the farm upon the economy.

The first method was ultimately rejected for two main reasons. The first was that, with the first approach, pressure on time and resources would have ruled out the study of the impact of both Bud farms, forcing me to choose between them. Since my aim was not to understand a single rural area, but to understand the effects of Bud, this would have seriously impoverished the study. I would have had to choose the Baobab farm, since it was the larger and longer established, while the Kirene farm was still experiencing 'teething troubles', and since Baobab was providing the bulk of the export produce and employing the bulk of Bud labour. Without studying Baobab – the farm, furthermore, which had the farm management offices on site – I could not have understood Bud. However Kirene, while new and small, was a part of Bud which suggested more clearly the directions in which Bud was likely to develop if it grew, and it was put forward as more nearly approximating the image that the Senegalese government and the Bud management had of the farm's integration into the rural areas, complementing the wet season agriculture.

My second reason for rejecting the comparison of villages affected and unaffected by Bud was that it proved difficult to find villages which could be reasonably regarded as similar except for the presence or absence of Bud. In particular, it was difficult to find villages which were similar in both ethnic composition and ecological characteristics. This was especially true for the area of the Baobab farm. The villages in the area of the Baobab 'forest' (after which the farm was named) with its heavy clay soil, were all affected by Bud to a considerable degree. To find a village out of Bud's orbit which was comparable to Bambilor in being a market gardening village, one would have had to go to the villages out towards the coast, where soil conditions, ethnic composition and village history were all different. And to go in the other direction from the Baobab 'forest', over behind Sebikotane, would take one into the ethnically and ecologically quite different area of the Serer.

I therefore concluded that to try compare villages affected and unaffected by Bud, though appealing in principle, was not superior to the alternative method of historical reconstruction of the recent economic changes in several villages close to Bud, since the former method would narrow the scope of the study, and the attribution of observed differences to the affects of Bud would be thrown into doubt by the ecological and historical diversity of the area near Dakar. The same problem, it turned out, arose for the Kirene area, despite the greater ethnic homogeneity of the area, because of the specific agricultural history of Kirene. I therefore decided that, given the short period of presence of the Bud estates, I could assess the impact of Bud more effecively by reconstruction of the history of a number of nearby villages.

I chose for study, therefore, three villages, two in the area of the Baobab farm and one near the Kirene farm. Near Kirene the village chose itself, as the main village supplying labour to the estate. Near Baobab, Bambilor and Ponty offered two contrasting cases: one village of recent migrants whose lives were dominated by the estate, and one longer-established, more diverse, and offering the possibility of assessing the impact of Bud on local market gardening. There existed, furthermore, a baseline study for Bambilor done in 1967 by students from the Ecole Nationale d'Economie Appliquée (ENEA) in Dakar. Throughout the study I lived in one of the villages near the Baobab estate.

Fieldwork Method

In the three villages the fieldwork method was a mixture of questionnaires and more open-ended interviewing. In each village I did a complete census of the resident population, using census forms modelled on those used or village studies by the ENEA, but containing more detailed occupational data. The census questionnaires were administered during August/September 1975 with the assistance of one research assistant who worked with me on the whole project.

On the basis of the census I chose a stratified sample of about one-tenth of the compounds (in Bambilor and Ponty) or households (in Kirene). Each household within the samples was intended to form a unit of subsequent analysis: some of the resulting conceptual problems have been discussed. In each village, the principles on which the sample was stratified differed: I used compound size in each village, plus participation in wage work (in Ponty), a classification by farming activity of the compound head (in Bambilor), and area of the village in Kirene. The reason for this difference in stratification methods was that each village, even at that stage of the research, posed rather different problems of analysis, and I wished to use the data to address rather different questions.

Thus I wished to use the Bambilor material to address the specific question of the impact of Bud upon indigenous market gardeners, and therefore needed a sub-group of the sample which consisted of market gardening compounds. In Ponty, I hoped to use the material amongst other things for a detailed analysis of participation in the Bud labour force, and in Kirene a marked feature of the village (poorly understood by me at the beginning) was that it was dispersed in small hamlets, so that I felt that the sample should be geographically representative. Retrospective tests of these samples as regards various variables of the village economy generally confirmed their representative nature for the villages from which they were drawn.

For each *household* in the sample I then did a plot by plot study of farming practices (labour use, seeds, fertiliser, tools used, dates of operations) for all the farm plots of all the people in the household, plus participation in various forms of communal agricultural labour. These involved repeated interviews and observation through the farming season. Further interviews concerned a reconstruction of the farming history of the household over the previous few years, told separately by various adult members of the household. I and a research assistant did studies of present income and expenditure patterns over the year of the study. We conducted interviews concerning changes in expenditure and participation in wage work, and collected work histories of all the adult household members. We also tried to identify other sources of cash income, the history of the acquisition of durable goods, and recent changes in household structure; and we engaged in more general discussions of the history of the household and the compound. I also spent two months with a woman research assistant interviewing separately the women in the sample households concerning their personal histories, domestic work, and the effects of Bud on work within the household.

It should be noted what information was not collected. The major omissions are crop yield data, plot measurements (except for the market gardens, which were accurately measured) and daily time budget and cash budget data. All of these omissions were due to lack of time and resources. Time and cash budget data consume enormous amounts of research time, and with only one research assistant who frequently worked as a translator as well as administering questionnaires independently, I did not have the resources for this. Crop yield and plot measurements data would have cut down considerably the number of farmers I could have studied and, given the aims of the study set out in the previous section, retaining the wider scope seemed more important. The data on planted areas of millet and groundnuts, cited in Tables 4.1 and 4.2 and in Chapter 7, are therefore estimates based by conventional methods on quantity of seed sown, and method of sowing. Not too much weight should be placed, therefore, on their absolute values; they have been used chiefly for comparisons of relative areas sown by different farmers within Kirene.

It remains to comment on the construction of the 'without Bud' farming income estimates, used particularly in the discussion of Kirene. For these, I used two types of information. First, area of each crop (vegetables or groundnuts) grown in the last reasonable farming year before the arrival of Bud (the 1971 wet season): these areas were expressed as proportions of the area farmed in that crop in the year of the study, not in hectares. And second, farmers' estimates of the volume of each crop sold in that year. This information gave two alternative estimates of 'without Bud' incomes, when the output estimates were multiplied by farm gate prices prevailing in the year of the study. When studying farmers who lost land to Bud, I used the lower of the two estimates. It is my general view on other evidence that these estimates understate rather than overstate the income lost through Bud's arrival.

Bibliography

Official and Statistical Publications

Le Sénégal en Chiffres, Société Africaine d'Edition, Dakar, 1976, 1982/3.
République du Sénégal, *Situation Economique du Sénégal*, 1974, 1983, 1985.
République du Sénégal, *6e Plan Quadriennal de Développement Economique et Social 1981–1985*, Dakar, 1982.
République du Sénégal, *Résultats Provisoires de la Recensement Général de la Population d'avril 1976*, Direction de la Statistique, Dakar, n.d.
Republic of Senegal, *Fifth Four Year Plan for Economic and Social Development* Ministry of Planning and Cooperation, Les Nouvelles Editions Africaines, Dakar, 1977.

Other Sources

Adams, A. 'The Senegal River valley', in Heyer, 1981.
Amin, S. 'Les mechanisms de l'extension de l'agriculture arachidière 1885–1970, Part I', Institut Africain de Développement Economique et de Planification (IDEP), Dakar, Mimeo, 1970.
Amin, S. *L'Afrique de l'Ouest Bloquée*, Editions de Minuit, 1971a.
Amin, S. 'Les mechanisms de l'extension arachidière 1885–1970, Part II: Les Difficultés de l'Industrialisation 1950–1969', IDEP, Dakar, Mimeo, 1971b.
Amin, S. (ed.) *Modern Migrations in West Africa*, Oxford University Press, 1974.
Amin, S. *Drought and Migration in the Sahel*, Oxford University Press, 1978.
Andrae, G. and Beckman, B. *The Wheat Trap*, Zed, 1985.
Angrand, A. *Les Lébous de la presqu'île du Cap Vert*, Dakar, 1947.
Anthony, J. *et al. Agricultural Change in Tropical Africa*, Cornell University Press, 1979.
Arnaud, J. *L'économie maraîchère et fruitière dans la Région du Cap Vert, Grand Banlieu de Dakar*, Thèse, Université de Strasbourg, 1970.
Ball, N. 'Understanding the causes of African famine', *Journal of Modern African Studies*, Vol. 14, 1976.
Banaji, J. 'Modes of production in a materialist conception of history', *Capital and Class*, No. 3, 1977.
Barry, B. *Le royaume du Waalo Le Sénégal avant la conquête*, Maspero, 1972.
Bates, R. *Markets and States in Tropical Africa*, University of California Press, 1981.
Batsch, C. 'Les mésaventures d'une entreprise de maraîchage au Sénégal', *Le Monde*

Diplomatique, September 1980.

Beckford, G. *Persistent Poverty: Underdevelopment in Plantation Economies of the Third World*, Oxford University Press, 1972.

Benoit-Cattin, M. and Faye J. *L'exploitation agricole familiale en Afrique Soudano-Sahelienne*, Presses Universitaires de France, 1982.

Berry, S. *Cocoa, Custom and Socio-Economic Change in Rural West Nigeria*, Oxford University Press, 1975.

Berry, S. 'The food crisis and agrarian change in Africa: a review essay', *African Studies Review*, Vol. 27/2, 1984.

Bettelheim, C. *Calcul économique et formes de propriété*, Maspero, 1970.

Brighton Labour Process Group, 'The capitalist labour process', *Capital and Class*, No. 1, 1977.

Bryceson, D. 'The proletarianisation of women in Tanzania', *Review of African Political Economy*, No. 17, 1980.

Burbach, R. and Flynn, P. *Agribusiness in the Americas*, Monthly Review, 1980.

Butterwick, M. and Neville-Rolf, E. *Food, Farming and the Common Market*, Oxford University Press, 1968.

Carney, J. 'Struggles over crop rights and labour within contract farming households in a Gambian irrigated rice project', *Journal of Peasant Studies*, Vol. 15/3, 1988.

Catala, D. *Le Controle des Investissements Etrangers au Sénégal*, Mémoire Institut Universitaire de Hautes Etudes Internationales de Genève, 1977.

CENECA, 'Role et dynamique des industries agricoles et alimentaires', *Les Cahiers du CENECA*, No. Spécial, 1969.

Chayanov, A. V. (ed.) Thorner, D. *The Theory of Peasant Economy*, Kerblay and Smith, 1966.

Chambers, R. *Rural Development: Putting the Last First*, Longman, 1983.

Cleave, J. *African Farmers. Labour Use in the Development of Smallholder Agriculture*, Praeger, 1974.

Cohen, R. *et al. African Labour History*, Sage, 1978.

Collier, P. and Lall D. 'Why poor people get rich: Kenya 1960–79', *World Development*, 1984.

Colvin, L. *et al. The Uprooted of the Western Sahel. Migrants' Quest for Cash in the Senegambia*, Praeger, 1981.

Comité Information Sahel, *Qui se nourrit de la famine en Afrique?* Maspero, 1974.

Copans, J. (ed.) *Sécheresses et Famines au Sahel*, Maspero, 1975.

Copans, J. 'From Senegambia to Senegal: the evolution of peasantries', in Klein, M. (ed.), *Peasants in Africa*, Sage, 1980.

Crowder, M. *Senegal A Study of French Assimilation Policy*, Methuen, 1967.

Crubelier, J. *Structures Agraires et Diffusion de L'économie Contractuelle en Agriculture 2. La Plaine Viticole du Gard*, CNRS, Paris, 1977.

Cruise O'Brien, D. *The Mourides of Senegal*, The Clarendon Press, 1970.

Cruise O'Brien, D. *Saints and Politicians*, Cambridge University Press, 1975.

Cruise O'Brien, D. 'Ruling class and peasantry in Senegal 1960–1976: the politics of a monocrop economy', in Cruise O'Brien, R., 1979.

Cruise O'Brien, R. (ed.) *The Political Economy of Underdevelopment, Dependence in Senegal*, Sage, 1979.

Curtin, P. *Economic Change in Pre-Colonial Africa: Senegambia in the Era of the Slave Trade*, University of Wisconsin Press, 1975.

Dalby, D. and Harrison Church, *Drought in Africa*, International African Institute, 1973.

Dalby, D. *et al. Drought in Africa 2*, International African Institute, 1977.
Davies, I. *African Trade Unions*, Penguin, 1966.
De Latour Dejean, E. 'La Transformation du régime foncier: appropriation des terres et formation de la classe dirigeante en pays Mawri (Niger)', in Amin, S. (ed.), *L'Agriculture Africaine et le Capitalisme*, Anthropos, 1975.
Derman, W. and Whitford, S. (eds) *Social Impact Analysis and Development Planning in the Third World*, Westview Press, 1985.
Deschamps, H. *Le Sénégal et La Gambie*, Presses Universitaires de France, 1968.
Dey, J. 'Gambian women: unequal partners in rice development projects', *Journal of Development Studies*, Vol. 17/3, 1981.
Dia, T. *La Propriété Foncière dans les Niayes*, IDEP, Dakar, n.d.
Diagne, P. *Pouvoir Politique Traditionel en Afrique Occidentale*, Présence Africaine, 1967.
Diarrassouba, V. *L'Evolution des Structures Agraires du Sénégal*, Cujas, 1968.
Dinham, B. and Hines, C. *Agribusiness in Africa*, Earth Resources Research, 1983.
Diop, A. *Société Toucouleur et Migration: L'immigration Toucouleur à Dakar*, IFAN, Dakar, 1965.
Dumont, R. *Paysanneries aux Abois*, Editions du Seuil, 1972.
Dupire, M. *et al.* 'Résidence, tenure foncière, alliance dans une société bilinéaire (Serer du Sine et du Baol, Sénégal)', *Cahiers d'Etudes Africaines*, Vol. 14/3, 1974.
Eicher, C. 'Facing up to Africa's food crisis', in Eicher, C. and Staatz, J. (eds), *Agricultural Development in the Third World*, Johns Hopkins University Press, 1984.
Eicher, C. and Baker D. 'Research on agricultural development in Sub-Saharan Africa', *International Development Papers*, Michigan State University, 1982.
EIU (Economist Intelligence Unit). *Country Profile: Senegal*, 1987/8.
EIU. *Country Report: Senegal, The Gambia, Guinea-Bissau*, 1987, 1988.
Elkan, W. 'Rural migration, agricultural practice and resettlement in Senegal', University of Durham, Department of Economics, *Working Paper* No. 4, 1975.
Faye, J. 'Zonal approach to migration in the Senegalese peanut basin', in Colvin *et al.*, 1981.
Feder, E. 'Strawberry imperialism', Institute of Social Studies, *Report Series* No. 1, The Hague, 1977.
Franke, R. and Chasin B. *The Political Economy of Ecological Destruction: Development in the West African Sahel*, Allanheld, 1980.
Fredericks, A. 'California agribusiness: a case study', Department of Community Studies, University of California, Santa Clara, Mimeo, 1978.
Friedland, W. *et al. Manufacturing Green Gold. The Conditions and Social Consequences of Lettuce Harvest Mechanization*, University of California, Davis, 1978.
Friedland, W. *et al.* 'Conditions and consequences of lettuce harvest mechanization', *HortScience*, Vol. 14/2, 1979.
Gakou, M. *The Crisis in African Agriculture*, Zed, 1987.
Gastellu, J-M. *et al. Maintenance Sociale et Changement Economique au Sénégal II: Pratique du Travail et Rééquilibres Sociaux en Milieu Serer*, Travaux et Documents de l'ORSTOM, No. 34, Paris, 1974.
Gastellu, J-M. '. . . Mais où sont donc ces unités économiques que nos amis cherchent tant en Afrique?' AMIRA, *Note du Travail*, Paris, 1978.
Gastellu, J-M. *L'égalitarianisme Economique du Serer du Sénégal*, Travaux et Documents de l'ORSTOM, Paris 1981.

Gellar, S. *Senegal: An African Nation between Islam and the West*, Westview Press, 1982.

Gentil, D. and Dufumier, M. 'Le suivi-évaluation dans les projets de développement rural: orientations méthodologiques', AMIRA, *Brochure* No. 44, Paris, 1984.

George, S. *How the Other Half Dies*, Penguin, 1976.

Goldberg, R. *Agribusiness Management for Developing Countries – Latin America*, Ballinger, 1974.

Goodman, D. and Redclift, M. *From Peasant to Proletarian: Capitalist Development and Agrarian Transitions*, Blackwell, 1981.

Goody, J. *Production and Reproduction: A Comparati. ᵔ Study of the Domestic Domain*, Cambridge University Press, 1976.

Gulliver, P. *Neighbours and Networks*, University of California Press, 1971.

Guyer, J. 'Household and community in African Studies', *African Studies Review*, Vol. 24, Nos 2/3, 1981.

Harle, V. (ed.) *The Political Economy of Food*, Saxon House, 1978.

Harrison, M. 'Chayanov and the economics of the Russian peasantry', *Journal of Peasant Studies*, Vol. 2/4, 1975.

Harriss, B. 'Going against the grain', *Development and Change*, Vol. 10, 1979.

Harvey, C. 'Conclusion', in Harvey, C. (ed.), *Agricultural Pricing Policy in Southern Africa: Four Country Case Studies*, Macmillan, 1988.

Haswell, M. *Economics of Agriculture in a Savanna Village*, U.K. Colonial Office Colonial Research Studies, No. 8, HMSO, 1953.

Haswell, M. *The Changing Pattern of Economic Activity in a Gambian Village*, Ministry of Overseas Development, Overseas Research Publications, No. 2, 1963.

Helleiner, G. *Peasant Agriculture, Government and Economic Growth in Nigeria*, Irwin, 1966.

Heyer, J. *et al. Rural Development in Tropical Africa*, St. Martin's Press, 1981.

Hill, P. *Migrant Cocoa Farmers of Southern Ghana*, Cambridge University Press, 1963.

Hill, P. *Rural Hausa. A Village and a Setting*, Cambridge University Press, 1972.

Hill, P. *Development Economics on Trial. The Anthropological Case for a Prosecution*, Cambridge University Press, 1986.

Hindess, B. and Hirst P. *Precapitalist Modes of Production*, Routledge and Kegan Paul, 1975.

Hinton, W. and Housden, R. *Economic Results from Horticulture: 1972 Harvest Year*, Agricultural Economics Unit, University of Cambridge, 1973.

Hopkins, A. G. *An Economic History of West Africa*, Longman, 1973.

Horst, T. *At Home Abroad: A Study of the Domestic and Foreign Operations of the American Food Processing Industry*, Ballinger, 1974.

Horton, J. 'Characteristics of the horticultural export enterprises utilizing contract farming schemes in Senegal', in Watts, 1986.

Hunt, D. 'Chayanov's model of peasant household resource allocation', *Journal of Peasant Studies*, Vol. 6/3, 1979.

IBRD (International Bank for Reconstruction and Development, World Bank). *Senegal: Tradition, Diversification and Economic Development*, 1974.

IBRD. *Accelerated Development in Sub-saharan Africa*, 1981.

IBRD. *World Development Report*, 1985.

IBRD. *Poverty and Hunger. Issues and Options for Food Security in Developing Countries*, 1986.

INRA. *Les 'Marchés Physiques' dans l'Économie des Fruits et Légumes*, Montpellier, 1974.

Jackson, S. 'Hausa women on strike', *Review of African Political Economy*, No. 13, 1979.

Kemp. C. and Little, A. 'Editorial introduction', in Kemp *et al.*, 1987.

Kemp, C. *et al.* 'People in plantations: means or ends', *IDS Bulletin*, Vol. 18/2, 1987.

Kirk, C. 'People in plantations: an annotated bibliography', *IDS Research Report*, No. 18, 1987.

Klein, M. *Islam and Imperialism in Senegal Sine-Saloum 1847–1914*, Stanford University Press, 1968.

Klein, M. 'Colonial rule and structural change: The case of the Sine-Saloum', in Cruise O'Brien, R.. 1979.

Lacombe, B. 'Fakao, (Sénégal): dépouillment des registres paroissaux et enquête démographique rétrospective: méthodologie et résultats', Travaux et Documents de l'ORSTOM, No. 7, Paris, 1970.

Lacombe, B. *et al.* 'Exode rural et urbanisation au Sénégal. Sociologie de la migration des Serer de Niakhar vers Dakar en 1970', Travaux et Documents de l'ORSTOM, No. 73, Paris, 1977.

Lappé, F. M. and Collins, J. *Food First. Beyond the Myth of Scarcity*, Houghton Mifflin, 1977.

Lauret, F. 'Le role économique des techniques de l'abri dans les diverses systèmes de production de légumes', INRA, *Série Notes et Documents*. No. 3, 1973.

Lauret, F. and Montigaud, J. 'L'économie des fruits et légumes', INRA, *Série Notes et Documents*, Montpellier, 1974a.

Lauret, F. and Montigaud, J. 'Systèmes de production légumières en France', *Revue Horticole*, Mai, 1974b.

Lawrence, P. (ed.) *World Recession and the Food Crisis In Africa*, James Currey, 1986.

LeBihan, J. *Etude de Quelques Grands Complex Industriels et Commerciaux de L'économie Alimentaire. Compte Rendu d'une Mission Effectuée en Suède*, INRA, Paris. 1964.

Lennihan, L. 'Agricultural wage labour in Northern Nigeria', in Watts, M. (ed.) *State, Oil and Agriculture in Nigeria*, Institute of International Studies, University of California, Berkeley, *Research Studies*, No. 66, 1987.

Lericollais. A. *Etude Géographique d'un Terroir Serer (Sénégal)*, Atlas des Structures Agraires au Sud du Sahara, No. 7, Mouton et Cie, 1972.

Lewis, W. A. *The Theory of Economic Growth*, Allen and Unwin, 1955.

Lindsay, B. (ed.) *African Migration and Rural Development*, Pennsylvania State University Press, 1985.

Lipton, M. 'The theory of the optimising peasant', *Journal of Development Studies*, Vol. 4/3, 1968.

Lipton. M. (ed.) 'Rural poverty and agribusiness', Institute of Development Studies, *Discussion Paper* No. 104, 1977.

Lloyd, P. *A Third World Proletariat?* Allen and Unwin, 1982.

Longhurst, R. 'The energy trap: work, nutrition and child malnutrition in Northern Nigeria', Cornell *International Nutrition Monograph Series*, No. 13, 1984.

Low, A. *Agricultural Development in Southern Africa. Farm Household Economics and the Food Crisis*, James Currey, 1986.

Mackintosh, M. 'Industrial relations in the Republic of Senegal', Institute of Development Studies, *Discussion Paper* No. 81, 1975.

Mackintosh, M. 'Fruit and vegetables as an international commodity. The relocation of horticultural production and its implications for the producers', *Food Policy*, 1977a.

Mackintosh, M. 'Reproduction and patriarchy: a critique of Meillassoux, "Femmes, Greniers et Capitaux"', *Capital and Class*, No. 2, 1977b.

Mackintosh, M. 'Domestic labour and the household', in Burman, S. (ed.), *Fit Work for Women*, Croom Helm, 1979.

Mackintosh, M. *The Impact of Newly-Introduced Estate Farming on the Surrounding Rural Economy: A Case Study of Bud Senegal 1971–1976*, D. Phil. Thesis, University of Sussex, 1980.

Maxwell, S. 'Food aid to Senegal: disincentive effects and commercial displacement', Institute of Development Studies, *Discussion Paper* No. 225, 1986.

Meillassoux, C. *Anthropologie Economique des Gouro de Côte d'Ivoire*, Mouton, 1964.

Meillassoux, C. (ed.) *The Development of Indigenous Trade and Markets in West Africa*, Oxford University Press for International African Institute, 1971.

Meillassoux, C. 'Development or exploitation: is the Sahel famine good for business?' *Review of African Political Economy*, No. 1, 1974.

Meillassoux, C. *Femmes, Greniers et Capitaux*, Maspero, 1975.

Meynaud, J. and Salah-Bey, A. *Le Syndicalisme Africaine*, Payot, 1963.

Montigaud, J. *Filières et Firmes Agro-alimentaires. Le Can des Fruits et Légumes Transformés*, Thèse Montpellier, 1975.

Morrissey, J. *Agricultural Modernisation through Production Contracting. The Role of the Fruit and Vegetable Processor in Mexico and Central America*, Praeger, 1974.

Moscardi, E. and de Janvry, A. 'Attitudes towards risk among peasants: an optimising approach', *American Journal of Agricultural Economics*, Vol. 59/4, 1977.

Navez, S. *Résultats et Considérations sur l'Enquête Techno-Sociale Effectuée dans la Zone Maraîchère de la Région du Cap Vert*, République du Sénégal, Ministère du Développement Rural, Dakar, 1974.

Norman, D. *An Economic Study of Three Villages in Zaria Province*, 2 Vols., Institute for Agricultural Research, Ahmadu Bello University, Zaria, 1967.

Obbo, C. *African Women: Their Struggle for Economic Independence*, Zed, 1980.

OECD. *Fruit and Vegetables Processing in OECD Member Countries*, 1974.

Painter, T. 'Migrations, social reproduction and development in Africa: critical notes from a case study in the western Sahel', *DPP Working Papers* No. 7, The Open University, Milton Keynes, 1987.

Pélissier, P. *Les Paysans du Sénégal: Les Civilisations Agraires du Cayor à la Casamance*, Saint-Yrieux, Haute-Vienne, 1966.

Price Gittinger, J. *Economic Analysis of Agricultural Projects*, Second Edition, IBRD, 1982.

Reboul, C. 'Structures agraires et problémes de développement au Sénégal', *Revue Tiers Monde*, Vol. 14/54, 1973.

Reverdy, J. *Une Société Rural au Sénégal. Les Structures Foncières, Familiales et Villageoises des Serer*, Collection des Travaux du Centre Africain des Sciences Humaines Appliquées, Aix-en-Provence, 1964.

Rey, P. *Colonialisme, Néo-Colonialisme et Transition au Capitalisme. Exemple de la "Comilog" au Congo-Brazzaville*, Maspero, 1971.

Rey, P. *Les Alliances de Classes*, Maspero, 1973.

Richards, A. *et al.* (eds) *Subsistence to Commercial Production in Present Day Buganda*, Cambridge University Press, 1973.

Richards P. *Indigenous Agricultural Revolution. Ecology and Food Production in West Africa*, Hutchinson Educational Books, 1985.

Richards P. *Coping with Hunger: Hazard and Experiment in an African Rice-Farming System*, Allen and Unwin, 1986.

Roberts P. 'Feminism in Africa: Feminism and Africa' *Review of African Political Economy*, No. 27/28, 1984.

Roch, J. 'Emploi du temps et organisation du travail agricole dans un village Wolof Mouride', in Copans *et al.*, *Maintenance Sociale et Changement Economique au Sénégal I: Doctrine Economique et Pratique du Travail Chez les Mourides*, Travaux et Documents de l'ORSTOM, No. 15, Paris, 1972.

Rodney, W. *A History of the Upper Guinea Coast 1545 to 1800*, Oxford University Press, 1970.

Rosaldo, M. and Lamphere, L. (eds.) *Women, Culture and Society*, Standford University Press, 1974.

Ross, C. 'A village level study of producer grain transactions in rural Senegal', University of Michigan, Centre for Research on Economic Development, *Discussion Paper* No. 81, 1979.

Sandbrook, R. and Cohen, R. *The Development of an African Working Class*, University of Toronto Press, 1975.

Schneider, D. and Gough, K. (eds) *Matrilineal Kinship*, University of California Press, 1961.

Sen, A. K. *Poverty and Famines. An Essay on Entitlement and Deprivation*, Oxford University Press, 1981.

Sen, G. and Grown, C. *Development Crises and Alternative Visions. Third World Women's Perspectives*, Earthscan Publications, 1988.

Sow, A. *L'évolution des structures agricoles dans les zones rurales dans la Cap Vert. Contribution à la problématique de la réforme agraire*, Thèse Maîtrise de Géographie, Dakar, 1975.

Stack, C. 'Sex roles and survival strategies in an urban black community', in Rosaldo and Lamphere, 1974.

Stichter, S. *Migrant Labourers*, Cambridge University Press, 1985.

Suret-Canale, J. *Afrique Noire Occidentale et Centrale. II: L'ère Coloniale*, Editions Sociales, 1964.

Suret-Canale, J. *Afrique Noire de la Colonisation aux Indépendances 1945–1960, I: Crise du Système Colonial et Capitalisme Monopoliste d'Etat*, Editions Sociales, 1972.

Swainson, N. *The Development of Corporate Capitalism in Kenya 1918–1977*, Heinemann Educational Books, 1980.

Swindell, K. 'From migrant farmer to permanent settler: the strange farmers of The Gambia', in Clark, J. and Kosinski, L. (eds), *Redistribution of Population in Africa*, Heinemann Educational Books, 1982.

Tanner, N. 'Matrifocality in Indonesia and Africa, and among black Americans', in Rosaldo and Lamphere, 1974.

Terray, E. *Le Marxisme devant les Sociétés 'primitives'*, Maspero, 1969.

Tosh, J. 'The cash crop revolution in tropical Africa: an agricultural reappraisal', *African Affairs*, Vol. 79, 1979.

Turner, L. *Multinational Corporations and the Third World*, Allan Lane, 1973.

Vaitsos, C. *Intercountry Income Distribution and Transnational Enterprise*, Oxford University Press, 1974.

Van Binsbergen M. and Meilink H. 'Migrations and the transformation of modern African society'. Special Issue of *African Perspectives*. No. 1. 1978.

Vanhaeverbeke, A. *Remunération du Travail et Commerce Extérieur*, Centre de Recherche des Pays en Développement, Louvain, 1970.

Vercambre, M. *Les Unités Experimentales du Sine Saloum. Revenues et Dépenses des Deux Carrés Wolofs (Enquêtes Effectuées de Juillet 1972 à Août 1973)*, CNRA-Bambey/IRAT, Senegal, 1973.

Wallace, T. 'The Kano River project, Nigeria: the impact of an irrigation scheme on productivity and welfare'. in Heyer (ed.). 1981.

Watts. M. *Silent Violence. Food, Famine and Peasantry in Northern Nigeria*, University of California Press, 1983.

Watts. M. (ed.) *Contract Farming in Sub-Saharan Africa*, Vols 1 and 2, Institute for Development Anthropology, Binghampton, and Clarke University, Worcester, 1986.

Whitehead, A. 'Some preliminary notes on the subordination of women', *IDS Bulletin*, Vol. 10/3, 1979.

Whitehead. A. '"I'm hungry, mum." The politics of domestic budgeting'. in Young *et al.*, 1981.

Young, K. *et al.* (eds) *Of Marriage and the Market*. CSE Books, 1981.

Zachariah, K. and Condé J. *Migration in West Africa*, Oxford University Press, 1981.

Index

absenteeism, of women, 173, 174
accumulation, patterns of, 182-200
agribusiness, 9, 181-200
agricultural equipment, 54, 58, 60, 63, 64
agriculture, commercial: and West
  African farming, 1; spread of, 1
aid agencies, 9
apprenticeship, 78
aubergines, 15, 22, 76, 149, 150, 151, 152

Bambilor, 120-32, 162, 202; labour use in,
  t160; landholdings in, t158
banabanas, 59, 94, 129, 141, 151, 153
bananas, 10, 12
Baobab estate, 21-4, 31, 47, 116-36, 137,
  172, 189, 201, 202; strike at, 37, 174-9
bird scaring, 144; children in, 139
boys, and domestic work, 165
Bud Antle company, 12-17
Bud estates: and cash incomes, 93; and
  compensation to villagers, 73; and
  decline of farming, 181; and male
  labour market, 123-8; appropriation
  of land by, 72; area of farmland, t43;
  attitudes to, 117; calendar conflicts
  with farming tasks, 81; cash income
  from, t113; composition of labour
  force, t89; conflict with Kirene
  villagers, 78; control of hiring, 104;
  demands made of, 104; dependence
  on, 175; employment at, 97, t23, t155;
  impact on agriculture in Kirene, 72-9;
  impact on class formation, 163; impact
  on communal labour, 82; impact on
  labour market, 33, 39, 72, 137, 150-2;
  impact on land use, 33; impact on
  market gardening, 152-4; impact on
  position of women, 107; impact on
  product market, 39, 150-2; impact on
  spending patterns, 99-101; impact on
  wage labour, 24-7; income losses

attributable to, 93-5; insecure nature
  of work on, 125; relation to Senegalese
  farmers, 20-4; sales of, t43; strikes at,
  t46, 105, 189; unpredictability of
  incomes at, 171; villagers' dependence
  on, 86; wage levels at, 96, 123; women
  in labour force, 78-80, t136; women's
  work at, 128-31; work conflicts with
  farm work, 80-2
Bud Senegal, 13-14, 181-7; bankruptcy of,
  xiv, 20, 181, 182, 191; employment at,
  118, 119; exempted from tax, 13;
  financial structure of, 182; ownership
  of, t199; return cash flow of, 182, t183
Bud-Baobab, labour market for, 162
Burkina Faso, 9, 11

Cap Vert, 38; agricultural labouring in,
  120-2; decline of farming in, 137-61;
  land tenure in, t159; wage labour in,
  137-61
capital, international, 41
cash: transfer of, 168, 170, t180; villagers'
  resistance to, 101
cash crops, 1, 2, 16, 30, 55, 74-5, 85, 196,
  197
cash incomes, 35, 38, 44, 60, 62, 75, 103,
  162, 195, 203; and women, 102;
  changes in, 93; control of, 167-72;
  from Bud estates; t113; in Kirene,
  t114, t115; women's disposition of, 167
cassava, 76, 142, 152
casual labour, 120, 196
cattle, 72, 125; as wealth, 63
cattle ranching, 9, 10, 125
cattle-herding, 7
ceremonies: attendance at, 149;
  expenditure on, 99
Chavez, Cesar, xv
childcare, 131, 173
class formation, 33-5, 35-7, 162-81, 178-9;

and individual work, 131-2
class structure, transformation of, 17
clothes, buying of, 101
co-operation, 30, 57, 58, 193, 197;
    household, 79, 165
co-operative labour, 45, 198;
    undermined, 72
co-operatives, 39, 55, 143, 188, 194
colonization, 1, 2, 45
commercialization of farming, 26, 33
communal labour parties, 31, 32, 57, 65,
    t71, 102, 138, 139
communal labour system, impact of Bud
    estates on, 82
*Compagnie Française de l'Afrique
    Occidentale*, 4
compound, structure of, 49-51
conditions of employment, 177
*Confédération Nationale des Travailleurs
    du Sénégal, 176*
conseil rural, 37
construction, 100
contracts, labour, 172
cotton plantations, 4
cotton production, 8, 9
credit, 39

dahira, 57, 58, 62, 83-4
debt, 40, 153, 195
demonstrations, xiv
deforestation, 4
desertification, 7
development funds, 9
development projects, xiii-xviii
differentials, skill, 168
diversification of exports, 15
division of labour, sexual, 30, 35, 36, 48,
    56, 59, 79, 80, 163, 165, 172, 196
divisions among villagers, prevention of,
    105
Domaine National, 37-8, 52, 54, 146, 164,
    188
domestic work, 30, 32, 47-9; adaptation
    of, 35; and household structure, 165-7;
    changes in, xiv; of women, 79, 130,
    131, 162, 163, 165, 170, 173;
    organization of, 164-5
drought, xiii, xv, 4-10, 34, 41, 44, 53, 76,
    77, 82, 86, 119, 139, 140, 181, 190
dry season farming, xiv, 17, 21, 74, 80, 85,
    116, 137
durable goods, 103, 203

Ecole Nationale d'Economie Appliquée
    (ENA), 202
economic crisis: in Senegal, t192; rural,
    181-200

egalitarianism, 65
equipment, agricultural, 141, 142, 164
estate farming, relation to small-scale
    farming, 2, 20
ethnic homogeneity of Kirene, 45
export crops, 21, 40, 189, 190, 193, t200

fallowing of fields, 53, 54
famine, xvi, 7, 86
farm labour, organization of, t68, t69, t70
farm plots, distribution of, in Kirene, t88
farm work, conflict with Bud estates
    work, 80-2
farmers, risks of, 181
farming: and women, 143; changing
    patterns in, 37; decline of, 92, 103 (in
    Cap Vert, 137-61); in West Africa,
    relation to commercial agriculture, 1;
    organization of, pre-Bud estates, 54-8;
    time spent in, t91; women in, 140, 196
farming systems, relation to households,
    30-3
farming tasks, calendar conflicts with Bud
    estates, 81
farming techniques, 139
female-centredness, 166, 167, 171; of
    households, 35
female-headed households, 166
fertilizer, chemical, 54
Findus, 11
firdus, 84
firewood, fetching of, 48, 164
Fonds Européens de Développement
    (FED), 13, 189
food: buying of, 41, 100, 102, 169;
    common consumption of, 30, 168;
    imports of, 5, 86
food crisis, xiii-xviii, 40-1, 190
food farming, decline in, 85-6
food security, necessity of, 197
France, 7, 117, 118
fruit trees, 60, 102

Gambia, 118
gender division, 162-81
Ghana, 7
GIPES, 194
glasshouse production, 10
green beans, 21, 150, 152, 193
groundnut farming, 38, 41, 54-8, 75, 80,
    84, 85, 94, 95, 120, 138, 141, 142, 191;
    in Kirene, t112
groundnut market, stagnation of, 5, t6
groundnut schemes, 193
groundnut trade, state monopoly of, 189
groundnuts, xiv, 2, 4, 5, 15, 32, 53, 54, t68,
    t69, t70, 74, 77, 82, t155, 197, 204;

output of, t89; prices of, 7, 119, 195; unprofitability of, 142-3
Guinea, 5

Heidematschappij, 186
Heinz, 11
henna, 76
herbicides, use of, 22
hierarchy, 163
hired labour, 27, 33-5, 77, 146, 147
hiring systems, 104, 105, 123, 127, 196; for women, 129, 172-3
hiring, control of, 93, 105, 106, 107
hoeing, 22, 54, 56, 58, t68, t69, t70, 80, t81, 94, 105, 119, 140, 143, 172, 177
hoes, animal-drawn, 63
horticulture in Europe, transformation of, 10
horticulture, export, 15
horticulture, international, 10-12
House of Bud SA (HOBSA), 12-14, 182-7; and Senegal state, 185
household expenditure, shift in, 109
household farming, 147, 153, 193, 195, 196, 198; concept of, xiv-xv
household groupings, 55, 56
household structure: and domestic work, 165-7; changes in, 203; transformation of, 179
household: and wage labour, 162-81; as centre of productive activity, 103; as economic unit, 171; concept of, 28-33, 37; head of, 29, 32, 55, 65, 74, 85, 162, 166, 171; incomes of, 96-8; propertyless, 163-4; relation to farming systems, 30-3; reorganization of, 117; social organization of, 47-9; structure of, 35, 137
housing, 47, 64, 121, 164

identification cards, introduction of, 173
income: distribution of, 96-8; t98; spent on food, 41
income losses: attributable to Bud estates, 93-5; distribution of, 95-6
incomes: drop in, 94; from market gardening, 152; rise in, 128; seasonal, 137
individualization, 26, 85, 92-115, 181, 197, 198
inheritance, 48, 65, 109; and women, 66; changing pattern of, 63-4; of land, 146, 147, 148; through female line, 51, 52
International Finance Corporation (IFC), xiv, 9, 13, 15, 184
investment, xiii, 12; agricultural, 11, 92, 102, 103; disappearance of, in Kirene,

102-3; horticultural, 10
irrigation, xiii, 8, 10, 16, 17, 32, 76, t81, 82, 139, 142, 145, 146, 148, 149, 172, 188, 190, 193, 194, 196, 198
Islam, 63, 64, 65
Israel, 186, 194
Ivory Coast, 2

job rights, 103-5

Kano River project, 186
Kirene, 29, 30, 38, 41; before arrival of Bud, 44-71; cash incomes in, t114, t115; currency of money in, 62-3; decline of vegetable growing in, 75; disappearance of investment in, 102-3; distribution of farm plots in, t88; economic transition in, 64-6; effects of land loss in, t87; groundnut farming in, t112; impact of Bud estates on, 72-91; income distribution in, t98; land loss in, 72-4; land shortage in, 53-4; vegetable growing in, 59, t111; wage labour in, 92-115
Kirene estate, 21-4, 189, 201, 202; strike on, 36, 105-6, 174
Kirene villagers, conflict with Bud estates, 78

labour: collective, 77; communal *see* communal labour; competition for, 150; organized, and Senegal state, 189; paid, 57; shortages of, 124, 150; unpaid, 29, 190, 195 *see also* hired labour
labour co-operation, 41, 56, 85; unpaid, 31
labour conflict, 35, 187
labour costs, 153
labour force, formation of, xiv
Labour Inspectorate, 189
labour laws, 177
labour market, 40, 181, 196; formation of, 116-36; impact of Bud estates on, 72, 137; male, and Bud estates, 123-8
labour use in market gardening, t160
labouring, agricultural, 137; in Cap Vert, 120-2
land: access to, 51-3; appropriation of, by Bud estates, 72; inheritance of, 51-2, 146, 147, 148; prices of, 153, 154; sale of, 37, 38
land holding, 51-3; fragmentation of, 54
land loss, 20, 51, 72, 77, 84, 94, 96, 97, 100, 102, 103, 204; effect of, on crops, 74-5; in Kirene, t87 (impact of, 72-4); resistance to, 103
land prices, 145, 146

land purchase, illegality of, 37, 146
land rights, 164, 103-5
land shortage, 44, 65, 73, 153, 198; in Kirene, 53-4
land tenure, 141, 145, 146; in Bambilor, t158; in Cap Vert, t159
land use, 27
lettuce, iceberg, 10
Libby McNeil, 10
Liberia, 2
lodgers, 167, 170

maize, 142
Mali, 7, 9, 11
mangoes, 95, 129
manuring, 53, 85
market gardening, 8, 10-12, 13, 14-17, 21, 39, 77, 82, 94, 97, 108, 118, 120, 124, 125, 126, 128, 138, 162, 187, 188, 189, 190, 194, 202; and women, 145; costs and returns of, t161; economic organization of, 144-52; impact of Bud estates on, 152; labour use in, t160
markets, 37-40; in Senegal, operation of, 38; protected, 7
marriage, 35, 48-9, 61, 63, 78-9, 100, 103, 122, 127, 166, 170
Marxism, 27, 33
matrilineal patterns, 32, 45, 49-51, 53, 63, 146
May Day parades, 177
meals, preparation of, 164
mechanization, 10, 22, 40
melons, 21
men: in relation to women, 107, 117, 174, 193, 196; instability of, 171
methodology, problems of, 20
migrant labour, xiv, 2, 4, 16, 24, 35, 38, 78, 104, 116-36, t134, 137, 147, 162, 175, 179, 181, 196; male, 142; women as, 122-3, 143, 165
migration, 1, 22, 33-5, 40, 60, 66, 100, 103, 117, 118, 148, 163, 166, 167, 169, 171; pattern of, 61
millet, 5, t6, 30, 49, 53, 54, t68, t69, t70, t81, 74, 95, t98, 99, 100, 102, 118, 139, 141, t155, 164, t200, 204; output of, t89; unprofitability of, 144
millet farmers, 78, 82, 96, 99
millet farming, 31, 32, 41, 54-8, 76, 77, 82-4, 85, 86, 138, 191
millet growing, social importance of, 75
minimum wage, legal, 174, 175, 178
mobility of residence, 53
modes of production, concept of, 25
monetization, xvi, 35, 37-40, 45, 60, 65, 66, 85, 103, 109, 137, 194

money, currency of, in Kirene, 62-3
monopoly, 39, 189
mosque, 47, 57, 62, 84
multinationals, control of, 185

nationalization of groundnut trade, 138
Nestlé, 10
New Agricultural Policy, 191, 193, 194
niayes, 15, 24, 144, 145, 149, 154, 190, 191
Niger, 7, 9
Nigeria, 2, 7, 9, 11, 186
night shift work, and women, 128, 130, 174

onions, 150, 151
organization, forms of, 103

packing shed work, 22; of men, 168; of women, 105, 128, 168, 172, 174
pawpaw trees, 76
peasant farming, 195
peasantry, 33, 40, 187
peppers, 21, 22, 149, 150, 151, 193
personnel delegates, 107
pesticides, 10
picking work, women in, 128
piece rates, 175, 177, 178; resistance to, 105
piece work, 128
plague, 138, 145
polygyny, 166
Ponty, 202; as company village, 162-79; cash transfers in, t180; composition by ethnic group, t133; households in, 171
potatoes, 149, 150, 151, 152
poverty, xv, 100
productivity, 144, 195, 197
profit, 181-200
proletarianization, 27, 93, 103, 117, 164, 197; rural, xv, 25, 26, 33, 34, 103, 109, 116, 187
public sector employees, 126

Réseau Africain pour le Développement Intégré, 194
railways, spread of, 4
redevance, 52
remittances from migrants, 61
research method, 201-4
rice, 5, 8, 86, t98, 99, 100, 139, 144, 164, t200
Richard Toll sugar plantation, 8
risks, xv, 181-200; of farmers, xvi, 181; of horticulture export, 15
Rural Council, 104
rural development strategy, 8, 187

Safen society, 50, 65

Sahel, xiii, xv, 12, 86
Sainsbury, 11
savings, 100
schooling, 78, 117, 118, 126, 139
seasonal labour, 21, 22, 84, 94, 150
seed, availability of, 55, 77
seeding, 143, t68, t69, t70, t81
Senegal state: and small farmers, 190-5; and HOBSA, 184-6; losses sustained by, 184, 187; provision of infrastructure by, 14
Senegal, economic crisis in, t192
Senegambia, 2
Senghor, Adrien, 188
Senprim, 191
Serer society, 50
shift work, for women, 128
Sierra Leone, 2
singing, religious, 108
skilled work, 62, 127, 168, 172
slave trade, 1, 4
small farmers, and Senegal state, 190-5
smallholder, concept of, 28
smallholdings, 14-17
SOCAS project, 8
Société Commerciale de l'Ouest Africaine, 4
Société Nationale Horticole, 188
social organisation, new forms of, 106-8
soil erosion, 7
solidarity, xv, xvi, 92-115; among women, 106, 175; economic, 44-5; men's lack of, 175, 176, 177; village, 37
sorghum, t6, 55, 141, t200
spending patterns, impact of Bud estates on, 99
state intervention in groundnut growing, 16
state responses, 187-90
strawberry production, 11, 93, 108, 189
strikes: at Baobab estate, 174-9; at Kirene, 105-6; by women, 36, 37
sugar cane, 8, 138
surgas, 120, 123-4, 141, 147, 148, 149, 150, 152-3; wages of, 123-4

tâcherons, 120, 141, 147, 153
tax exemptions, 13
team leaders, 172, 173
Tesco, 11
Thiam, Habib, 8, 188
tomato prices, ruined by Bud, 151
tomatoes, 8, 15, 21, 22, 53, 74, 142, 149, 151, 152
tractor driving, 172
trade unions, 27, 36, 176-8, 187; organization of, 106-8

trade, agricultural, 1
traders, women as, 128-9
transition, 37-40; agrarian, 40-1, 195-8; analysis of, 24-8; economic, in Kirene, 64-6; indicators of, 39
transportation: costs of, 12; private, 39

unemployed workers, xiv, 104, 140, 178
unemployment, concept of, 127
Unilever, 10
union delegates, 176-8; and women's concerns, 177
Union Progressiste Sénégalaise, 176
unionization, 35
United Africa Company, 2
United Farm Workers (UFW), 12
United States of America (USA), 10
unskilled work, 171, 172
US AID, 9
US subsidies, 9

vegetable production, 15, 65, 80, t81, 82, 94, 95, 97, 101, 181, 189; decline of, 92, 102; in Kirene, 59-60, 75, t111
village studies tradition, 27, 28, 201, 202
Volta River Project, 2

wage differentials, 103, 196; between men and women, 174, 175
wage labour, 14-17, 16, 26, 34, 39, 44, 60, 83, 85, 92-115, 116, 126, 127, 131, 137-61, 165, 190, 193, 197, 198; agricultural, 96; and girls, 80; and household, 162-81; and women, 116, 122-3, 175, 179; as stimulus for change, 92; by Kirene villagers, 60; by wives, 130; combined with domestic work, 173; dependence on, 33, 35, 41, 181; dominance of, 137; participation in, t90; use of, 8
wages, 148; dependence on, 24
water: carrying of, 48, 101, 102, 164; sale of, 14, 101, 102, 188; supply of, 21, 184
watering, by hand, 148, 149
wealth, changing pattern of, 63-4
wet season farming, xiv, 41, 59, 72, 74, 76, 77, 80, 118, 121, 123; cash costs and returns of, t156, t157; decline of, 24, 35, 137-40; individualization of, 140-4; unproductiveness of, 140-4
wheat, 8; imports of, 5
William Ponty school, 117, 119
women's earnings, 93, 95, 96, 100, 102; control of, 36
women's militancy, 174
women's work, 35-7, 41, 56, 82, 85, 105, 117, 163; at Bud estates, 128-31;

category of, 36, 172; in Bambilor, t135
women: and absenteeism, 174; and
  buying clothes, 101; and buying food,
  100; and carrying of water, 101; and
  domestic work, 79, 163, 170; and
  farming, 143; and inheritance, 66; and
  market gardening, 77, 145; and night
  shift work, 174; and packing shed
  work, 22, 105, 128, 168, 172, 174; and
  picking work, 22, 128; and trade
  unions, 177; and wage labour, 122-3,
  175, 179; as agricultural wage labour,
  116; as market gardeners, 94; as
  migrants, 122-3; as traders, 128-9; as

unskilled labour, 174; cash incomes of,
  96; change in position of, 35; economic
  autonomy of, 167; effects of Bud
  estates on, 107; hiring conditions for,
  172; in Bud labour force, 78-80, t136;
  in farm work, 140, 196; in relation to
  men, 107, 117, 174, 196; interviews
  with, 203; older, and strikes, 176; on
  strike, 36; organization of, 106-8;
  solidarity among, 106; subordination
  of, 36; young, subordination of, 107
World Bank, xiv, 9

young people, organization of, 106-8